THE RAGE OF REPLACEMENT

THE RAGE OF REPLACEMENT

Far Right Politics and Demographic Fear

MICHAEL FEOLA

University of Minnesota Press
Minneapolis — London

Chapter 1 was published in a different form as "'You Will Not Replace Us': The Melancholic Nationalism of Whiteness," *Political Theory* 49, no. 4 (2021): 528–53; copyright Michael Feola. Chapter 3 was published in a different form as "Metapolitics and Demographic Anxiety on the New Right: Using and Abusing the Language of Equality," *Perspectives on Politics* 20, no. 3 (September 2022): 1012–23; copyright Michael Feola.

Published by the University of Minnesota Press
111 Third Avenue South, Suite 290
Minneapolis, MN 55401-2520
http://www.upress.umn.edu

ISBN 978-1-5179-1679-4 (hc)
ISBN 978-1-5179-1680-0 (pb)

A Cataloging-in-Publication record for this book is available from the Library of Congress.

Printed in the United States of America on acid-free paper

33 32 31 30 29 28 27 26 25 24 10 9 8 7 6 5 4 3 2 1

CONTENTS

INTRODUCTION
THE RAGE OF REPLACEMENT vii

CHAPTER 1
"YOU WILL NOT REPLACE US" 1
The Melancholic Nationalism of Whiteness

CHAPTER 2
THE CATASTROPHIST VISION OF THE FAR RIGHT 27
Race War, Crisis, and Violence

CHAPTER 3
METAPOLITICS AND DEMOGRAPHIC FEAR 55
The New Right's "War of Ideas"

CHAPTER 4
VISIONS OF ESCAPE 79
The Ethnostate and the Secessionist Dream of the Far Right

CHAPTER 5
THE REPRODUCTIVE POLITICS OF A "NICE, WHITE NATION" 103
The Biopolitics of the Far Right

CODA
THE SPREAD OF THE NARRATIVE AND ITS CIVIC COSTS 131

Acknowledgments 143

Notes 145

Index 199

INTRODUCTION

THE RAGE OF REPLACEMENT

It is often said that our time is defined by rage. Indeed, many of the iconic images of contemporary politics amount to gestures of anger. Recent years have been defined by protesters spilling into the streets, overturning cars, tearing down monuments, and storming the halls of power. Nations have seen uprisings of rage in response to police brutality, contested elections, and judicial decisions.[1] Public officials stage spectacles of fury when their decisions or characters are questioned. And there is perhaps no better way to describe the current far right than as a movement of rage, oriented against a broad variety of targets: elites, progressives, women, nonwhite populations, LGBTQ+ movements, the state.[2] The recent upsurge of populism, for instance, has been described as the "rage of the left behind"—a defensive expression of anger on the part of all those who believe they have been abandoned by the state and its ruling class.[3]

Though many observers have identified rage as a primal emotion, any effort to render this emotion in archetypal terms tends to miss how rage is activated under specific circumstances, directed toward specific aims, and turned away from others.[4] Such an approach obscures how some groups use rage to secure benefits while this same rage leads to conditions of violence and vulnerability for others. It misses the distinct publics that are formed by rage and the dangers of binding a public in this way. And it likewise fails to inquire into how the contemporary politics of rage is stoked, guided, and maintained by a media ecosystem in which rage is the key to maintaining audience engagement. Indeed, rage has become the central currency of contemporary political media, driving clicks, pushing distribution, and keeping eyes on screens.

This book tackles a specific politics of rage that increasingly defines and mobilizes the far right across the global stage. Consider the following scenes:

- August 2017. Various groups of the far right gather in Charlottesville, Virginia, to protest the removal of a Confederate statue—though the grievance runs deeper. They claim that such an act of removal would erase their very customs, history, and traditions. It would, they claim, erase *them* from the nation they claim as their own. They parade through the night bearing torches, screaming in unison, their faces twisted with rage, "You will not replace us! Jews will not replace us!" The next day sees widespread, violent conflict throughout the city, which culminates when a white supremacist drives his car into a crowd of people, killing Heather Heyer, a thirty-two-year-old counterprotester.
- May 2022. An angry white extremist drives more than two hundred miles to Buffalo, New York, with multiple firearms to target an area he knows to be majority Black. He begins his violence in the parking lot of a grocery store, shooting four people. He then moves inside the supermarket, where he shoots eight more, killing ten Black shoppers and workers in total. His online manifesto explains his act as motivated by racial resentments toward nonwhites "invading" the country, and he explicitly invokes the eclipse of white majorities as the source of his rage.

What binds these episodes is not rage in the abstract or even populist rage against governments. Instead, the rage on display is stoked by a carefully cultivated anxiety over demographic change in Europe and North America. More specifically, this panic is organized around fears of racial "replacement" associated with immigration—that is, the idea that white citizens (particularly white males) are being deposed from their "rightful" place at the top of the social and cultural hierarchy.

A symptomatic version of this narrative appeared in 2022 in the official publication of the National Vanguard, an influential neo-Nazi organization in the United States: "About sixty years ago in this country the Establishment made a decision to drastically reduce the percentage of white people in the population. This was not done by chance. It was not accidental. . . . It was a deliberate, well thought out, and intentional plan—and it was done in a concerted way, by design."[5] This conspiratorial vision is not limited to the movement literature of American white supremacy; it defines much of the far right across Europe as well. For instance, the French far right author Guillaume Faye claims that European civilization currently faces the existential threat of being "replaced on its own soil by the rejects of other nations."[6] In sum, the anger that fuels and mobilizes major sectors of the far right is the rage that attends what has come to be named "the Great Replacement" (or, in an alternate rendering that stresses its racial resentments, "white replacement"). For the far right, "replacement" is not simply a decline in the status or numbers of white citizens across the nations of the global North. Rather, it is a process of substitution in which traditional majorities are pushed aside so that other ethnic and cultural groups can take their place.

An essential feature of the Great Replacement narrative is its spread across the far right. The name is typically tracked to the work of the French literary theorist Renaud Camus, who first posed it to describe the "brutal change of population" that stems from the "submerging wave of ethnic substitution" associated with mass immigration.[7] Though the formula was popularized through Camus's 2011 book *Le Grand Remplacement,* its use has hardly been confined to scholarly debates over population change. The phrase crystallizes a wide range of anxieties around cultural, economic, and political change in global times. It sums up a concept that is easily passed through extremist forums, chat rooms, and the popular media. And it provides ample fodder for the posters, stickers, and memes that make up much of the far right's political culture. The popularity of the formula goes beyond its transmissibility: it also provides a ready-made cognitive framework to lend meaning to a wide array of social and cultural changes associated with globalization. This work is reflected in how quickly the narrative has passed from the elite sphere into the dark corners of the Internet, only to be mainstreamed through major media personalities and elected officials in both Europe and North America.[8]

One source of the narrative's power is its ability to channel an established literature on demographic trends. Population scholars have long expressed concerns over what has been termed "demographic winter"—a situation in which fertility rates in nation after nation have slipped below replacement level and deaths outpace births.[9] To borrow the hyperbolic language of this diagnosis, the core problem of the West might not be a military, economic, or spiritual crisis, but rather an "epidemic of empty cradles" that will eventually threaten civilizational collapse if birthrates cannot be stimulated to reach the level of population replacement.[10] This ostensible fertility crisis rests at the heart of white replacement narratives. A familiar version runs as follows: because many advanced industrial nations cannot meet their economic or population needs through their own reproduction, they have been forced to import populations for labor. And for those gripped by replacement fears, the enhanced reproductive rates of cultural newcomers mean that white majorities are being swamped by an "invasion" of nonwhite immigrants. As a result, present demographic trends exert a kind of gravitational pull that draws nations inexorably toward nonwhite population majorities. These anxieties over an increasingly diverse population are illustrated by a prominent feature on the home page of the notorious white extremist website the Daily Stormer: an image of a globe that displays the current white percentage of the population in both the United States and the world.[11] To drive the point home, the infographic projects the ongoing decline of the white population share and offers a numeric countdown, ticking down toward the exact moment of perceived white racial eclipse.

By emphasizing a story of deep demographic change, the Great Replacement narrative sounds familiar notes. Though the coinage has recently surged into prominence, its major concerns were prominently featured in Jean Raspail's 1973 novel *Le Camp des saints (The Camp of the Saints),* a xenophobic work now lauded across the far right.[12] At the heart of the book rests a narrative of racial eclipse: a fleet of refugees leaves from India, travels the world, and arrives on the shores of France. What begins as a surge of immigration ends with the overrunning of the nation. Eventually, the broader white world is overcome by the uncultured, nonwhite "horde." And the precedents for Great Replacement thinking are hardly confined to the sphere of fiction. To press beyond literary speculation, far right figures have likewise posited a number of sinister, long-standing plots for racial replacement, supposedly targeting the European arena (e.g., the Hooton Plan or the Kalergi Plan). Take, for instance, the Kalergi Plan, named after Richard von Coudenhove-Kalergi, a politician and founder of the Paneuropean Union. This demographic conspiracy theory arises from a distorted reading of von Coudenhove-Kalergi's *Practical Idealism* (1925), in which he predicts that "the man of the future will be of mixed race."[13] Where this book forecasts that immigration and intermarriage will transform the character of Europe, figures from the racialist right focus on this prediction as evidence of a plan to undermine the distinction of European cultures. In this paranoiac vision, the threat that faces Europe is not simply heightened migration but rather a conscious effort to engineer immigration policy so "that the nationalities of Europe should be destroyed by mixing them all up to become a single homogenous undifferentiated people."[14]

The United States has its own considerable history of panics over population change (e.g., nineteenth-century fears of "Chinese invasion"). Recent controversies have centered on the specter of a migrant "caravan" or an "invasion" pouring across the nation's borders—perhaps best exemplified by calls to build a wall along the southern border. This insistence on the need for a physical boundary echoes a long line of xenophobic campaigns and policies, some of which have explicitly invoked the threat of racial replacement. At the beginning of the twentieth century, for instance, the nation was gripped by fears over what was termed "race suicide." This panic, which was promoted by a wide range of social elites, involved similar issues: rising immigration rates, changes in patterns of immigration, and a decline in reproduction among members of the so-called Nordic race, viewed as the ethnic core of the nation. Perhaps the most notorious articulation of this panic came from the American conservationist Madison Grant, who was widely lauded as an inspiration for Adolf Hitler's own race thought. As Grant argued in his influential *The Passing of the Great Race* (1916): "These immigrants adopt the language of the native American, they wear his clothes, they steal his name and they are beginning to take his women . . . and while he is being elbowed out of his own home the American looks calmly abroad and urges on others the suicidal ethics which are exterminating his own race."[15] The central terms of this historical episode resonate with the present narrative of demographic fear. Those who feared the process of "race suicide" argued not only that the "ethnic core" of the nation would be engulfed by a tide of ethnic competitors but also that this process would yield the disappearance of the "native American" (a phrase that figures the so-called Nordic subject as native, eliding the violent history of settler colonialism through which white majorities were forged). These fears were anticipated by the stark diagnosis of Francis Amasa Walker, an economist and director of the U.S. Census, who forecast in 1891 that increased immigration would lead "not to a re-inforcement of our population, but to a *replacement* of native by foreign stock."[16]

The contemporary politics of demographic fear adopts many of these established themes: nativism, race panic, xenophobia, fertility anxieties, and economic pressures. It magnifies the urgency, however, with a more pointed line of argument: the demographic changes unfolding across the globe are not simply the far-reaching effects of labor migration, global trade, and comparative fertility rates. Rather, the decline of white majorities has been engineered deliberately by political and economic elites (an assertion that persistently draws from the long-standing tropes of anti-Semitic conspiracy theory).[17] The more elaborate presentations of replacement theory are accordingly peppered with out-of-context phrases pulled from the documents of international organizations (e.g., the United Nations, the European Union, the International Monetary Fund), which supposedly provide "smoking gun" evidence of these plots for ethnic substitution.[18]

This claim that white population decline is the result of an intentional plan hatched in elite circles does significant work to politicize population change as an antagonistic process, where the members of one group ("globalist" elites) benefit and those of another (white, native-born subjects) are "dispossessed of their inheritance as the majority in the nation their ancestors built."[19] This theme of dispossession by shadowy elites reflects how the replacement narrative draws from the lineage of what is often termed a "paranoid" politics. In the canonical formulation of the American historian Richard Hofstadter, the paranoid style of politics is one that tracks social changes to a "vast and sinister conspiracy, a gigantic and yet subtle machinery of influence set in motion to undermine and destroy a way of life."[20] In this vision, the ills that beset the nation go beyond accident, luck, or ineptitude. Instead, national decline is read as evidence of an intentional design, devised by enemies.[21] For those gripped by the replacement narrative, however, the agents and objectives are distinctive. Where the canonical articulation of the paranoid style was forged in the anticommunist obsessions of the Cold War, the replacement narrative identifies a more diffuse range of antagonists. Commentators in the conservative popular media, for instance, have persistently accused the center-left Democratic Party in the United States of working to import nonwhite populations from the global South (presented as a faithful base of Democratic support) for purposes of electoral gain.[22] In other renderings the culprits are figured as economic elites or multinational corporations who import nonwhite populations in order to enrich themselves at the expense of native-born laborers (under the reasoning that nonwhite migrants will work for lower wages).[23] What binds these figures is their contribution to a situation of perceived emergency. These elites are depicted as betraying the "true nation," and, in doing so, they commit a deeper sin: eroding the identity of the nation by promoting population mixture.

At bottom, this narrative arrives at one conclusion: elite policy decisions have produced a situation in which nation after nation is being stripped away from its rightful holders and turned over to more fertile nonwhite groups—thus ensuring that these nations will remain majority nonwhite for the foreseeable future. It is for this reason that the replacement narrative is often accompanied by more lurid variants that stress its antiwhite intentions. In the far right media ecology, these projects of racial substitution are described as "white replacement," "white extermination," "white erasure," or "white genocide."[24] This insistence on a conscious plan for ethnic substitution reflects the currents of grievance that define white reaction politics. The replacement narrative asserts that native-born white citizens are not simply experiencing far-reaching cultural shifts; rather, they are "losing their nation" because of prevailing currents of "antiwhite hatred" or "antiwhite racism." Far right forums persistently detail how white citizens are targeted for irrelevance, their children are taught to hate them, and their history is being erased in educational settings. In the formula often cited in white extremist circles, the "straight, white man" is the most oppressed member of contemporary liberal democracies—defamed for his identity, his beliefs, and his accomplishments. These various lines of argument come to a head for Jared Taylor, the self-described "white advocate" who heads the New Century Foundation, located in the United States: "What we are witnessing is one of the great tragedies in human history. Powerful forces are in motion that, if left unchecked, will slowly push aside European man and European civilization and then dance a victory jig on their collective grave. If we do nothing, the nation we leave to our children and grandchildren will be a desolated, third-world failure, in which whites will be a despised minority."[25]

It is this emphasis on the intentional aspect of demographic change that feeds the affectual core of the far right—the rage that attends this narrative of replacement. The narrative does not simply track shifting population trends; rather, it typically paints these changes in lurid terms designed to elicit anger toward a specified set of targets. Given the currents detailed above, much of the replacement literature is defined by rage against the elites who have ostensibly engineered the displacement of native-born subjects from the nation viewed as their birthright. As Patrick Buchanan, two-time former candidate for the Republican presidential nomination, asks, "Is it not treason to bring in foreigners, deceitfully, to swamp a people and dispossess them of their culture and country?"[26] That said, this fulmination against elites hardly exhausts the currents of rage that run through the far right politics of demographic fear. White reaction movements turn this anger against other prominent targets as well, including nonwhite, non-Christian populations, presented as usurpers of the nation that properly belongs to "legacy" (i.e., white) citizens. What defines the recent generations of immigrants, we are told, is that they have no wish or need to integrate into their new cultural landscapes. A staple of the narrative is that these immigrants worship their own gods, listen to their own music, and follow their own traditions. According to the ethnonationalist prime minister of Hungary, Viktor Orbán, these immigrants "don't speak our language, don't respect our culture, our laws or lifestyle and . . . want to exchange ours for their own."[27] One prominent example of this fear is the Islamophobic vision of a Europe overrun by specifically Muslim immigration—what has been termed the specter of "Eurabia" by the British far right author Bat Ye'or.[28] It is not just the scope of recent immigration, then, but also its supposed character that feeds the politics of demographic panic. As a result, these foreign-born inheritors of the nation become a lightning rod for xenophobic anger, fomented by a narrative that figures them as hostile invaders.[29]

The Rage in Question

A prevailing atmosphere of rage, then, defines the contemporary far right. Where other formations of the far right have dedicated themselves to rage over tax burdens, entitlement systems, or the expansion of the state, much of the rage that drives the contemporary far right stems from the organized perception of their displacement.[30] Although this book is rooted in the narrative of racial and ethnic displacement that is dubbed the Great Replacement, the rage of the far right spills well beyond the terrain of demography. Indeed, in the chapters that follow, I will periodically address how this narrative spawns much broader fears of replacement or erasure—for instance, the dislocation of maleness as the source of social and political authority. These overlapping fears are captured in a formula that circulates widely across the far right: there is an ongoing "war against white men" or a "war against white working-class men." The thread that links these categories is their representation as remnants of a disappearing age—they have all been pushed aside or "left behind" by a world that is increasingly globalized in economic, social, and political terms.

As a result, the character of this rage merits scrutiny. There is a wide literature on rage as a feeling that may have rich political utility.[31] This is a rage that arises from witnessing cruelty, the violation of moral norms, the breaking of bodies, or the abandonment of vulnerable populations.[32] Feeling here signals a rich set of moral commitments—an embodied reservoir of moral intuitions and lessons. This rage is what we *feel* in the face of patent injustice. The utility of this rage is not limited to judgment, however; it also undergirds movements for emancipation, driving people into the streets to confront unjust institutions.[33] This practical dimension reflects how the politics of rage must be situated in a landscape of power, in terms of its raced, gendered, and classed features. As the Black feminist Audre Lorde argues, for instance, anger can provide a rich set of practical potentials for those who have been silenced and disenfranchised by hierarchical distributions of power. For those who confront the indignities of racism and feel these injustices register in their everyday, embodied experience, anger is a justified response. It is the mode in which the oppressed experience a world that is designed to deny their equality. And this rage is a potential source of emancipatory energies. Not only is anger an "appropriate reaction" to racist attitudes and structures, Lorde notes, but when properly focused, "it can become a powerful source of energy, serving progress and change . . . a radical alteration in all those assumptions underlining our lives."[34]

The rage that occupies this book possesses a different character. The rage of replacement stems from the belief that one is entitled to a given set of goods and the aggrievement that results when these goods are no longer exclusively one's own.[35] This rage fixates upon changing social roles and hierarchies—what the political theorist Wendy Brown terms "the anger of the dethroned." The anger of the far right targets a world that has found increasing space for nonwhite narratives, values, histories, and practices. And ultimately, this rage mobilizes a politics dedicated to shoring up traditional hierarchies of power and the racial order that such hierarchies serve.[36]

As I will detail in the chapters that follow, this rage is not just expressed through a diffuse set of feelings that hang over the contemporary political scene. And it is not just stoked through a media ecosphere designed to remind its audience of all the ways they have been betrayed or abandoned by their own institutions. Rather, this affect binds its bearers in toxic forms of solidarity, animated by felt losses, resentments, and imagined adversaries. Further yet, this anger mobilizes action in the world, often against movements for civic and social equality. It is, in short, a *politics* of rage. The recent controversies over the purported teaching of critical race theory in American schools, for instance, reflect anxieties over a changing racial terrain and changing narratives surrounding the racial violence that has defined the United States from its inception. When a variety of schools introduced works into their curricula designed to address the nation's long history of white supremacy, this move was met with outrage by white parent groups (guided by well-funded think tanks and conservative activist networks) who decried these critical histories as "antiwhite indoctrination" or, more simply, "antiwhite racism."[37] Captured in video clips that were widely replayed on the social media circuit, parents disrupted meetings of their local boards of education to decry how their children were being "taught to hate whites" or to be "ashamed of their race." These orchestrated campaigns of racial anger encouraged a number of conservative-majority statehouses to pursue legislation constraining how history could be taught in public schools, what texts could be assigned, and the degree to which classroom conversations could address the ongoing reverberations of white supremacy.

The most notorious cases of replacement rage, however, have taken the form of racial violence carried out explicitly in reaction to the Great Replacement narrative. In March 2019, a white supremacist entered two different mosques in Christchurch, New Zealand, and killed fifty-one unarmed Muslims at their places of worship, wounding forty more. In August 2019, a white supremacist went to a Walmart in El Paso, Texas, for the express purpose of targeting "Hispanics." Upon arrival, he killed twenty-three people and injured twenty-three more. In 2018, a white supremacist entered a Pittsburgh synagogue during morning services. He killed eleven people and injured six more. And in May 2022, a white supremacist drove more than two hundred miles to a supermarket in Buffalo, New York, in order to target Black Americans. He killed ten people and injured three more. What connects these mass killings is that all of the shooters explicitly named the Great Replacement narrative as their inspiration, and all viewed their actions as justified responses to the perceived displacement of white population majorities. Across the manifestos left by these shooters, one theme rises to the top: a rage based in the belief that the shooter's nation was being taken from white natives and given over to more fertile nonwhite populations. The shooters likewise turned their rage toward fellow white subjects whose "weakness" or "cowardice" allowed their nations to be "taken" from them. The episodes noted above hardly exhaust the record. Recent years have seen a surge of violence by white extremists, many of whom have stated their aim to spark a race war, which they believe will bring about a reconstituted, majority-white nation.[38] As the following chapters will clarify, this violence cannot be viewed as the work of isolated, "lone wolf" actors, motivated by individual delusions or mental illness. Rather, these episodes stem from networks of rage, founded within narratives of racial grievance that are circulated within the cultural spaces and media ecology of the far right.[39]

One of the central interests of this book, then, is how the politics of demographic anxiety is tied to such episodes of racial violence. These concerns give rise to an interlocking series of questions: What are the fears and anxieties conjured up by the replacement narrative? How does the replacement narrative focus wide-ranging resentments on the distinct axis of race? What civic futures does this politics of rage open or foreclose? And what are the democratic and civic costs to this spreading narrative? As I will detail in the chapters that follow, many of the pathologies that define the contemporary far right stem from this constellation of race, nation, and futurity. More specifically, this politics of rage is rooted in the widespread insistence that the white nation (or the white race more broadly) no longer *has* a legible future, given the perceived assaults on its demographic majorities and cultural strongholds. The far right politics of demographic fear is thus defined by a rage against the present and the desire to recapture a mythic past in which whiteness supposedly held sway.

By asking these questions about race, nation, and violence, this book roots itself in the political work of narrative. Extremist reactions to demographic change are not, after all, unvarnished takes on population trends. Rather, these responses are shaped and directed by a story that gives a name, intelligibility, and direction to dynamics experienced in the world: a supposed "Great Replacement." According to the replacement narrative, population changes are the outcome of a design with one intention: the racial replacement of white majorities. For broad sectors of the far right, the effects of this process run considerably deeper. Once racial or ethnic replacement reaches sufficient velocity, they believe, the vitality of "white" or "European" culture will be lost. It is the power of this narrative, encapsulated in a simple formula, that has allowed this paranoiac worldview to circulate so widely and to spread across mainstream political culture. What might have otherwise been diffuse resentments over social change have crystallized into a formula that allows rage to be sustained and communicated through the right-wing media ecosystem. Significantly, the narrative allows the bearers of resentment to find one another through the extremist media ecology, affirm the rage they have been trained to feel, and direct this anger at the approved targets. Because of the replacement narrative, these subjects do not merely express individual, private resentments. Instead, white reaction politics channels a public economy of anger that is reinforced and magnified through network participation.[40] Thus, throughout the book, I follow scholars such as Ruth Wodak and Kurt Braddock to attend to the role of political narratives in shaping perception, delimiting imagination, and directing action.[41]

To address the questions noted above, the book's chapters move through a range of issues that define the far right's politics of demographic anxiety. The first, "'You Will Not Replace Us': The Melancholic Nationalism of Whiteness," is rooted in the psychodynamics that drive the narrative of the Great Replacement. Centering on the anxieties of loss that mobilize the contemporary politics of whiteness, the chapter makes two main arguments. The first is that the contemporary politics of whiteness must be understood as a melancholic politics—one forged by a narrative of loss and grievance. In this narrative, the nation is not simply changing at the demographic level; instead, it is framed as *taken* from the white subject to whom it properly belongs. The second argument is that this melancholic narrative helps to forge the subject of nationalist rage. The subject of white nationalism is a subject paralyzed by a fear of displacement and fixated on those groups and agents that have ostensibly taken the nation from the native. By extension, this is a subject who cannot think in terms of political futurity, but rather fixates on an imagined national past.

Chapter 2, "The Catastrophist Vision of the Far Right: Race War, Crisis, and Violence," pursues the guiding narrative of the Great Replacement in a different sense. Where the opening chapter highlights the psychodynamics that forge white rage, this chapter focuses on the violence embedded in the far right's catastrophist vision—where the present can be understood only as an unfolding disaster that demands extreme responses if the nation is not to be lost altogether. This narrative is tracked through a pervasive trope of the far right in which the present is defined not simply by demographic change but rather by an underlying ethnic or racial "war." The chapter shows how this discourse of war served as the ideological impetus behind recent acts of violence (e.g., the mass shootings at Christchurch, El Paso, and Buffalo) by figures seeking to inaugurate widespread conflict (and ultimately to redeem the white nation). Overall, the chapter argues that such spectacular acts of violence are both facilitated and prepared by the white replacement/genocide narrative. At its deepest level, this narrative roots conflict into the "nature" of racial relations and therefore forecloses the possibility of politics.

Chapter 3, "Metapolitics and Demographic Fear: The New Right's 'War of Ideas,'" takes a step back from the practice of white extremism to detail how the far right has expanded throughout civil society through what it describes as "metapolitics." Put briefly, the new right seeks political gains by transforming the symbols, vocabularies, and narratives that structure civil society and shape public opinion. The chapter pursues this line of cultural politics to address a specific object of anxiety on the far right: how large-scale demographic change is supposedly being engineered through the egalitarian ideals at the heart of liberalism. In response, figures of the far right hope to shift civil society toward ethnonationalist ideals by taking over the liberal vocabulary of equality and diversity. The chapter argues that this political strategy hollows out the normative substance of liberal values to justify the mandates for expulsion that have defined the far right. In doing so, this cultural politics seeds civil society with antiliberal ideals and commitments.

Chapter 4, "Visions of Escape: The Ethnostate and the Secessionist Dream of the Far Right," moves beyond the themes of the preceding chapters to explore the positive ideals that organize the far right imagination. Perhaps the far right's most notorious vision of the future is what has come to be known as the "ethnostate"—an ethnically homogeneous homeland. In the North American context, this dream of an ethnic homeland is rooted in the imagined racial bond of whiteness. As the chapter details, this political ideal must be situated within a longer secessionist tradition that informs the political imagination of the far right. For a wide variety of far right figures, the possibility of saving the "true nation" hinges on a secessionist impulse to craft new geopolitical spaces that can resist the population changes associated with globalization. The racial fears of the far right thus lead it away from libertarian-individualist ideals, in favor of a violent ideal of cultural and racial homogeneity. More ominously, the far right vision of the ethnostate reserves a strong role for the state that would carry out this "rebirth" of a racial nation, thus drawing from the political imagination of fascism.

Where chapter 4 pursues the secessionist impulse of the far right, chapter 5, "The Reproductive Politics of a Nice, White Nation: The Biopolitics of the Far Right," takes on the "natalist" imperative that drives the vision of the ethnostate. As various figures argue, establishment of the ethnostate will demand not only a moment of "purification" (i.e., the expulsion of "inharmonious" groups or populations) but also a forward-looking reproductive strategy; that is, reproductive rates must be stimulated in order to project an authentically "white" nation into the future. This imperative channels a longer history of panic in the far right over declines in the birthrates of Western liberal democracies (e.g., "race suicide," "demographic winter") and the meaning of these declines for "white" nations. By placing this project in dialogue with the literature on biopolitics, this chapter details both the violence of a racialized reproductive politics and the politics of gender that subtends much of the recent far right. As white supremacists have long argued, the path to save the nation rests on the "wombs of its women." Accordingly, the chapter details how the natal politics of the far right rests on a violent constellation of gender and reproduction that is hostile toward women's reproductive autonomy.

Finally, the book ends with brief concluding thoughts that chart the evolution of the replacement narrative, along with its abiding civic costs. As the replacement narrative continues to expand into new contexts, it serves to stoke the persecution complex that defines much far right literature: the belief that traditional social and political majorities are under attack by enemies who seek to take what is "rightfully" theirs. By placing white majorities in the position of victimhood, the replacement narrative fuels the dangerous politics of rage that has come to define the far right.

Before moving to the book proper, a quick note on terminology may be useful. Scholarship on white and nativist extremism is characterized by a wide range of categories and descriptors for the actors and groups in question. At the specifically political level, the taxonomy cycles through the far right, extreme right, and radical right. The scholarship on extremism points to white power, white supremacy, and white nationalist movements (among other things). There are important differences across these categories. For instance, the scholar of the far right Cas Mudde distinguishes between the far right and the extreme right on the basis of their stances toward basic democratic institutions—and whether they wish to discard democratic processes entirely to bring about their violent dreams.[42] The term that I use most often throughout this book is *far right*—largely to mark how the movements in question tend to embrace one of the most fundamental commitments of the far right: the rejection of human equality. As should be clear from this Introduction, this book is not intended to provide an exhaustive history of the far right; it does not trace the development of this political tradition or track the full range of its concerns.[43] The binding thread of this text is instead a more focused concern: how much of the far right in Europe and North

America has converged around one powerful narrative—that the most formidable threat facing cultures and nations in global times is demographic change, engineered by a broad variety of antagonists. This narrative of racial and demographic panic has achieved considerable organizing power throughout the right-wing thought ecology, from dedicated extremist forums to the legacy media to politicians on the highest electoral stages. Where other scholars might be keen to draw bright-line distinctions between various geographic schools of the far right, in this book I am more interested in how this narrative of demographic panic serves to unite various schools of the far right into something closer to a far right international.

There are undoubtedly narrower formulations I could have chosen to describe the book's central object. For instance, I could have opted for "the far right politics of white racial reaction" or "the far right politics of demographic fear." And in the following pages, where these more restrictive formulations are appropriate, I use them. These are, however, fairly unwieldy phrases, and their overuse would both bloat the text and tax the reader. For purposes of economy and readability, in the remainder of the book I typically refer simply to far right actors and movements.

CHAPTER 1

"YOU WILL NOT REPLACE US"

The Melancholic Nationalism of Whiteness

By now the details are well known. In August 2017, the eyes of the nation turned to Charlottesville, Virginia, where a variety of white nationalists and other far right organizations gathered for the "Unite the Right" rally. The rally was ostensibly organized to protest the removal of a statue memorializing the Confederacy, though the events quickly took an aggressive turn. Over the course of two days, clashes between protesters and counterprotesters occurred throughout the city, punctuated by cries of "White Lives Matter." These skirmishes culminated in the death of a counter-protester when a white supremacist drove his car into a crowd of bodies. But the scene that burned itself into the public imagination came on the opening night, when these angry white men gathered en masse, lit torches, and marched through the local university campus while chanting "You will not replace us" (and the anti-Semitic variant, "Jews will not replace us").

The central question addressed in this chapter stems from the infamous chant that came to define this episode. What anxieties are conveyed through this claim—that replacement is under way, something to be indicted or contested? The theme of replacing has, after all, long troubled observers of industrial modernity. Many critics have lamented the growth of "throwaway culture" and the seamless field of exchangeable objects, all rendered identical by a manufacturing apparatus that produces without distinction or variance. As Renaud Camus, the French author who popularized the replacement formula in his 2011 book *Le Grand Remplacement,* argues, "*Replacing* is the central gesture of contemporary societies. For better or worse, everything is being replaced by something else: something simpler, more convenient, more practical, easier to produce, more at hand, and, of course, cheaper."[1] This interchangeability characterizes not only the objects that roll off the assembly line but also the cultural icons that are reproduced in ever more places, torn from the historical or geographic milieus in which they originally appeared (e.g., the replica monuments that now appear in places such as Disney World and Las Vegas).

If these examples convey long-standing discomfort toward a society defined by mass production, they do not capture the rage that defined the "Unite the Right" rally, where angry men filled the streets to rail against a supposed process of social replacement. It was not replaceability as such that animated this demonstration, but rather the replacement of a specified *us* by a specified *them* within the space of the nation. According to a growing ethnonationalist literature, recent decades have seen a "Great Replacement" in liberal democracies, where immigration has produced a wholesale transformation in the nation's demographic characteristics. This is the phenomenon that the political scientist Eric Kaufmann describes as "whiteshift"—a process in which "white majorities absorb an admixture of different peoples" and are thus consumed by "an existential insecurity channeled by the lightning rod of immigration."[2] This analysis is regularly confirmed by the movement literature of demographic fear. In characteristically lurid terms, Camus argues that "the flow of migrants has taken such proportions that *immigration* has become a misnomer for what it is: it is more akin to an invasion, a migratory tsunami, a submerging wave of ethnic substitution."[3]

At one level, this rage against demographic change reflects currents of a resurgent nationalism. Even casual observers have noted that ethnic nationalism is on the rise across the globe, reflecting a wide set of anxieties over global modernity. In an age when national borders seem unable to stop the movement of bodies, the spread of pathogens, or the flows of capital, far right figures increasingly appeal to a traditional ethnic core as a bed-

Advertisement for the "Unite the Right" rally in Charlottesville, Virginia, August 2017.

rock of cultural stability.[4] Even when all other social bonds are thought to be disintegrating, the ethnonationalist commits to an organic basis for true community: an ethnicity or race that defines a given people at the brutely biological level.[5] The American alt-right writer Gregory Hood, for instance, argues that "race is the key building block of any real community and the farthest meaningful grouping to which we can give our loyalty."[6] In the European context, the French far right author Guillaume Faye argues that the heart of any coherent nation is its *germen*—its "biological identity," which underpins its expressions of culture.[7] Many such statements may seem to channel those populisms that have gripped the recent political imagination. When the material and cultural forces of the nation are perceived to be in crisis, the populist persistently answers by asserting the rights of the group that is ostensibly most under attack: the people.[8] And yet what distinguishes this brand of ethnonationalism is the composition of "the people" that rests at its heart. In this case, the people are defined not through an appeal to race or ethnicity in the abstract but as indelibly *white*.[9]

These appeals to whiteness hardly require demonstration. Indeed, in one multicultural nation after another, political and social change has been met with the reassertion of a distinctively white *ethnos*. There are ample instances of this reactionary racial politics—for example, Rick Tyler, a 2016 Tennessee candidate for the U.S. Congress, campaigned with the slogan "Make America White Again" (a nostalgic vision of racial history, conjuring a time when the nation was safe, trusting, and "in excess of 85% white").[10] This dynamic represents a noticeable shift in the social meaning of white identity, such that whiteness becomes more than the invisible set of expectations for social respectability—it is instead thematized and presented as a good to be celebrated.[11] This is the intuition that motivates the now-familiar exhortation to embrace "white pride" across the far right, as well as the more recent "It's OK to be white" meme campaign. The important question, then, is something like the following: Are these renewed appeals to a white nation an expression of an eternal white supremacy, or can they be historicized within the tensions, pressures, and material conditions of the present?

Though scholars have identified the threads that connect contemporary white extremism to the long history of white supremacy, this chapter will read these demands for irreplaceability as reaction formations toward perceived loss on the part of historically white majorities.[12] As the political scientist Juliet Hooker argues, "White grievance, particularly the inability to accept loss (both material and symbolic), continues to be the dominant force shaping contemporary racial politics."[13] This verdict reflects how the far right routinely frames the present through sentiments of loss or mourning. The pseudonymous author Wilmot Robertson, an American advertising executive who turned to a far right literary career, offers a symptomatic eulogy for the United States as an ethnically white nation: "As far as millions of Americans are concerned, their country has already passed into alien hands. All that is left to them is the remembrance of better times, some history."[14]

"Make America White Again." Advertisement for Rick Tyler's 2016 campaign for U.S. Congress from Tennessee. From RickTylerForCongress.com.

This chapter is devoted to unpacking the character, meaning, and political implications of this loss narrative. More specifically, it asks how the perception of loss has been mobilized and guided by the narrative of ethnic or racial replacement—and how this narrative produces a distinct public, bound by rage toward those thought to engineer or profit from demographic change. To pursue these questions, the chapter begins by approaching the iconic demand "We will not be replaced" as an effort by far right figures to preserve the historic privileges of white racial citizenship within a changing nation. As I will argue in subsequent sections, however, we cannot fully understand this politics of irreplaceability without exploring its underlying psychodynamics. It is not simply a situation of loss (whether real or imagined) that animates contemporary far right politics. Rather, it is necessary to recognize white grievance politics as a form of political melancholia in order to grasp its costs and pathologies.[15] This melancholic character is evinced, for instance, in the trope that defines much of the literature of white anxiety: the nation is not just slipping away from its racial core but is being *taken* from its rightful heirs and *given* to undeserving others. Stated differently, the narrative of white replacement does not simply target a process of change rooted in migration or labor flows; it is the story of a displacement enacted *against* a certain group for the benefit of others. The subject of whiteness is, accordingly, formed as the subject of melancholic rage. As I will go on to argue later in this chapter, however, the more fundamental pathology of this enraged, melancholic nationalism rests in how it forecloses the futurity essential to democratic politics.

The Whiteness in Question: The Politics of White Dominion

It may be useful to begin with some guiding questions: If the politics of white grievance is founded in perceived loss, then what sorts of attachments could mobilize these expressions of grief and rage? What, in short, is the threatened good of *whiteness* that motivates such rearguard projects of white reassertion? In the context of the United States, these questions cannot be understood apart from the American legacy of white settler colonialism, in which an imagined republic of liberty was historically predicated on the violent dispossession of Indigenous and Black populations. This linkage of freedom and subordination reflects what the legal scholar Aziz Rana terms the "two faces" of American freedom—a relationship that founds the right to white dominion upon the normative disqualification of the nonwhite.[16] The order of whiteness was not founded simply on a right to command; instead, it justified this right on the grounds that nonwhite populations lack the capacity to exercise their own autonomy. This grammar of domination found its foremost anti-Black articulation in the institution of chattel slavery, where racialized others were reduced to property, fungible objects to be used according to white desires and white pleasures.[17]

In broad terms, then, white racial formation is rooted in a field of power that naturalizes relationships of domination through the category of race.[18] To understand the abiding investment in whiteness as a structure of civic membership, however, it is necessary to track how white identification has been institutionalized to provide a wide-ranging set of civic benefits. In this connection, scholars have dedicated particular attention to the compensatory role of whiteness within the class structure that attended the U.S. slave economy—particularly for those white subjects who occupied a class world far from that of the wealthy planters of the U.S. South. In the face of these class divides, whiteness was not simply an abstract identity category distinguishing its bearer from nonwhite populations. Rather, it provided the grounds for full membership within the republic, thereby compensating for the status wounds of material inequalities. As the political scientist Joel Olson notes: "Poor English colonists came to identify themselves as 'white.' They shared this new identity with the planters, further elevating their status and self-esteem."[19] In the famous phrase of the philosopher and sociologist W. E. B. Du Bois, in the Reconstruction South, whiteness served as a kind of "psychological wage" that both compensated for material dispossession and foreclosed the possibility of class-based solidarities across racial lines.[20] The privileges that attended white identification were significant, ranging from "titles of courtesy" to a racial monopoly on public office to full access to public space (among other things). Moreover, historians have demonstrated that the political work of whiteness was hardly exhausted as a regional compromise within a particular historical moment. Indeed, the history of labor immigration to the United States has routinely reflected efforts by European immigrants to leverage their whiteness to facilitate social inclusion and secure political capital.[21] Migrants who began as "ethnics" (e.g., Germans, Italians, Irish) were eventually able to melt away these distinctions to integrate within a generalized whiteness and gain the benefits that attended that status.

Minimally, then, whiteness (as an axis of citizenship) is a *political creation* that has been misrecognized as a natural heritage, and this status has historically provided access to a range of goods within civil society. Accordingly, the benefits of white citizenship extend beyond a privileged status in civic life.[22] The symbolic advantages of white identification are redoubled by a legal organization that allots protections, liberties, and opportunities to white subjects while exposing populations of color to rightlessness, labor predation, and extrajudicial violence. Even in times of economic duress, these civic advantages have been amplified by a broad set of material benefits reserved for white citizens: preferential access to employment, legal rights for union organization, opportunities for wealth creation, and subsidies for homeownership (among other things).[23] For the legal scholar Cheryl Harris, this means that whiteness has historically provided a kind of "consolation prize" on the field of class—a guarantee that whites, even when suffering relative losses, will never sink to the social position allotted for Blackness.[24]

Major strains of the far right draw from this history of white racial citizenship to pursue a more aggressive politics of reaction: the effort to *claim* the nation as a white nation, even as demographic shifts erode white numerical majorities. Richard Spencer, the alt-right figurehead and onetime leader of the white nationalist National Policy Institute, voiced this position in a 2016 address at Texas A&M University: "Our bones are in the ground, we own it, and at the end of the day, America cannot exist without us. We defined it. This country does belong to white people, culturally, politically, socially, everything. We defined what America is."[25] This logic of dominion follows a line that recurs throughout the literature of the far right. Because the nation was shaped by white violence, white subjects assert an enduring claim to ownership, no matter the passage of time, civil rights gains, or shifting demographic tides. This is a vision of founding as possession, in which imagined authorship (and erasure of Indigenous claims to authorship) entails a permanent right to the nation.

The language of belonging pervades the ethnonationalist literature, though it often floats among a number of meanings.[26] On the one hand, these appeals signify a symbolic good—a claim to be "at home" in the nation.[27] In programmatic terms: "I belong in this civic space because it contains the traditions, beliefs, and cultures that have formed my identity, sensibilities, and aspirations. This nation is my ancestral home." On the other hand, the appeal to belonging shifts in meaning: the nation "belongs to me/us," which means that "I/we" have an enduring right to direct its resources and institutions. As the anthropologist Ghassan Hage unpacks the possessive logic of white supremacy, "The belief that one has a right over the nation, involves the belief in one's possession of the right to contribute . . . to its management such that it remains 'one's home.'"[28] This point reflects a more politically substantive vision of white ownership and a more visceral fantasy of loss within the politics of white reaction. An insistence on white irreplaceability reflects a claim to political supremacy, a right to manage the nation in accordance with white interests—to ensure white material advantage, to maintain white traditions, and to preserve a culture understood as meaningfully white. This right to order the nation is *owed* to the white citizen, regardless of how the demographic terrain of the nation is reshaped under conditions of globalization.

At this point, some questions can be posed. To insist on the irreplaceability of a historically dominant group is not simply to assert that group's essential role within a given nation's culture; rather, it is to claim that members of the group have a present and future right to shape the nation in accordance with their own interests. In making this claim, the politics of white dominion demands an enduring right to mastery that is contrary to core democratic ideals. The political theorist Danielle Allen has argued, in Aristotelian terms, that democratic practice is founded in a reciprocal process of ruling and being ruled, in turn. To engage in the activity of collective self-rule is not to be a figure of untroubled sovereignty whose own wants, needs, and preferences always win out. Pluralist nations are, instead, divided in terms of needs, interests, and values. This means that democratic citizenship just as often means a minority status—experiencing defeat on decisions concerning one's deepest commitments and inhabiting such disappointments against the promise of citizen rule.[29] Accordingly, a healthy democratic polity demands a certain virtue of its citizens: to endure these frustrations and allot them more equitably among the groups that share the nation.[30]

This ideal throws into relief some of the most obvious pathologies bound up with the far right politics of white reaction. Where democratic communities rely on a reciprocal process of citizen rule, a wealth of ethnographic and survey evidence demonstrates that the ethnonationalist position is founded on a twofold refusal: a refusal to acknowledge the pluralism of a democratic polity, coupled with a refusal to accept the guiding ideal of democratic equality. Within its zero-sum accounting of civic life, the far right views the gains of other groups as its own intolerable losses.[31] Further, white reaction movements persistently read efforts to repair historical wrongs or expand civic equality as evidence that the historical priority of whiteness is in a state of terminal decline.[32] It is this possessive, antipluralist calculus that motivates the far right's claim to white dominion, no matter the shifting demographic realities. Within the political imaginary of white supremacy, the alternative can only represent what the American paleoconservative politician and author Patrick Buchanan derides as "ethnomasochism"—a "disease of the heart" that would celebrate the disappearance of one's own group from the historical stage.[33] For the far right, the compliance of white majorities with their own decline ultimately reflects a will to die out.[34] Indifference to the prospect of a more diverse national population—or an unwillingness to defend a future for white nations—is condemned as a form of collective suicide.

From Loss to Rage: White Political Melancholia

Minimally, then, the ethnonationalist response to perceived replacement reflects a deeply antidemocratic, antipluralist vision. To assert a permanent claim to mastery is to substitute the historic privileges of racial citizenship for the demands of a democratic polity—particularly one shaped by demographic change. As I will detail in the remainder of this chapter, however, such a diagnosis is nevertheless incomplete, as it neglects the psychodynamics that drive replacement fears and the political pathologies that follow. For instance, it leaves out why so many across the far right attach so deeply to this racial logic of ownership and irreplaceability. And likewise, it passes over the visceral investment in this far right narrative of white dispossession. Indeed, a desire for political supremacy is hardly sufficient to account for the lurid fantasies of "white genocide" or "white extermination" invoked by those who fear that white populations will be dispossessed of their supposed inheritance.[35] Moreover, such a diagnosis is doubly inadequate to capture the disorientation and rage that define the politics of white reaction.

In the literature of demographic panic, there is no shortage of examples designed to highlight the racial and ethnic transformations unfolding in civic life—typically figured through the rhetoric of an immigration "invasion," "reverse colonization," or "genocide by replacement."[36] For some, the symptoms of replacement are evinced by the unfamiliar cultural forms that are inserted into public spaces or the displacement of holidays that previously enjoyed unquestioned cultural centrality.[37] For the political scientist Samuel Huntington, the symptoms of national erosion are found in the proliferation of non-English languages, the clustering of ethnic groups within residential microworlds (a process he describes in the militarized terms of ethnic "beachheads"), and the heightened presence of political symbols from other nations (flags, anthems, and the like).[38] Others see the primary signs of an ethnic "invasion" in the "occupation" of neighborhoods and public space by nonwhite populations—where the occupation takes the form of everyday crime and supposed antiwhite aggression.[39] For yet others, the true motor of cultural displacement rests in comparative rates of fertility and reproduction (a diagnosis that draws from long-standing currents of white racial anxiety over nonwhite reproduction).[40] For those who describe ongoing population change as a process of "white genocide" or "white extermination," the fundamental site of warfare is located within the enhanced reproductive rates of nonwhite populations, who have undertaken a slow-paced demographic transformation that will eventually enable them to capture both cultural and political institutions.[41]

These sorts of claims are staples of far right literature. Their power can be understood, however, only through an interrogation of the psychodynamics that lend them such force within the far right imagination. For instance, any reading that is limited to the political history of white supremacy would miss the atmosphere of loss that pervades far right discourse, feeding its tendencies toward rage and resentment. As the sociologist Arlie Hochschild argues, a fundamental grievance of radicalized whites is that the nation has become alien to them—it "no longer feels like their own."[42] Television news personality Laura Ingraham has given public voice to this story of alienation; speaking on the conservative Fox News network, she lamented that "in some parts of the country, it does seem like the America we know and love doesn't exist anymore. Massive demographic changes have been foisted upon the American people. And they're changes that none of us ever voted for and most of us don't like."[43] To grasp the force behind these lamentations, it is necessary to conceptualize the nation as more than a set of institutions that can fall into one set of hands or another. Rather, in this literature of estrangement, the nation takes on a distinct character. It is figured less as a geopolitical entity than as a source of meaning through which the subject understands itself—a horizon of practices and values in light of which the subject connects to a tradition it embraces as its own. And increasingly it is presented as a primordial site of identity that is besieged, slipping away from its "true" owners.[44] A recruitment video for the English chapter of the pan-European identitarian group Generation Identity stages these sentiments clearly. As the video displays a montage of images of national greatness, accompanied by swelling orchestral music, a voice-over intones: "You are descended from the builders of nations, from the greatest explorers, artists, inventors, and innovators the world has ever known. You are the sons and daughters, the heart, the soul, the living, beating culmination of your heritage. Are you really going to let it all just fade away?"[45]

This fear of loss is well illustrated by the zero-sum accounting of the replacement narrative. Simply put, much of the far right construes white displacement comparatively, in relation to *others*—more specifically, those groups that are ostensibly gaining while the white, native-born subject is losing (a decline typically linked to decades of economic restructuring, the loss of traditional manufacturing centers, outsourcing practices, and changes in the technologies of labor).[46] As the logic goes: *they* are on the rise, while *we* are displaced, ignored, and humiliated. And this displacement takes symbolic form, we are told, when the identity category of whiteness can no longer be asserted as a source of pride, even as all other identities are celebrated through commitments to diversity and multiculturalism. Instead, white subjects are supposedly taught to hate themselves, their racial history, and their traditions.[47] Accordingly, accounts of white replacement typically invoke a double loss. In a multicultural society, white subjects suffer not only the loss of material and political advantages but also symbolic denigration—within a "politically correct" landscape, the assertion of whiteness is met with derision, categorized as backward or racist. This narrative of displacement is not, however, simply a tale of relative gain or decline, indifferent to questions of agency. As Hochschild elaborates, the anger that animates many on the far right stems from a certain "deep story": the economic and social losses of the white subject cannot be reduced to the accidents of history or the unplanned consequences of economic globalization, nor is it merely that others are "cutting in line" for the status and benefits formerly reserved for "hardworking Americans" (itself a deeply racialized category); rather, these losses are engineered by elite decisions to promote other groups and cultures over the native white subject.[48] These losses are not simply losses, then, but *what has been taken from* the white subject and *given to* others. This narrative took particularly virulent form in the wake of the election of the first Black U.S. president, Barack Obama, who embodied a source of agency for what would otherwise have remained faceless shifts in the racial topography of power and privilege.[49]

Although these themes usefully illustrate the resentment that drives white reaction politics, they only begin to explore its orienting psychodynamics.[50] More substantive inroads can be made through the resources of psychoanalytic theory, where the subject is defined not through its mastery or sovereignty but rather in relation to a field of loss—the job one did not get, the parent who withdrew, the death that left one bereft, the lover who found another.[51] Perhaps most famously, Sigmund Freud offers that there are importantly different ways of understanding the experience of loss and how this experience shapes the subject.[52] In mourning, the subject undertakes a project of libidinal untangling, where the object can be reflectively understood as lost and new connections are enabled. This is a process of *working through* loss, so that the subject might invest its libidinal energies anew, forge new attachments, and become other than what it has been. In contrast, the melancholic subject is the one that cannot let go of the lost object. The wound of loss is instead interiorized into the ego so that the object, in its absence, becomes ever more central to the subject's identity.

Where this Freudian story begins in the therapeutic scene—the individual relationship between therapist and patient—scholars have expanded these resources to propose what might be termed melancholic *social* experiences. The literary theorist Seth Moglen, for example, calls attention to a form of melancholy associated with social trauma. What distinguishes social trauma is a broadened stage for understanding and feeling loss—specifically, its effort to grasp the responsibility or source of collective harm. Social melancholia is thus defined by its socially mediated character. Not only do collective losses typically stem from social processes and institutions, but this grief assumes a distinctly social presence as well. Specifically, social trauma turns upon a core demand: to identify the source of suffering—to develop public narratives that make this dispossession intelligible by identifying a culprit that has *done this to* the group in question.[53]

This turn to narrative sheds helpful light on the central trope of far right demographic politics: that a historically white nation is on the verge of being lost, handed over to others. This story of decline, familiar from far right forums, can be paraphrased in rough strokes: "We white natives, of a certain class, have suffered a series of losses that explain our degraded social position today. Not only have other (raced, gendered, ethnic) groups been promoted ahead of us, but we have also been deprived of opportunities to feel and assert pride in our own white identity. We have suffered losses that go unrecognized and unappreciated while other groups are celebrated. This country no longer resembles the land we were promised as our birthright. We are strangers in our own land."[54] It would be easy to read this narrative as a vernacular history of felt cultural decline. What is most noteworthy about this story, however, is the work that it performs in constituting subjects of whiteness as aggrieved, melancholic subjects. Such a reading is informed by the sociologist Jeffrey Alexander's argument that narrative is essential for constructing trauma as an enduring social form that can bind communities of shared suffering. It is only through publicly circulated "scripts about who did what to whom" that injury (whether real or perceived) can transcend the status of passing event, enter into social memory, and structure a group's "sense of who they are, where they came from, and where they want to go."[55]

The central script of white reaction politics, then, performs an important double duty. What is presented as a story of decline doubles as a narrative through which the far right subject is formed around the pathos of loss, now rendered in distinctly politicized terms—as the conscious endeavor of other groups.[56] In this story, the nation and its history are not just slipping away from the white subject but are rather *taken* by elites and given to undeserving others. This narrative shift from loss to displacement helps to explain the affectual reflex characteristic of the far right literature: a rage against those who have surpassed the white subject, as well as those political institutions and elites who facilitate the rise of these others. A poster distributed by the now-diminished white fascist organization Vanguard America (a major presence at the "Unite the Right" rally) puts this charge clearly, "YOU'RE LOSING YOUR COUNTRY, WHITE MAN! . . . The same people who buy out your government are using it to replace White Americans with migrants who will undermine your sovereignty and way of life."[57] This wording highlights the overlap of race and gender in what has become an increasingly intersectional story of persecution. The viewer is hailed not simply as white, or even as a white native, but specifically as a *white man*—a gendering of the addressee that reveals the gendered order of whiteness and the gendered character of replacement rage. As detailed earlier, the order of whiteness is not just a structure of hierarchy but also one of possession. In this structure, white *men* manage, possess, and direct the nation—what it is, what it has been, and what it will become. It is the white man who is to venture forth, shape the nation through his labor (itself enabled by the uncompensated work of women), and control it as his birthright. To believe that the nation is passing into the hands of others threatens not only a dream of belonging but also a gendered fantasy of control. And this loss of control reverberates most broadly for those shaped by the mythology and institutional structures of masculinity, in which the world is ordered by male decisions for male benefit.[58]

It is now possible to unpack more fully the meaning of the rallying cry of the far right: "You will not replace us." Important cues can be found in the grammar of the call that resounded in the streets of Charlottesville. The chant did not simply demand that a given "we" not be replaced (a formulation in which agency retreats into the passive voice); rather, it insisted that a specified "you" will not replace the "us" that properly defines the nation. The power of the slogan draws from its ambiguity. At one level, the rallying cry of white reaction casts the agent of replacement in explicitly anti-Semitic terms—Jewish elites, enacting policies to erode white cultural and demographic majorities.[59] Here it is significant that the demonstrators at Charlottesville periodically revised the chant to fill in the indeterminate "you" with a more specific subject: "Jews will not replace us." This version of the slogan demonstrates the polemical fiction of "the Jew" within the white extremist literature—the agent of "globalism" working to destroy the nation in favor of transnational loyalties, abstract circuits of capital, and global institutions (themselves ostensibly controlled by Jewish interests).[60] These anti-Semitic currents help connect the discourse of white replacement to long-standing fears of a "white genocide." In one of the central tenets of the racialist far right, ongoing demographic changes represent generations of design by Jewish elites, who have supposedly devised a far-reaching plan to undermine majority-white nations.[61] And yet the full resonance of this slogan can be appreciated only if the "you" is read in yet another sense, also drawn from the far right literature. This "you" is not the imagined source of replacement policies, but rather the amorphous set of agents who are ostensibly displacing white males as the privileged national subject (e.g., feminists, liberals, nonwhites, Muslims, multiculturalists, globalists, corrupt political elites, and cosmopolitans of all stripes), all the while promoting a discourse of "diversity" through which this displacement is celebrated.[62]

If the resentments and anxieties at the heart of this slogan are now legible, what remains to be explored are the distinct politics of a melancholic nationalism. To do so is to confront both its torsions and its political costs.

YOU'RE LOSING YOUR COUNTRY,

WHITE MAN!

DEMOCRACY HAS FAILED YOU

Corrupt and bought out politicians have sold out your homeland to Third World immigrants, and globalist corporations. They did all this without a vote, without a referendum. Democracy has failed you, and your people. It will soon fail America as a whole.

YOU ARE BEING REPLACED

The same people who buy out your government are using it to replace White Americans with migrants who will undermine your sovereignty and way of life. People are used and thought of as nothing more than units of production to the corporate elite that has betrayed you.

ONE QUARTER OF MEXICO'S POPULATION HAS RELOCATED TO THE U.S.

- ILLEGAL IMMIGRATION COSTS THE US $6.3 TRILLION ANNUALLY
- THE WHITE PERCENTAGE OF AMERICA IS AT AN ALL TIME LOW AT 63% AND DROPPING
- SINCE 1940, TEXAS' WHITE POPULATION HAS DROPPED 25%, AND IS FALLING EXPONENTIALLY

- AFRICANS WILL MAKE UP 40% OF THE WORLD'S POPULATION BY 2100, WITH WHITES AT ONLY 9%

EVERY RACE DESERVES A NATION. WHITES ARE NO DIFFERENT. FIGHT BACK AGAINST THE SYSTEM THAT HAS NEGLECTED YOU FOR SO LONG. WHITE AMERICA NEEDS A VANGUARD. FIND US AT BLOODANDSOIL.ORG

Poster from the Vanguard America organization, challenging the "replacement" of white Americans at the hands of "corrupt politicians" and "globalist corporations."

The Pathologies of a Melancholic Politics

Other scholars have approached social movements through the framework of melancholia.[63] The art historian Douglas Crimp, for instance, identifies melancholia as a factor that inhibits queer movements in their efforts to mobilize against violence and abandonment.[64] The psychoanalysts Alexander and Margarete Mitscherlich famously characterize the melancholy of postwar Germany, where the shame of National Socialism was too quickly sidestepped in favor of national pride.[65] And in the closest parallel to current concerns, the British social theorist Paul Gilroy diagnoses nativist resentment toward multiculturalism as a token of Britain's "postcolonial melancholia"—that is, an inability to own up to the violence embedded within the nation's colonial past.[66]

The distinctiveness of white racial melancholia can be recognized, however, through an interrogation of what undergirds the fear of replacement. It would be easy to identify a white or Anglo nation as the object in a state of perceived loss—the love object no longer under the subject's control. This loss yields the rage of humiliation, where the beloved shares with another what once exclusively *belonged* to the subject. In narratives of white replacement, however, the good that is threatened is more fundamental to the meaning of white racial citizenship: the loss of a social order where whiteness functions as an entitlement to social goods. From this point, it is possible to cast the rage of white reaction in more substantive terms.[67] When the melancholic nationalist rages over a nation in a state of loss, they rage over something more than the loss of political sovereignty or cherished traditions. Rather, this subject targets the loss of those cultural conditions under which whiteness yields the status to which they have historically been entitled. The sociologist Michael Kimmel describes this outrage as a situation of "aggrieved entitlement." As he puts it: "It is that sense that those benefits to which you believed yourself entitled have been snatched away from you by unseen forces larger and more powerful. You feel yourself to be the heir to a great promise, the American Dream, which has turned into an impossible fantasy for the very people who were *supposed* to inherit it."[68] The core grievance of white reaction movements is thus rooted in the organized perception of unfairness—what you (the white subject) were *owed* has been snatched away. Likewise, this narrative of white dispossession does not simply translate into grievance over the loss of entitlement; further yet, it encourages rage toward the perceived authors of this displacement. As a staple of the narrative, these "enemies of whiteness" have transformed not only the racial hierarchy of white dominion but also the norms and languages through which white losses can be memorialized as losses (e.g., the characteristic far right scorn toward discourses of equality, diversity, and multiculturalism).[69]

It is for this reason that far right figures persistently invoke a language of indigeneity and colonization. The aim is to place their own fortunes in analogy to the forced displacement, humiliation, and violence suffered by Indigenous peoples under settler colonialism. Jared Taylor, the American head of the white nationalist New Century Foundation, makes this link explicit in detailing the ostensible threats posed to white majorities by immigration and diversity policies. According to Taylor, the analogy is clear: just as the European colonization of North America was a catastrophe for the Indigenous peoples of the continent, mass immigration today yields catastrophe for historic white majorities. And just as the Indigenous peoples were justified in fighting to preserve their way of life against European settlers, so are white populations justified in fighting to preserve their way of life against immigration, integration, and multiculturalism.[70] This claim to justified resistance is a widely shared trope across the far right. By foregrounding the immigration-based "threat" to white culture, white reactionaries attempt to compare their losses to the cultural devastation faced by Indigenous peoples under colonial rule.[71] Even a superficial approach to the historical politics of whiteness, however, demonstrates that it is grotesque to claim a moral equivalence between these two situations, or to analogize white racial melancholy to the historical trauma of the colonized.[72] Though the politics of white rage persistently invokes a situation of loss, what it laments goes well beyond the possibility of losing a recognizably "white" life (presented as a matter of culture, distinct from questions of power). To revisit a point detailed above, it is racially inscribed advantage (i.e., a claim to deserve *more*), founded within symbolic and material power, that forges the historical meaning of whiteness in the American context.[73]

And yet, within the prevailing narratives of white reaction, this position of advantage is often figured as pride in a cultural identity, detached from any expectations of enhanced power, resources, or standing. Instead, the movement literature persistently encourages white subjects to "feel white pride" or "celebrate the achievements of your people." Although it is tempting to diagnose this oversight as a simple instance of bad faith, the difficulty may be rooted more deeply within racial hierarchies of power. The philosopher Charles Mills, for instance, has proposed that this misrecognition reflects the "inverted" epistemology characteristic of white dominance.[74] Where white reaction movements explicitly demand the preservation of traditions and culture, the appeal rests on an incapacity to recognize the histories of domination through which this subject enjoys its identity as status. This compromised historical knowledge helps to explain one of the hallmarks of melancholic nationalism: an inability to come to terms with the violence that forged its pathways of material and symbolic benefit. As Mills proposes, this form of racial power "produc[es] the ironic outcome that whites will in general be unable to understand the world they themselves have made."[75] Within this distorted economy of knowledge, the historical violence that forged and maintained the privileges of whiteness does not rise to the level of "productive shame"; instead, this violence remains unavowable within far right narratives of white accomplishment or white pride.[76] Structures of white racial advantage are misrecognized as deserved, merited solely through individual or group initiative. Even when histories of domination are noted, these episodes are assigned to the distant past, construed as the sins of long-dead forefathers, severed from the presentist lens for calculating moral or political culpability.[77] Above all, the far right literature enjoins white subjects to refuse guilt for histories of racial violence, and instead to embrace their white identity as a source of pride. This line of argument is well represented by the New Century Foundation's poster campaign featuring messages instructing white subjects to "never apologize" for histories of white violence, but instead to "love who you are."

To account fully for the melancholic character of this politics, however, it is necessary to press further into its iconic demand ("You will not replace us"). The political legacy of this formula rests in the future tense of the appeal: that the dominance of the white subject *must be carried into the future,* no matter the demographic and cultural shifts that are under way in the nation. To flesh out this imperative, the politics of white reaction pursues a variety of projects. For some, the perceived crisis demands a project of restoration (e.g., to return to the immigration protocols of previous generations). For others, it demands "natalist" policies to bolster the reproductive rates of white populations, to keep pace with the reproduction of ethnic competitors.[78] And for yet others, it calls for the establishment of a white "ethnostate": a monumental effort of social engineering that would involve "repatriating" nonwhites to their nations of heritage or to competing ethnostates.[79] In this connection, no small effort has been dedicated to delineating the locations and constituencies of these racialized territories (e.g., Northwest Territorial Imperative, New Albion, Ozarkia) within a partitioned national geography.[80] I will address each of these projects at length in upcoming chapters. What rests at the heart of this melancholic nationalism, however, is a desire to "return" to a mythic past in which white culture ostensibly had its meaning and place. The subject of white anxiety does not simply inhabit a framework of loss in the abstract; rather, this subject is defined by the melancholic identification with the lost object and the related demand to restore that attachment so that it can be whole again.[81]

This insistence on racial indispensability sheds light on the core pathology of white reaction politics: a refusal of the futurity that is essential to politics. To recall the psychoanalytic resources introduced above, the crucial distinction between mourning and melancholia is not simply whether one has suffered loss or has come to terms with the ongoing reverberations of trauma within the present. Rather, the distinction reflects diverging relationships to temporality and political imagination. Mourning represents a mode of *working through* the experience of loss so as to enable different investments in the future. In contrast, the melancholic failure to work through loss yields a fundamental inability to live in the present as a field with its own constraints and possibilities.[82] In Jeffrey Prager's pithy formulation, "Melancholia disables individuals from living currently."[83] Reading contemporary white nationalism as a form of aggrieved melancholy thus reveals a wider range of its political pathologies. Many observers have noted how far right movements are founded in hatred, anxiety, and resentment—often masked by assertions that ethnonationalist projects are actually motivated by the deepest possible "love of our own people."[84] What too often goes unacknowledged, however, is how the psychodynamics of melancholia cut these nationalist movements off from a politics that would mobilize new solidarities to forge new, common futures.[85] Instead, the politics of white reaction is essentially revanchist, seeking to return to a time when white interests held sway in the nation and this hegemony could be enjoyed as a birthright, insulated from challenge.[86] And, for segments of white reaction politics, this drive is equipped with a willingness to engage in violence in order to regain this lost golden age.

The Material Resonance of White Melancholia

To this point, this chapter has tracked how the Great Replacement narrative focuses on a major current of far right rage. At the heart of the narrative rests one insistence: that the demographic and cultural shifts unfolding across the global North are part of an extended project to displace white majorities and strip them of their political birthright. This story serves a variety of aims as it expands through civil society. Minimally, it facilitates a cognitive grasp of vast causal processes and lends them a simplified, coherent order. The framework translates broad-scale population changes into terms that allow a politicized vision of confrontation. This is a story with clear villains ("globalist" elites and their multiculturalist standard-bearers) and victims (white subjects, particularly white males, described as the group that is "most discriminated against" in multicultural societies). By framing social change in these terms, the narrative ultimately helps forge an antidemocratic public whose members are bound by rage against their imagined adversaries.

For many observers of the far right, the core question is how the white political imagination could be diverted from the antipolitics of melancholic fixation driven by a desire for white dominion. There is no shortage of proposals in the literature. For instance, Juliet Hooker contends that if democratic nations are to live up to their egalitarian commitments, "white citizens will need to accept the loss of political mastery. They will have to accept being ruled in turn."[87] Others have proposed an "abolitionist" approach that calls on white citizens to "abandon" their whiteness and dismantle institutional arrangements that treat whiteness as a basis for entitlement, status, and power.[88] These proposals address important features of white grievance politics, and the abolitionist approach has evolved into an important, wide-ranging movement for civic equality. As the discussion in this chapter has demonstrated, however, any effort to contest the destructive politics of white rage must engage the forms of political subjectivity forged by loss, the narrative construction of white victimhood, and the politics that stem from the stunted imagination of melancholic rage. To fail to grasp these currents is to miss the depth of the far right's *investment* in white grievance and how deeply this rage is rooted in the civic landscape.

At its heart, replacement discourse figures the white subject as the target of an aggressive campaign—stripped of its birthright, its nation, and its future.[89] Within this framework, a changing nation can only be experienced as a pure loss that yields rage against perceived adversaries and a desire to reclaim an idealized past. This politics of nostalgia is well illustrated by an episode noted earlier: Rick Tyler, the candidate for national office who depicted his racialized nationalism ("Make America White Again") as a return to Norman Rockwell's America—safe, trusting, and whole.[90] And this trope is more broadly reflected in the white nationalist literature that points back to a mythic time when the nation was truly unified, shared a core set of civic values, and committed itself to a shared purpose.

To concentrate solely on these appeals to culture and identity, however, would undersell the full tug toward white melancholia. As detailed earlier, the historic benefits of whiteness go well beyond symbolic or status rewards. Whiteness has historically come with access to a wide variety of material securities (e.g., guarantees of employment, industry rights to union organization, subsidies for education or homeownership). These guarantees undergird the mythology of the "white workingman"—the one who provides for his (nuclear) family through "self-making" initiative (a form of "self-making" that is underwritten by a wide variety of race-based subsidies).[91] And yet this racialized structure of economic advantage has been profoundly disrupted in neoliberal times. Decades of economic restructuring, technological change, outsourcing of labor, union declines, and job loss have eroded many of these guarantees for large sectors of the white working and middle classes. Increasingly, white workers find themselves in situations of material precarity from which they were previously sheltered. And their promised avenues to a stable future are increasingly experienced as closed off. Recent investments in the retrenched politics of whiteness, then, become more fully legible by accounting for the material conditions of the neoliberal present. As the sociologist Daniel Martinez HoSang and the political scientist Joseph Lowndes have helpfully argued, the fixation on loss that characterizes white reaction politics can productively be read "as reaction to the declining guarantees that whiteness has provided."[92] From this perspective, one pathway to white melancholia is staunchly material: the felt loss of those protections that buffered white workers from the full brunt of economic exposure.

This is not to say that far right energies are reducible to economic grievances, as many commentators argued in the wake of Donald Trump's 2016 presidential election victory.[93] Indeed, fully separating material from racial considerations would miss how economic practice is already a racialized space that has historically structured access, exploitation, and benefit along racial lines.[94] Furthermore, any such antiseptic divide would also miss how experiences of white economic precarity are routinely processed through far right narratives that assign responsibility to nonwhite groups, who have supposedly inherited the jobs that once furnished access to white security and respect.[95] These economic considerations instead highlight the richly materialist dimension to white melancholic politics when it demands a return to a time of past national greatness. Along with its desire for a time of unchallenged white culture, it seeks to recapture the material *world* that whiteness previously provided—a set of institutions that subsidized white security and advancement.

These material impulses are reflected in how the politics of white reaction focuses so intensely on the material infrastructure of memory—those monuments and architectural works that memorialize a time when whiteness was the unquestioned cultural medium and the pinnacle of the racial hierarchy (e.g., the near obsession with the monuments of the American Confederacy).[96] Recall that the infamous "Unite the Right" rally was organized around the planned removal of a Confederate monument—specifically, a statue of Robert E. Lee, the lead general of the Confederate Army. Opposition to the removal turned on the charge that it was designed to erase the memory of the American South (a linguistic proxy for a distinctly white national heritage). In the aftermath of the rally, President Donald Trump weighed in with a characteristic nod to white grievance politics: "They're trying to take away our culture. They're trying to take away our history."[97] In the eyes of the far right, such monuments are more than odes to a shared past or even memorials to a way of life. These statues are tangible remnants of a bygone culture, a white order that was celebrated without shame or fear. In the terms of neo-Confederate thought, these monuments represent the nobility of a different way of life, defined by the customs and agrarian gentility of the Old South. This effort to elide the racial violence of the Confederacy is central to the "Lost Cause" narrative that whitewashes the violence of slavery and instead portrays the Civil War as a noble fight to defend states' rights.[98] In the far right imagination, these material structures do something more than mourn a lost set of traditions. They allow the racial values of the Confederate South to live on in spectral form. And, in doing so, they authorize dreams of a different way of life, where supposed natural hierarchies were observed and whiteness sat at the pinnacle of the social order.[99]

The fixations of white reaction politics are thus rooted in a broad field of felt losses where symbolic, cultural, and material factors overlap. Outspoken fears of racial replacement speak to demographic changes that are unfolding across the global North—though they resonate with a wider range of privileges and protections that are perceived to be slipping away from those who view the nation as their birthright. What is grieved is the multivariate *order* of whiteness that historically protected and rewarded white subjects. And it is the replacement narrative that purports to make sense of these losses, by synthesizing them into a simplified story with clear plotlines, interests, and antagonists. It is not just that material insecurity has scrambled expectations of a legible future, or that public spaces now resonate with multiple, unfamiliar languages. Rather, these civic changes are depicted as a violent process of dispossession and betrayal. In this story, it is the dark-skinned other, aided by treacherous elites, who is taking the nation, eroding its culture, and claiming the material security previously reserved for the bearers of whiteness. And for the melancholic imagination, it is only by *getting these goods back* that the white subject (and the broader white world) can be whole again.

Accordingly, the remaining chapters focus on a number of interests. Most urgently, what are the consequences and implications of this politics of melancholic rage? What forms of politics follow from this narrative of rage and the communities it creates? By the end of the book, these questions will be joined by two others that speak to possible civic futures: Are narratives of loss available that would not end with a revanchist effort to recapture an idealized "golden age"? Could such a narrative yet be imagined?

CHAPTER 2

THE CATASTROPHIST VISION OF THE FAR RIGHT

Race War, Crisis, and Violence

> White America stands on the cusp of oblivion, of annihilation in the most literal sense; it is no hyperbole to state that the white race is facing extinction—not just demographic conquest and dispossession, not just humiliation, discrimination, and civil rights abuses, but extinction, with all of the violence which that word evokes.
>
> — *Neil Kumar, "White Identity Nationalism, Part 1," May 25, 2022*

Far right forums regularly obsess over preparations for widespread social collapse—what they often refer to as SHTF (when the "shit hits the fan"). At times, the acronym is meant to signal the collapse of the economy as a result of market crashes or currency instability. At other times, it stands for civic breakdown caused by misgovernance, social polarization, or a catastrophic pandemic event. At their most hectoring, these dreams of civic chaos stoke widespread fears about a "second civil war"—a topic that has been breathlessly distributed by the popular political media.[1] Indeed, nearly every major political controversy (e.g., Covid vaccine mandates, gun control regulations, the criminal indictment of Donald Trump) is met in the forums with predictions that *this* will be the precipitating factor to shift the nation's "cold civil war" into outright conflict.

In sum, it would be difficult to ignore the apocalyptic tone that defines recent political discourse. And this theme looms with particular prominence over the recent conservative imagination. The resurgence of interest in archconservative philosophers such as Oswald Spengler, René Guénon, and Julius Evola, for instance, reflects a vision of history as decline—a story in which the wisdom of the past or the vitality of culture has fallen into grave danger.[2] This is the situation that Evola describes as "men among the ruins," where the faithful lack the guidance of tradition and thus abide in a state of radical disorientation.[3] What defines much far right thought, however, is not simply a pessimism about the present but a foreboding sense of disaster that threatens to destroy peoples and cultures. In short, this is a political literature defined by the narrative form of catastrophism.[4]

To illustrate, it will be useful to begin with the vision of culture war that hangs over the contemporary political landscape. Indeed, even the phrase "culture war" suggests a catastrophic framing of cultural differences, in which shifts in civic culture are viewed not simply as representing changing mores or beliefs, but rather as a kind of existential battle fought to promote certain values while eliminating others. It is for this reason that the conservative literature on culture war so persistently takes a militaristic tone. It is only by recognizing the values at stake, we are told, that "true defenders" of the culture will be able to slow civic corrosion, retake the cultural ground, and preserve the traditions that properly define the nation.[5] This imperative tracks with what the writer and filmmaker James Davis describes as the distinction between "disease" and "cure" catastrophism. On the one hand, a catastrophist lens depicts the present as a time defined by pathology or degeneration—an ongoing disaster that has, to this point, gone unnoticed or underappreciated. On the other hand, catastrophe offers the opportunity for "cure." In this moment when the established order is unsettled, new possibilities may arise to halt the process of decay. It is by recognizing and acting on these possibilities that the nation might yet be saved or repaired. While the conservative literature often pushes tropes of renewal or preservation, the catastrophist lens of the far right yields a more antagonistic approach to resolving the perceived cultural crisis—one in which, in Davis's words, "enemies are confronted and vanquished in a final apocalyptic conflagration."[6]

Recent developments have pushed this supposed crisis into more fraught terrain.[7] Most clearly, a dominant strain of the far right tracks the most urgent crisis for liberal democracies below the level of ideologies and beliefs, to changes in the "demographic stock" of nations. Patrick Buchanan, the American paleoconservative and two-time candidate for the Republican presidential nomination, for instance, argues that the decline in reproductive rates across Western democracies portends a "death" of these nations as coherent forms of life: "First World nations are dying. They face a moral crisis, not because of something that is happening in the Third World, but because of what is not happening at home and in the homes of the First World. Western fertility rates have been falling for decades."[8] The "death" of nations is thus presented as twofold in cause. Not only have reproductive rates declined across advanced industrial nations, but this situation has also led these nations to suffer an influx of migration that is fundamentally changing their demographic character. The catastrophe thus exceeds an abstract decline in numbers and reflects a process in which historic majorities are being threatened by the rise, expansion, or arrival of others. This vision of displacement quickly gives way to more hyperbolic renderings that paint demographic change as an existential threat to white populations. To shift to the European context, the French far right author Guillaume Faye argues that recent immigration policies have produced an "ethnocide" against white majorities, amounting to "the destruction of a people through . . . progressive immigrational flooding; the destruction of one's cultural identity and historical memory; repressive measures; spoliation; and, last but not least, the relegation of the indigenous population to a lower status."[9]

Such references to ethnocide or genocide are hardly rare in the far right politics of demographic "replacement." Indeed, they reflect the central role of conflict within this narrative of population change. Essential to replacement discourse is a theme that has fueled the resurgence of nativist currents across Europe and North America: the insistence that these demographic shifts represent the deepest front in a war between cultural and ethnic groups under conditions of globalization. This "replacement" is depicted as a violent dispossession that has reached the current point of crisis because the displaced population has been largely blinded to the fact that it is occurring.[10] Figures within the far right argue that these developments have been masked under the guises of multiculturalism and diversity—values used to obscure (or even celebrate) the violence of ethnic substitution.

While the opening chapter addressed how the Great Replacement narrative helps to forge a subject of rage, this chapter pushes the dangers of this narrative in a different direction. First, I will situate far right appeals to a "demographic war" within a longer tradition that casts social conflict in distinctly racial terms (i.e., "race war"). After detailing how the politics of demographic panic both overlaps with and diverges from these earlier models of race war, I will elaborate how the far right political imagination increasingly presents extreme action as the path to racial and political redemption. Ultimately, one point will come to the fore by the end of this chapter: this far right conflict narrative yields a dangerous foreclosure of politics—one that reduces possibilities for democratic negotiation and instead trends toward a violent ossification of social conflict.

The Political Imagination of Race War

The linkage of population, war, and crisis is not without precedents. Perhaps most relevant for the American far right is the discourse of race war that has long haunted the United States as a racial polity. Narratives of racial supremacy played a central role in shaping the nation's imperialist imagination and crafting a racialized space of citizenship. The racial imaginary of the United States originated in a belief in the profound racial *difference* of Black slaves and Indigenous peoples—a difference that was used to justify colonial campaigns of violence and extermination.[11] This ideology of racial hierarchy was, moreover, instrumental to the order of whiteness that forged the United States as a racial state, organized around white needs, white power, and white benefits. This structure of racial dominance was hardly untroubled, however. It was plagued by anxieties over its undoing, particularly fears concerning the threat of slave insurrections.[12] For the racial imagination of the United States, the specter of uprising was fundamentally filtered through the fear that Black and Indigenous people would refuse their subordination and take arms against a violent racial order. Such an insurrection would upend not only an agrarian economy built on slavery but also the broader social order based in white supremacy.

These historical fears of racial insurgency are central to replacement thought, though far right figures also draw from a parallel lineage that evokes the wellsprings of European fascism. Michel Foucault, the French social theorist, observes how a framework of race war fundamentally shaped the fascist approach to nationhood. As he argues, their concern for war exceeds familiar Hobbesian presumptions, where the law of the sovereign puts an end (if provisional) to the ceaseless struggle of self-interested individuals. Instead, "beneath the law, war continues to rage in all the mechanisms of power, even in the most regular. . . . We are therefore at war with one another; a battlefront runs through the whole of society, continuously and permanently, and it is this battlefront that puts us all on one side or the other."[13] Minimally, this argument offers a stark challenge to models that view societies as systems of cooperation or consensus. Instead, society is figured as a collection of inharmonious groups struggling for social primacy. And if the theme of war casts a long shadow over modern political thought, Foucault marks an important shift in these antagonisms—one where the underlying war is conducted at the level of race. Within the fascist worldview, this struggle is conducted not over territory, power, or wealth, but over the fundamental determination of *who* exactly constitutes a given people and what racial composition will enable this people to actualize its destiny.

This fascist narrative of war accordingly casts its eye on racial differences rooted within the body politic. The enemy, in this story, is a biological potential—the hidden presence of racial influences that might spread through the body politic and corrupt the genetic inheritance of the nation.[14] As Foucault argues, these racial anxieties help to explain the violence endemic to fascist projects of nation building. Because the nation was supposedly in the grips of an internal, biological war, fascist regimes aimed to eliminate those elements that would pollute the ethnic or racial core of the nation "proper." To this end, fascist programs of "racial hygiene" *(Rassenhygiene)* attempted to prune or excise "lower" racial strains so that the body of the nation (now dedicated to the "superior" race) could flourish.[15] As Foucault concludes, this politics of "permanent purification" explains the central role of racism for fascist programs of population management—where race was used to distinguish those lives that belonged in the nation proper from those "lesser" or "degenerate" lives that had to be eliminated for the nation to be protected from elements that could threaten it from within.[16]

Though brief, the above discussion helps to clarify how replacement narratives both borrow and diverge from these classic visions of racial conflict. To begin, it is necessary to attend to the location of the perceived threat. Where the fascist imaginary fixates on a threat of impurity from within (i.e., an "internal" source of racial pollution),[17] the far right politics of demographic fear fulminates against global movements of labor and migration that are changing nations across Europe and North America. Guillaume Faye, for instance, describes the present state of immigration as "a massive colonisation by alien peoples, which makes it the greatest tragedy in [Europe's] history, because it threatens to destroy her ethnic stock."[18] And the American alt-right figure Richard Spencer claims: "It isn't just a great erasure of white people. It isn't just an invasion of Europe, an invasion of the United States by the third world, it is ultimately the destruction of all peoples and all cultures around the globe."[19] Accordingly, contemporary renderings of an ongoing racial war must be situated within the anxieties of a globalized time. The nation, in this reading, is not a sovereign actor, asserting its strength on the global stage; rather, it is subjected to transnational forces and breached by a flow of outsiders.[20] As a result, European and North American nations are inundated by "invaders" who fill public spaces with their own languages, symbols, holidays, and cultures. And the depth of this crisis is magnified by the supposed betrayal of "collaborationist" elites who enact permissive immigration policies to benefit multinational corporations at the expense of their own citizens.[21]

To grasp the scope of this crisis narrative, it is necessary to distinguish the multiple registers of the disaster that it portrays. At one level, the catastrophe is rooted in a story of population mixture, where heightened immigration erodes cultural integrity by "flooding" a nation that was previously defined by a coherent set of values, symbols, and practices. This outcome is what the American white nationalist Greg Johnson terms the problem of "habitat loss" for native-born white subjects, thus fusing nativist politics with an ecological discourse (a fusion that has come to characterize "ecofascist" movements across the far right).[22] At another level, however, many who invoke the Great Replacement target developments that exceed the comparative sizes of group populations. This crisis goes beyond the supposed flood of cultural newcomers to fasten upon the reproductive mixture of native and nonnative populations. Here, the discourse of invasion evokes the central fear of fascist race thought: the slow, internal transformation of the "demographic stock" that is thought to define a given nation. Pierre Krebs, the leader of Germany's far right Thule-Seminar, argues that the admixture of populations augurs the "biological implosion" of a given people. As he describes this process (channeling the anthropologist Ilse Schwidetzky): "'The foreign hereditary stock which now circulates in the new organism acts henceforth on the genotype of the mongrelised people at the physical and psychological levels.' . . . Unlike a colonised people who can return to their roots as soon as they free themselves from the foreign yoke, a mongrelised people are a genetically manipulated people that no longer have any roots."[23] These anxieties are based in the far right's persistent tendency to negotiate national and cultural identity through biological terms. The logic can be stated simply: if a people (understood as a unified cultural entity) has its roots in common biological resources, then the adulteration of this biological core will cut that people off from its nature and prevent it from continuing into the future.[24]

This fixation on a nation's supposed biological roots plays a major role in the politics of demographic fear. For those drawn to evolutionary strains of thought, the biological mingling of groups threatens something more than the purity of the nation: such mixture risks "dysgenic" outcomes that could erode the nation's cultural and intellectual capacities.[25] The charge of "mongrelization" that runs throughout the far right, then, shifts from a focus on traditions or customs to fasten on the supposed degradation of the genetic resources that define the nation and its future.[26] These fears over reproductive mixture are persistently invoked by those strains of the far right that draw from ecological and conservationist thought to cast nativist commitments in more user-friendly terms.[27] It is for this reason that far right forums often describe immigrants as a form of "invasive species" that will spread boundlessly and deplete the cultural ecosystem of the host nation. These arguments are given exemplary voice by the Carrying Capacity Network, the far right organization that promotes the notion of "cultural carrying capacity" to offer a putatively scientific justification for nativist policy. Drawing on the biologist Garrett Hardin's well-known concept of ecological carrying capacity (i.e., how much population a given biosystem can sustain), this organization promotes a parallel diagnosis from a cultural perspective—how much immigration-based strain the cultural terrain can sustain before it is degraded beyond repair.[28] Far right activists frequently employ the language of ecological protection to push a singular conclusion: at present rates of migration, European and North American nations are nearing this point of no return. There are simply too many new imports, pulling at the nation's cultural fabric, imposing a strain too great for the nation to bear. Only a committed effort to halt this influx will enable the cultural biosystem to heal itself.

Although the far right literature on demographic war draws from a variety of precedents, its guiding arguments take a distinctive shape. As detailed to this point, fascist race politics aims at a fundamental objective: to secure the racial core of the nation against forces that might "corrupt" it from within. Such projects have a long history, stretching from fascist campaigns of genocide to the eugenics programs through which a wide range of liberal democracies have historically pursued campaigns to "remove impurities" and thus improve the "national stock."[29] For the recent far right, however, the concerns tend to be framed as issues of national integrity or survival, which lends their arguments a militaristic resonance, oriented against invading influences. To render this threat narrative quickly: the perceived forces of biological and cultural "colonization" do more than simply displace historic population majorities in terms of sheer numbers; rather, these newcomers enter the biological composition of the nation and, in doing so, cut off its most essential roots.[30] From these threads, the prophets of demographic fear arrive at one conclusion: the current state of cultural and ethnic "panmixia" is not the multicultural dream that was promised by advocates of globalization but a process of "ethnocide" or "culturecide" that has largely gone unrecognized as such.[31]

Narratives of Catastrophe, Outcomes of Violence

For much of the far right, then, the present is defined by a singular crisis: the fate of nations subjected to the global movements of bodies, labor, and capital. And the pervasive references to war ultimately rest upon a grammar of dispossession, where traditional population majorities are stripped of their rightful inheritance by a variety of others (a story in which Muslims and migrants from the global South loom with particular urgency).[32] For those who promote this narrative of catastrophe, the nation no longer has a legible future, owing to the collapse of the biological and cultural conditions under which it has historically reproduced itself.[33] The situation goes beyond a hostile takeover by external forces; instead, demographic change is seen as a process of "ethnosuicide" or "ethnomasochism," in which the nations of the West hasten their own demise by welcoming ethnic and cultural "invaders" under the guise of humanitarian values or economic benefits.[34] For Jared Taylor, the intellectual leader of the far right New Century Foundation and editor of its online magazine, *American Renaissance,* this openness to a majority nonwhite nation represents a perverse form of autodestruction: "Whites . . . have the power to keep our lands for ourselves, but we are throwing them open to aliens, aliens who despise us as they take what is ours. . . . This is a mental illness unique to whites and unique to our era."[35]

This demographic panic takes on a more strident cast among those who push the themes of dispossession to their extreme conclusions. For such figures, the ultimate threat of immigration is not simply a culture that must be renegotiated in light of multiple constituencies. Rather, the greatest danger is reflected in the fate of existing demographic majorities. In the European context, for instance, Pierre Krebs decries the "assassination" of a race "when a people are subjected to negative cultural influences or when their demography declines."[36] And the British far right author Alex Kurtagic claims that the "unique biological entity" of "the White race faces complete erasure from the Earth" as a result of the "settler colonialism" that defines contemporary immigration practice.[37] These anxieties of effacement are especially virulent for those who argue that ethnic "replacement" is not a threat that faces cultures or races equally, but one that is meant to target white populations specifically. This narrative of an embattled white population has spawned the most notorious neologisms of the demographic panic literature, where the supposed replacement of white majorities is described as "white genocide," "white extinction," "white erasure," or "white extermination." As Greg Johnson argues: "For two or more generations now, whites have been subjected to mass ethnic cleansing in our homelands. . . . Whites have found a way to 'live with' a system in which we, as a race, have no future. Unless the present political, economic, and cultural system is fundamentally transformed, whites will become extinct in all of our homelands, and we will be replaced by non-whites. We are being subjected to a slow, cold process of genocide."[38] Here, the diagnosis of ethnic and cultural threat slides from "cultures" or "identity" broadly put and highlights the white race as an ethnic core that is purposefully marked for erasure—a displacement hastened by "antiwhite" dynamics that ostensibly prohibit white people from valuing or avowing their racial identity, even while other cultures are celebrated in the name of multiculturalism.[39] As a result, figures of the far right typically describe the general tenor of a multicultural society as founded in "antiwhite hatred."

The heart of this accusation lies in its insistence that global population change does not simply have winners (the previously subaltern populations that are entering and proliferating throughout liberal democracies); rather, the winners' gains are built on the sacrifice of white populations. This panic over the demographic eclipse of ethnic whites (a category that is assumed to be both existent and coherent) is redoubled by the political and cultural shifts that are associated with the broader process of "white extermination." According to this narrative, not only are white citizens soon to be outnumbered in their own nations by nonwhite populations, but their displacement is coupled with a campaign to make white subjects economically and culturally irrelevant. This antiwhite campaign is supposedly evidenced by the disappearance of white cultural monuments, the "war" against white public holidays, and school curricula that highlight the violent history of white dominion. Neil Kumar, an American white nationalist who unsuccessfully ran for national office in 2022, puts these developments in characteristically militaristic terms: "Cultural genocide is always the forerunner to physical genocide; you see, before they slaughter us, they wish to grind our heroes to dust, shatter our idols, strip us of our roots, and turn our children against us and against themselves. By denying us our history, they deny us our identity, and thus deny us our humanity."[40] This argument turns upon a characteristic trope of recent far right literature: even if the guiding precepts of liberal democracies prohibit discrimination against the members of any group, it remains permissible to discriminate against white people for purposes of erasing them from the national landscape.[41]

It would not be difficult to detail how the category of "genocide" is evacuated of moral content when applied to a process in which traditional demographic majorities find their numbers shrinking in relation to other groups within a specified geopolitical space.[42] What is more significant at present, however, is how this rhetoric of "colonization" or "extermination" structures perceptions, guides estimations of threat, and shapes the range of responses to match the perception of emergency. Once these demographic shifts are framed as an existential danger, only radical courses of action will suffice. For some, the path to restore the proper cultural habitat is through a project of "repatriation," in which the cultural "invaders" would be relocated beyond the space of the nation. Pierre Vial, leader of the French far right Terre et Peuple movement, has famously described the options that should be offered to migrants as "the suitcase or the coffin."[43] Others present this proposal for removal in more sanitized terms, designed to soften the message. For Greg Johnson, the path to a majority-white nation would be forged through a "racial divorce," in which white Americans would create "homogeneously white homelands" while allotting similar homelands for other ethnic and racial groups.[44] For a large portion of the far right, however the depth of the conflict is expressed in the stark alternatives of "expulsion or mass exodus."[45] Indeed, for the more militant wings of the ethnonationalist right, the ostensible demographic "war" unfolding across liberal democracies demands the response of *outright* war, with "native" ethnic groups using any and all means to resecure their cultural and racial domains. In the uncompromising terms of Guillaume Faye, "An open outbreak of ethnic civil war may be necessary."[46]

The implications of this militant discourse are considerable. To begin, it is necessary to consider how such proposals have found traction within civil society—more specifically, in projects of extremist violence designed to spark such an ethnic civil war. In 2019, a white extremist named Brenton Tarrant carried out mass shootings at two mosques in Christchurch, New Zealand. To publicize the violence, Tarrant not only livestreamed the shootings on Facebook but also posted a manifesto—titled simply "The Great Replacement"—detailing his motives for murdering fifty-one Muslims at their places of worship.[47] At one level, the manifesto strikes a tone of racialized, masculinist defiance against perceived demographic colonization. In the shooter's terms, the attack was intended to "show the invaders that our lands will never be their lands . . . and that, as long as a white man still lives, they will NEVER conquer our lands and they will never replace our people."[48] This performance of a specifically masculine defiance reflects the gendered character of far right demographic panic, where control and defense of the nation are committed to male hands. Quickly, however, this appeal to male resistance gives way to a program of explicitly racial violence—one meant to inaugurate a broader insurgence on the part of a besieged white majority. As Tarrant continues, the broader aim of the mass murder was "to show the effect of direct action, lighting a path forward for those that wish to follow" and eventually "to incite violence, retaliation and further divide between the European people and the invaders currently occupying European soil."[49]

This vision of violent direct action enjoys significant currency across the landscape of white extremism. In 2011, a Norwegian extremist, Anders Breivik, killed seventy-seven people on a single day to strike against the perceived Islamic "colonization" of Europe. In subsequent court appearances, Breivik doubled down on this xenophobic argument when he displayed a sign that read "Stop your genocide against our white nations."[50] In 2015, Dylann Roof killed nine Black worshipers in a historic Black church in Charleston, South Carolina, in a self-described effort to inaugurate a race war. And in 2019, when Patrick Crusius killed twenty-three shoppers in a Texas Walmart, he claimed that the Latinx victims of his assault "are the instigators, not me. I am simply defending my country from cultural and ethnic replacement brought on by an invasion. . . . I am honored to head the fight to reclaim my country from destruction."[51] In all of these cases, one theme runs through the speech and writings of these white extremists: not only are spectacular acts of race violence justified by a demographic "invasion" that has placed the native population in a defensive position, but, in a more active sense, such acts are necessary to spark reactions against the "soft genocide" of a white population that scarcely notices its own effacement.[52]

As the historian Kathleen Belew has argued, it would be a mistake to reduce these violent acts to the efforts of unhinged, radicalized individuals (i.e., the classic media figure of the "lone wolf").[53] The race violence of the far right is not limited to isolated figures who spiral into violence through their own devices; rather, these campaigns of violence are prepared by a considerable media ecology that (a) insists the contemporary political scene is already defined by a situation of unacknowledged race war and (b) equates cultural or racial survival with the "reconquest" of occupied terrain. This insistence on a surreptitious war already unleashed on traditional majorities has become a core element in the far right politics of demographic fear. Pierre Krebs, for instance, asserts that the conditions of war are not simply on the horizon but are already upon Europeans, who have not yet recognized the extent of the ongoing hostilities. As he describes this supposed emergency: "We are already in a war, a war that is infinitely more dangerous than classic wars. We are the witnesses of a change of population, the witnesses of a genetic war."[54] The character of this war takes on a more ominous cast when framed in these biological terms. Where a territorial war might be over terrain or jurisdiction (something that could be reclaimed at some future point), a "genetic" war threatens the deepest identity of a people (something that, once lost, supposedly cannot be restored). In the face of this war, one proposal comes to the fore in the racialist literature: the true heirs to the nation will survive only by reconquering their lands and nations.

The language of "reconquest" is pervasive across the European far right, where it is used to evoke the cultural memory of the campaign to expel Islamic "invaders" from the Iberian Peninsula. For instance, a core slogan of European Action, a German identitarian movement, simply states, "We have a choice: Reconquista or Requiem!"[55] The posters and stickers produced by the European far right regularly invoke both the language and the imagery of reconquest, enjoining native Europeans to "defend Europe" while figuring them as knights drawn from the iconography of the historical Crusades (when they are not figured as ancient Greek citizen-soldiers, tasked with defending their people and traditions). The popularity of this trope goes beyond the ubiquitous media campaigns that solicit European natives to "take back" their nations from what is perceived as a new Islamic threat, borne by tides of immigration. Indeed, the extent to which reconquest has been mainstreamed by far right actors is reflected in the name chosen by the French far right political party headed by the ultranationalist Éric Zemmour: Reconquête! The moniker is telling, as Zemmour organized his 2022 presidential campaign around "saving" France from the so-called Great Replacement.

A particularly notorious fantasy of reconquest in the American context stems from the white supremacist Church of the Creator (later rebranded the World Church of the Creator), an extremist organization that rose to prominence in the second half of the twentieth century.[56] In Creativity thought, the politics of redemption is based within an invidious theology that holds that racial salvation

Sticker from the German identitarian organization Identitäre Bewegung. The image enjoins viewers to "defend Europe," using the militant imagery of the ancient Greek hoplite soldier.

Poster from Identity England, an organization that defines itself in opposition to so-called demographic replacement. The print imagines contemporary English identitarians as heirs to Alfred the Great, the Anglo-Saxon king idealized for defending against Viking invasion.

can be secured only through "RAHOWA"—meaning "racial holy war." The idea of RAHOWA has become something of a rallying cry across the racial far right, with the term regularly appearing on bumper stickers, in white supremacist tattoos, and even in the name of a white power rock band. According to Creativity theology, the white race is in the end stages of a war engineered by Jewish interests to eliminate whites from their own nations. In the classic version of this narrative, the prime mover of this demographic threat is not "reverse colonization" but rather a hidden cabal of elites, familiar from anti-Semitic conspiracy theory. And the vision of RAHOWA comes equipped with a call to action: only by taking on this hidden war in kind can the white race ensure its biological and cultural survival.[57] For instance, Ben Klassen, the intellectual source of the Creativity movement, argues: "Whether you like it or not, my dear White Comrades, you are locked into a vicious racial war, whether you realize it or not. The Jews have decided for you, they have locked you into it, and you cannot escape it. . . . There is only one way out: fight your way out!"[58] This call to violent action has been met by a variety of assaults and murders committed by members of the Creativity movement. By taking on this fight, movement actors believe, they are not simply pursuing racial self-preservation; more significantly, they believe they are working to restore what Creativity theology presents as the divine intention: an order of separation in which the races were originally created and located apart from one another.[59]

Although it is tempting to slot this vision into the category of a fringe anti-Semitic ideology, its explicit appeals to ethnic war reflect the violence more centrally embedded in the far right's catastrophe narrative. Through this narrative lens, the present cannot be recognized as a time of change or negotiation, but only as an emergency or disaster. To expand a theme from above, the French identitarian Guillaume Faye makes this call explicit when he describes heightened tensions in Europe between native and immigrant populations. In contrast to those who propose multiculturalist approaches to negotiating the tensions of a pluralist society, Faye embraces conflagration as the path to racial and cultural redemption: "My position is an entirely different one: a confrontation has become indispensable if we are to resolve the problem, remediate the situation and free ourselves."[60] Ultimately, he argues, the true sign that European natives are serious about defending their culture "would be their readiness to shed blood."[61]

The stark character of this verdict is magnified by those strains of the far right that cloak their positions in the spuriously scientific discourse of "race realism." The stance of race realism is based within the troubled legacy of "race science" and has been promoted by a variety of far right foundations (e.g., the Pioneer Fund, the New Century Foundation) seeking legitimacy for their invidious racial beliefs. More recently, it has taken on new life in the Internet age through what advertises itself as the "human biodiversity network." Minimally, those who present themselves as "race realists" push a broadly shared commitment: that race reflects genetically inscribed, natural differences between human beings.[62] Beyond this insistence on the "reality" of race, a further claim speaks directly to the interests of this chapter: a "realistic" approach to racial relations asserts a history of zero-sum competition between groups—that is, any outcomes that are gains for one racial group represent losses for others. From this perspective, racial interaction takes on a singular character: necessary conflict that undermines any possibility of the multiculturalist harmony promised by advocates of globalism.[63] This position is given voice by Pierre Krebs, who argues: "There are no examples of the peaceful cultural integration of one people into the culture of another. The multiracial project leads directly to the 'soft genocide' of which the biologist Erlung Kohl speaks. It is the expression of a 'society that despises races insofar as it destroys them.'"[64] And the American face of race realism, Jared Taylor, derides "the idea that 'diversity is a strength.' Diversity of language, religion, but especially of race bring conflict and tension."[65] For race realists, the supposed fact of conflict is founded less in contingent, historical tensions between groups and more in broadly ecological premises, according to which racial collectives exist, *by their very nature,* in a state of biological competition. Given the depth of this antagonism, the far right literature of demographic fear frequently pushes a single conclusion: members of imperiled majority cultures are faced with a stark decision—to fight to preserve their way of life or capitulate to their own disappearance.

Fight or Die: Replacement Language and the Closure of Politics

One theme, then, pervades much writing of the far right: large-scale demographic change poses an existential threat to white nations. To recall the distinction introduced at the opening of this chapter, however, the framework of catastrophe does something more than detail a set of threats to white majorities or white culture—it renders a situation where conditions are ripe for a final conflict. Specifically, this would be a conflict in which embattled, white natives take back their cultural spaces, protect their ethnic identities, and secure their futures. The catastrophe that defines the present is thus not an unmitigated disaster but "a dark interregnum" that might yet give way to "the dawn of a radiant future."[66] These appeals to loss, possibility, and victory reflect the philosophy of history adopted by many figures of the far right. Here, the present is to be understood as what the Italian protofascist thinker Julius Evola refers to as the Kali Yuga—a stage in a cyclical history, drawn from Hindu sources.[67] Within this mythic history, the present represents the lowest historical point, when the possibilities of tradition have been lost, moral guideposts have dissolved, and chaos reigns.[68] The cyclical nature of history means, however, that this time of social darkness is not a terminal state; rather, the losses of the present can be endured for the possibility of rebirth. By stressing this possibility, the historiography of the far right evokes what the historian Roger Griffin has identified as one of the deepest commitments of the fascist political imaginary: *palingenesis*—the ideal of "rebirth . . . destined to put an end to a process of decline, decadence, or dissolution."[69]

This vision of rebirth animates far right narratives of conflict.[70] When taken at face value, the movement literature often presents conflict in diagnostic terms. The more that the process of "reverse colonization" continues, the more that white majorities experience cultural loss, resource competition, and resentment—all of which (we are told) naturally give rise to violence. This is what might be termed the mechanistic vision of conflict, where violence represents the natural outgrowth of social frustration, which builds until it reaches the point of necessary eruption.[71] Violence, in this narrative, arises with near necessity, just as surely as a bridge span will snap given a certain amount of strain. When competing groups are forced to live in proximity, there is only one possible outcome to their natural frustrations. As the foregoing details, however, this pervasive language of race war (along with its rhetorical nods to invasion, colonization, and genocide) pursues aims that go well beyond a description of growing social tensions. Rather, this discourse reflects an effort to engineer perception, guide responses, and seed emotions that could serve militant projects of "cultural defense."[72] Narrative, here, is less an act of description than an effort to forge a new political imaginary, steeped in outrage and disposed toward aggressive action.

There are obvious ways to track this strategy through the far right's pervasive appeals to colonization, extermination, and invasion—each of which primes the subject to experience immigration-based population change as a campaign of violence that demands violence in response. As the extremism scholar Paul Jackson argues, for instance, the rhetoric of "white genocide" or "ethnic cleansing" is not simply a hyperbolic response to demographic panic; rather, it creates a situation in which a community believes that it "needs to fight an existential conflict for its survival and continued 'purity.'"[73] The overriding rhetoric of emergency (invasion, cultural collapse, racial death) crafts a militant imaginary of cultural defense and disqualifies responses that would not operate with a similar degree of urgency. If demographic transformations are presented as a one-sided war that is under way against the true heirs of the nation, then the survival of a people hinges on their willingness to recognize this violence and take it on in kind.[74] This imperative is expressed along a number of avenues in the movement literature. To begin, much far right literature looks inward, to indict those white subjects who have supposedly stood by and allowed demographic changes to go unchallenged. In the manifesto of the Christchurch shooter, the perceived crisis of ethnic replacement ultimately reflects a

The cover of the far right French magazine *Réfléchir & Agir* raises the specter of an imminent race war.

crisis of masculinity. Mapping masculinized ideals of strength onto national integrity, Tarrant states: "Strong men do not get ethnically replaced, strong men do not allow their culture to degrade, strong men do not allow their people to die. Weak men have created this situation and strong men are needed to fix it."[75] It is for this reason that white reaction movements often promote a heroizing stance, with Promethean efforts by "great men" presented as necessary to turn the tides of white demographic losses and take back the nation for white interests.[76] Patriot Front, the American white nationalist organization that arose in the wake of the 2017 Charlottesville rally, puts this imperative in blunt terms: "America needs a generation of brave men to fearlessly rise to face all threats to their collective interests."[77]

At one level, then, the far right narrative of demographic catastrophe shapes an atmosphere of crisis. It forges a subject who sees the world as a state of emergency, demanding hard action to confront the perceived threat. The formula that is often bandied about in far right forums, "Hard times create strong men," encapsulates this vision, as it fuses the imperative of defense with the masculinist vision of hardness and strength.[78] The intuition can be parsed quickly: a state of cultural and moral decline cannot help but produce exemplary types, capable of enduring such chaotic times, and it is only these "strong men" who can turn the tide of history. Though this appeal to masculine hardness characterizes debates over so-called ethnic replacement, the manufactured air of crisis is magnified by two further features of the far right imaginary. These features lead white reaction movements toward a more foreboding set of conclusions, radicalizing the call to action and fueling trends of white extremist violence.

First, the push toward conflict is amplified by the biological undercurrents that run through the literature of demographic fear. As detailed above, significant strains of the far right root their population anxieties within a "race realist" framework. From this vantage point, forms of life are defined by an inexorable desire to propagate and consume, embedded at a brutely biological level. These expansionist tendencies of nature are then used to craft an analogy to current immigration practice: in an invasion of cultural habitats by "nonnative species," foreign life-forms flourish at the expense of the native species (a line of argument that reflects the far right's long-standing practice of borrowing from conservationist and ecological movements).[79] By rooting demographic conflict in the biological terrain of racial competition, the far right catastrophe narrative does something more than track conflict or advocate for resistance; rather, it commits what the anthropologist Verena Stolcke terms the "ideological subterfuge" of presenting "what is the outcome of specific politico-economic relationships and conflicts of interest as natural and hence incontestable because it, as it were, 'comes naturally.'"[80] More simply put, this biological rhetoric naturalizes social conflicts and heightens the perception of competition to an all-or-nothing struggle. Such a framing petrifies ethnic or racial conflict into the ostensibly immutable order of nature, set against a background of life or extinction. Because competition is supposedly rooted within basic biological drives, nonviolent responses are increasingly unavailable within this political imaginary. Instead, the mortal threat must be contested through equally extreme means.[81]

Such conclusions are common throughout the politics of demographic fear. The manifesto of the Christchurch shooter, for example, offers a stark illustration of how this catastrophist imaginary naturalizes demographic conflict and short-circuits possibilities for political resolution. As Tarrant asserts, "Understand here and now, there is no democratic solution, any attempt to vote your way out of ethnic replacement will be met at first with derision, then contempt and finally by force."[82] In light of this closure of political channels, one conclusion is presented as inevitable: "Radical, explosive action is the only desired, and required, response to an attempted genocide. . . . Prepare for war, prepare for violence and prepare for risk, loss, struggle, death. Force is the only path to power and the only path to true victory."[83] Though it may be tempting to read these formulations as isolated, extremist meditations, they are echoed by a variety of leading voices on the far right. Jean Thiriart, the Belgian political thinker who founded the Young Europe identitarian organization, makes this insurrectionist logic explicit: "One does not create a nation with speeches, pious talk, and banquets. One creates a nation with rifles, martyrs, jointly lived dangers."[84] And Guillaume Faye, one of the most prominent intellectual figures of the global far right to promote violent action, argues that the necessary "reconquest" of Europe "can only be accomplished through blood and pain."[85] As he elaborates: "Faced with a *state of emergency,* one can no longer espouse the conventional means one would use in times of peace and amiable discussion. War is inevitable, and in the face of such a state of affairs, it is the law of the strongest, the most determined, the most intelligent and the most strategically capable ones that prevails, not, sadly, that of democracy."[86] What characteristically defines these calls to action, moreover, is a deflection of responsibility for the violence to come. Because conflict is supposedly rooted within basic biological drives for survival, neither the individual who takes up arms nor the theorist who solicits action is considered responsible for the violence that must unfold. Rather, responsibility is assigned to those political elites who have created a situation where incompatible ethnic groups are forced to share the space of the nation, thus generating a battle for cultural and racial supremacy. In the stark terms of Markus Willinger, the Austrian identitarian associated with the Generation Identity network: "He who drives all cultures and peoples together into one territory will cause the bloodiest wars in the long term. . . . You [elites] will bear the guilt for these conflicts, not the combatants!"[87]

These tendencies to naturalize social conflict thus close off nonviolent alternatives in the far right imagination. And this push toward violence is magnified by another strain of the far right thought ecology: accelerationism. Though accelerationism has a long history in the materialist tradition, its central themes can be rendered quickly. As a broad thesis on politics and history, accelerationism holds that the present is not simply a time of darkness or loss but a time when social contradictions are reaching a point of unsustainability. The tensions are simply too great to be contained within the present set of institutions. Where this language of contradiction and crisis conveys a familiar materialist vision of history, the turn toward militant accelerationism is founded on the belief that actions can be taken to amplify these contradictions, "accelerate'" the ongoing crisis, and usher in a new age that will redeem the present.[88] These themes run throughout the landscape of militant white extremism.[89] For instance, Atomwaffen Division, an American neo-Nazi organization that has now spread to international chapters, has long promoted accelerationist ideals as a justification for militant violence. The extremist commitments of Atomwaffen members are evidenced by their links to a number of targeted killings and conspiracies to commit further violence against people and civic infrastructure. More recently, the loosely organized, Internet-based coalition known as the Boogaloo Bois has come to attention for advocating acts of mass public violence as a means to spark a second civil war in the United States.[90] Such commitments to violence are not limited to extremist militias acting on antistate paranoia or racial hatred. Rather, leading figures of the ethnonationalist right have also pushed accelerationist positions as part of their efforts to build an extremist thought ecology. As the American far right author Wilmot Robertson argues: "If whites really believed that the present trend of political, economic and social decay was irreversible, they would not try to slow the downhill rush, but accelerate it. With the arrival of total chaos, proposals for drastic solutions would become less censored and more popular. Whites would have a better chance of surviving if they could start with a clear slate, provided enough whites still remained to build on the ruins."[91]

Accelerationist themes feature prominently in the manifestos of extremists who commit violence in response to perceived racial replacement. These screeds do not simply present acts of violence as the natural outcome of mounting social conflicts. And the upshot of the extremists' violence is not reducible to the death tolls of their specific acts. Instead, these writings present campaigns of racial violence in tactical terms—as catalyzing acts intended to inspire widespread conflict that will end in a reconstituted racial nation.[92] Within the far right media ecology, the Christchurch shooter is known as "Saint Tarrant" for inspiring other white extremists to pursue violent action in the hopes of inaugurating a racial war. (The extremist forums routinely apply the "Saint" moniker to racially motivated mass shooters.) As his manifesto maintains, in addition to "show[ing] the effect of direct action," his violence served a patently accelerationist objective: "to add momentum to the pendulum swings of history, further destabilizing and polarizing Western society in order to eventually destroy the current nihilistic, hedonistic, individualistic insanity that has taken control of Western thought."[93] Such commitments have been taken up more broadly by extremists hoping to follow this lead. In 2019, John Earnest opened fire in a synagogue in Poway, California, killing one. In his anti-Semitic manifesto, he explicitly notes Tarrant's attack as an inspiration and asserts that "every anon reading this must attack a target while doing his best to avoid getting caught. Every anon must play his part in this revolution. . . . This momentum we currently have may very well be the last chance that the European man has to spark a revolution."[94] In this vision, it is not simply that there are no possibilities for change through political channels, making violence an act of last resort. Instead, according to an accelerationist model of praxis, the perpetrator of racial violence stands at the levers of history, capable of inaugurating a complete system breakdown from which a radical new order can emerge.

These stark formulations permit a final accounting of the catastrophism that defines far right demographic narratives. On its face, the Great Replacement narrative purports to unmask the truth of multicultural society and expose the hidden violence of demographic change. This work of unmasking is often described as "red-pilling" by the online variants of the far right—evoking the central metaphor of the 1999 film *The Matrix,* where the red pill allows the protagonist to see beyond the virtual reality in which he (along with everyone else) has been trapped. It is this enlightening function that helps explain the replacement narrative's histrionic language of colonization, genocide, and invasion. This hyperbolic rhetoric seeks to "awaken" its audience, pull back the curtain that veils social practice (in the classic vein of conspiracy theories), and reveal the truth that is supposedly obscured by the prevailing language of diversity or multiculturalism.

And yet, to grasp the full political work of this narrative, it is necessary to account for what it *does* as it reframes and represents ongoing demographic change. To ask this question is to highlight the most far-reaching and dangerous outcomes of replacement thought. In this narrative, cultural and political anxieties are translated into a register where politics is no longer possible. Instead, the present is rendered as a moment of emergency, where cultural extinction can be avoided only through extreme action by "brave men." Overall, this call to extreme action rests on an insistence that race war is not an eventuality toward which current trends point; rather, the present is figured as a state of already existing race war that poses an existential threat to the host nation's way of life. Broadly put, then, the narrative forges for its audience a new political imaginary, structured around a situation of radical threat that can be resolved only through radical means.[95] Not only is extremist action justified on grounds of "cultural self-defense," but this call to action resonates with one of the most cherished elements of far right mythology: rebirth through violence. If the racial nation is to be reborn, then its passage can be enabled only through the work of strong men who are willing to do what is necessary to break the grip of the present. This work is persistently pressed upon the audience as a personal responsibility. In the phrase that often floats through far right meme culture, the addressee is hailed to be a figure of action, tasked with defending the nation, culture, or race: "If not you, who? If not now, when?"

Recent episodes of extremist violence in response to perceived racial replacement are thus hardly accidental. They represent the efflorescence of a narrative ecosystem in which the present is systematically framed in terms of radical, growing danger. According to this narrative, war has already been unleashed on traditional cultural majorities (particularly white majorities) whether they recognize it or not. The thought ecology that surrounds the replacement narrative does more than simply detail an ongoing situation of radical threat—it also routinely forecloses the possibility of political solutions. The danger of this narrative thus goes beyond its emotional appeals to outrage and fear. Because politics can no longer be perceived as useful, the present is displaced into a different register entirely, where only violence can halt the catastrophe that looms.

CHAPTER 3

METAPOLITICS AND DEMOGRAPHIC FEAR

The New Right's "War of Ideas"

Metapolitics is the occupation of culture, politics is the occupation of a territory.

— *Guillaume Faye,* Why We Fight: Manifesto of the European Resistance, *2011*

Whoever controls the language controls the minds of the people.

— *GreekIdentitarian (@GIdentitarian), Twitter, September 6, 2020*

Visitors to far right forums can often be bewildered by the terms and phrases on display. People absorbed in consumer pleasures, lacking any appreciation for transcendent cultural ideals, are maligned as "bugmen." The present state of society, where natural differences and hierarchies are supposedly no longer recognized, is described as "clown world." And Covid vaccine holdouts draw from the long history of fascist race theory (as well as the Harry Potter fantasy franchise) to describe themselves as "purebloods." The far right politics of demographic fear is no exception. At the center of its narrative world rests the coinage of the "Great Replacement" that has captured the extremist imagination. This formula is hardly the only linguistic invention of note. Even a casual glance at far right immigration debates finds lurid references to "invaders," "colonizers," and "occupiers." Elites who have ostensibly engineered these developments are routinely described as "traitors" and "collaborators." And the effects of these immigration policies on white demographic majorities are consistently rendered as "genocide," "erasure," or "extermination."

The polemical work of this language is not accidental. As Christopher Rufo, an activist affiliated with the ultraconservative Manhattan Institute for Policy Research, has argued, "Politics is a form of conflict and rhetoric is its primary weapon."[1] By extension, a militant right "[has] to fight at two levels: we need to win on the issues directly, but we also need to start shifting the deeper structures. This means subverting the existing language, creating our own frames, building our own aesthetic, and contesting institutional power."[2] It would be easy to view these imperatives as simple culture war sloganeering from a provocateur seeking to steer public opinion. The more interesting element to these claims is how this motivated politics of language reflects strategies that define the new right across the global scene.

A staple of new right thought (in both the European and North American contexts) is that political power is ultimately rooted at the cultural level, below the level of institutions or policies. Pierre Krebs, the leader of the far right Thule-Seminar in Germany, puts this insight in brute terms: "In order to exist at all, political power is thus dependent on a cultural power diffused within the masses."[3] This commitment reflects the abiding legacy of the European New Right for the present—a lineage that is typically traced back to the French GRECE Institute (Groupement de Recherche et d'Études pour la Civilisation Européenne). The institute was formed in the late 1960s to reconsider the fortunes of a right that had been outstripped by the new politics and countercultural energies of the left.[4] From the first seminars and publications of the GRECE Institute, the European New Right committed itself to a central premise: the right could contest its losses only by recognizing the importance of what they came to term "metapolitics." Minimally, the concept of metapolitics can be understood as an effort to channel the intuition, articulated by the Italian Marxist Antonio Gramsci, that every community is rooted within a reservoir of beliefs, values, symbols, and sentiments.[5] This field of "common sense" structures what is taken for normal or natural within a given society. It guides which policies can be reasonably proposed or supported, shapes the perception of appropriate social roles, and constrains what the community in question can legitimately hope for or pursue.

These early commitments of the GRECE Institute have shaped the politics of what is now broadly termed the new right. For the new right, deep political change cannot limit itself to shifts in power achieved through institutions, elections, or policies. Instead, efforts to transform society must also set their sights on the symbols, discourse, and culture that form that society's political imaginary. Politicians come and go, policies may be overturned, but the beliefs, sentiments, and values of civil society provide an enduring basis for social power. Accordingly, the new right stakes its public work on a positive metapolitics—a committed project to transform civic symbols and vocabularies to provide resources for an antiliberal public sphere. This commitment to a "Gramscianism of the right" helps to explain the upsurge in far right publishing, broadcasting, and media houses, viewed as the organs that can help to secure abiding political change. And for what has come to be known as the alt-right (or the more recent "dissident right"), this cultural politics accounts for the investment in visual memes that flood the far right online ecosphere. As Daniel Friberg, the head of the far right publishing house Arktos, argues, this metapolitical project pursues "the process of disseminating and anchoring a particular set of cultural ideas, attitudes, and values in a society, which eventually leads to deeper political change."[6]

Though these commitments came to notoriety through European figures, they have been widely taken up across North America.[7] The American alt-right figurehead Richard Spencer, for instance, asserts that "metapolitics is more important than politics" for an alt-right movement that seeks to "capture the imaginations of our people (or the best of our people) and shock them out of their current assumption of what they think is possible."[8] This metapolitical intuition rests at the heart of the far right media platform associated with Andrew Breitbart.[9] And the white nationalist Greg Johnson (himself the leader of the far right Counter-Currents media organization) argues that the task of a meaningful right politics is to disseminate ideas in order to reorient what is thought to be politically possible. As he proposes: "We must create our own metapolitical organizations—new media, new educational institutions, and new forms of community. . . . We must fight bad ideas with better ideas. . . . This is not to say that there is no room for street activism today, but it has to be understood as a metapolitical activity, a form of propaganda, not as a battle to control the streets. Actual politics comes later, once we have laid the metapolitical groundwork."[10]

This program has particular relevance for the far right politics of demographic fear. For those gripped by fears of racial replacement, the politics of culture helps account for what would otherwise remain inexplicable: how native-born citizens could reconcile themselves to the ongoing loss of their demographic majorities and cultures.[11] According to much of the "antireplacement" literature, major demographic changes are not an accidental outgrowth of economic necessity or elite decisions that open nations up to a "flood" of immigration. Rather, the policies that enable these demographic shifts are facilitated by a sprawling media apparatus that shapes the beliefs, judgments, and reactions of civil society. More specifically, new right figures insist that long-standing white majorities have been rendered compliant with their own demographic "replacement" by a motivated media campaign that celebrates ethnic diversity and a multicultural future. The effect is what Dominique Venner, the French historian and far right activist, termed the "zombification" of citizens in liberal democracies—their inability to recognize or grasp the crisis ostensibly taking place around them.[12]

The preceding summary, though brief, helps to situate the concerns of this chapter. For much of the new right, support for (or at least compliance with) demographic change is the result of a significant ideological labor conducted by "globalist" interests (a term that draws on familiar anti-Semitic tropes involving a global cabal of "rootless" financial and media elites).[13] To this end, the new right dedicates particular attention to how the beliefs and sentiments of civil society have been shaped by a cluster of values associated with liberal democracy: diversity, multiculturalism, and equality. Within this constellation, equality takes on particular significance.[14] Pierre Krebs argues that "the egalitarian lie has turned on their heads the last two ways in which states retained their integrity; the most essential and, therefore, the most difficult to constrain: *territorial integrity* and the ethnic integrity that depends on it."[15] For the new right, then, the true costs of an egalitarian political culture lie in how it threatens national identity by engineering support for immigration and diversity initiatives. For Renaud Camus, the French author who popularized the Great Replacement label, egalitarian values go further, to pacify or anesthetize those long-standing majorities who are supposedly losing their cultures through population change. As he puts it: "This numbness had to be created, organized. . . . The principal ideal involved is *equality*. The principal interest at work is *normalisation, standardization, similarity, sameness*—needless to say, *equality* is the condition to those."[16]

The central aims of this chapter take a number of shapes. Most broadly, the chapter examines how deeply the politics of demographic fear draws from new right cultural politics. At one level, a metapolitical perspective is meant to explain why existing cultural majorities acquiesce to policies that engineer their demographic displacement. At another level, the new right responds by pursuing its own project to seed civil society with antiliberal values, symbols, and languages. In detailing this cultural politics, the chapter explores the legacy of the new right to chart its influence on the broader landscape of the recent far right. To do so, the chapter devotes particular attention to what the new right and its identitarian allies term the "principal menace" of liberal modernity: egalitarian values and vocabularies.[17] In the words of the pseudonymous alt-right author Gregory Hood, "Egalitarianism today is a mortal threat not just to white racial survival, but to human greatness itself."[18] The chapter demonstrates how, when enlisted as part of a new right cultural counteroffensive, core liberal terms (e.g., equality, diversity) are not simply targeted for irrelevance. Instead, these terms are infused with new meanings and fashioned into "linguistic weapons" designed to reengineer civil society toward antiliberal ideals. In this way, the metapolitics of the new right threatens to destabilize the normative resources of civil society toward antiegalitarian ends.

The Egalitarian Disaster: From Equality to Fungibility

The far right has long been defined by a resistance to egalitarian commitments. For some, the founding error of egalitarianism rests in how it obscures natural differences in rank between human types (whether individual or collective); for others, egalitarian ideals interfere with the outcomes of free economic competition.[19] To winnow this array of critiques, it is helpful to begin with the asserted link between egalitarian commitments and demographic change. Though the figures associated with the new right diverge in emphasis, they typically converge on the following insistence: the presumption of equality allots moral value to human beings on the basis of what they abstractly share. All individuals and groups are to be valued equally. From this premise, a more ominous conclusion is drawn: if there are no normatively meaningful distinctions between human beings, then there can be no compelling reasons to prevent the mixture of existing populations.[20] And these broad propositions in turn lead to a more pointed conclusion: equality is not simply a core aspiration for the liberal moral universe but rather the ideological basis for policies that have (a) opened nations to widespread immigration and (b) decimated the integrity of culture.[21]

In programmatic form, much new right literature targets one core element of the liberal moral universe: the commitment to human beings as rights-bearers, meriting equal protections by virtue of their equal humanity. Where an egalitarian moral grammar is often presented as a historic accomplishment of modernity, the new right typically insists that the true legacy of liberalism is a stark individualism that elides the historical and social contexts that lend meaning to human life.[22] In this vision, it is the individual that has moral standing, regardless of institutional, cultural, or social memberships. According to the far right author Michael O'Meara, liberalism is therefore not only atomistic but also fundamentally destructive toward traditional markers of identity. It "promote[s] a standardizing uniformity that seeks to eliminate national, racial, and historical differences for the sake of a borderless, color-blind order subject to one law, one market, and one humanitarian creed."[23] Alain de Benoist, the most prominent intellectual figure of the European New Right, argues that this homogenizing dynamic yields an important moral incoherence: "If all men are equal, if they are all fundamentally the same, if they are all 'men like others,' far from the unique personality of each of them being able to be recognised, they will appear, not as irreplaceable, but on the contrary as interchangeable."[24]

At one level, then, many new right figures pursue a well-worn communitarian rejoinder toward the impulses of liberal modernity—a tradition that questions whether it is meaningful to speak of "humanity" as such, outside of its social and cultural memberships.[25] Human life, for much of the new right, becomes intelligible only within particular communities and the traditions that lend these communities their distinct styles of life. That said, the new right critique goes beyond theoretical reservations to argue that liberal premises yield disastrous political consequences. Because the liberal moral universe is meant to render subjects exchangeable, new right theorists propose that liberal modernity has arrived at its logical conclusion in the globalizing present: the large-scale intermingling of populations and the related erosion of their cultural differences. As Daniel Friberg argues: "Universalism is . . . a view of the world in which humanity is represented as a homogeneous whole, one extended family, in which terms such as 'people' and 'identity' lose their relevance. . . . Universalist doctrine demands that all cultures should intermix, and thus vanish, since no relevant differences between them exist."[26]

The new right expands its lens, however, as it argues for another significant motor behind "population replacement": global capitalism. Just as liberal commitments abstract from culture, so does market society diminish the differences among cultures and peoples. Alain de Benoist offers a symptomatic rendering: "In the name of the capitalist system, the ideology of the Same reduces all meaning to market prices and transforms the world into a vast, homogeneous marketplace where men, reduced to the roles of producers and consumers—soon to become commodities themselves—must all adopt the mentality of *Homo economicus*."[27] As the language of this passage conveys, the difficulty is the distinct reshaping of economic and social life characteristic of neoliberalism capitalism. A variety of scholars have demonstrated, for instance, that one of the defining features of neoliberalism is the pursuit of a "globalist" project, where local forms of sovereignty are dismantled to permit capital to operate at a transnational level.[28] Minimally, then, much of the new right indicts neoliberalism as a form of economic imperialism, where the interests of multinational corporations are expanded across national borders through trade agreements and international organizations. In the process, international flows of capital are immunized against the interests of nonmarket actors or individual nation-states.

Here is not the place to reconstruct the full range of new right anxieties toward capitalism or its characteristic desire to tame market organizations toward nationalist ends.[29] What is most significant at present is how new right figures challenge the perceived costs of what they term "market imperialism." As they persistently argue, the expansion of global capitalism yields a deeper, "anthropological disfigurement" of human beings as market principles organize ever more spheres of life. From this perspective, efforts to universalize market forms and ideals represent what new right figures term a form of "soft totalitarianism," where culture after culture sees the rich variance of values reduced to common icons or tastes and the homogenizing rewards of mass consumption.[30] As John Bruce Leonard, editor at the far right publishing house Arktos, elaborates: "When a man gets his culture from HuffPost and his cuisine at MacDonalds, his friends from Facebook and his recreation from Hollywood, his garb from Abercrombie & Fitch and his dialect from Twitter, what is he? . . . He has grown cosmopolitan, this lucky son of modernity; he is a man of the neither here nor there, the great placeless one."[31] Though European new right figures often indict the reign of market value as a form of "Americanization," much of the North American alt-right takes a similar stance to indict the effects of market society.[32] Richard Spencer, for instance, proposes that promoters of neoliberal globalization "want an undifferentiated global population, raceless, genderless, identityless, meaningless population. . . . They want a flat grey-on-grey world, one economic market for them to manipulate."[33] This diagnosis sets aside the considerations of national sovereignty or democratic accountability that guide many critiques of global capitalism.[34] Rather, the new right channels the concerns that define neoconservative and paleoconservative thought, in which market ideals are feared to corrode or crowd out local cultures, transcendent ideals, and extramarket values—leaving subjects increasingly homogenized in their values and aspirations.[35]

Some provisional conclusions can now be posed. Under the terms of replacement thought, large-scale demographic transformation (and the cultural changes it ostensibly brings) is not a historical accident that follows from global flows of migration or labor, nor does it result from a patchwork of ad hoc policy decisions. Rather, this movement has been prepared by ideological currents and material practices that melt away cultural difference.[36] At the heart of this process rest the egalitarian commitments that define liberalism.[37] In programmatic form: within global modernity, the moral commitment to equality has effectively become a governing logic of *equalization* that promotes a decultured, deracinated equivalence between human beings. As Pierre Krebs argues, for example, the universal consumer represents "abstract, transparent, neutral copies, models bearing no identity and consisting of pure, formless projections of a universal, archetypal man."[38] Renaud Camus argues that this subject offers little more than "Undifferentiated Human Matter"—a bare unit of labor or consuming power that can be moved indiscriminately through geopolitical space.[39] For the new right, this push toward population mixture is only radicalized by the multicultural initiatives that have shaped demographic policies across the global North. From the multicultural perspective, cultural or ethnic interchange is not simply an unintended by-product of economic or humanitarian forces but an ideal to be celebrated.[40]

This line of argument has been adopted and set to work across the far right. A wide range of figures argue that large-scale demographic change rests on a cultural politics that conditions native-born citizens to support policies that yield their displacement. And egalitarian norms are thought to form the core of this process—rooted in the logic that all subjects and groups are normatively equal and thus, ultimately, exchangeable.[41] Human populations become, in Renaud Camus's rendering, little more than "human Nutella," capable of being spread widely across the earth.[42] Because human tastes and wants are increasingly standardized by global media and consumer culture, they can be plugged into new national contexts without friction or loss. If the scope of new right challenges toward egalitarian commitments is now legible, it is necessary to account for the other side of new right metapolitics: its offensive strategy to reconfigure the political imaginary toward antiliberal aims and objectives.

Metapolitics as Cultural Counteroffensive: Language as Battleground

There are many ways to contest these assertions. One might, for instance, reject the logic under which ethnic mixing constitutes a "destruction" of a host culture rather than a process of negotiation, exchange, or enrichment. Or one could expose the paranoiac element of the analysis—the insistence that these demographic changes are the result of motivated policy interventions by a shadowy set of actors behind the scenes (e.g., finance capitalists, the "Davocracy," Jewish elites, the technocratic "New Class") designed to erode national or racial integrity.[43] The most fundamental political questions, however, arise from how the new right uses these cultural insights to forge its own contribution to the politics of demographic fear.

To pursue this lead, it is necessary to set aside the new right's antiliberal polemics and instead engage how its central figures have pursued a cultural offensive of their own, designed to inspire a politics of cultural, ethnic, or racial defense. Pierre Krebs, for instance, announces this mission in bold terms when he argues: "We want to take over the laboratories of thinking. Hence our task is to oppose the egalitarian ethos and egalitarian socio-economic thinking with a world-view based on differentiation. . . . We want to create the system of values and attitudes necessary for gaining control of cultural power."[44] While these formulations may simply seem to oppose the values of equality and difference, the cultural politics of the new right does not discard the language of equality (as characterizes the hardened, antiegalitarian camps of the far right); instead, it seeks to take over these central liberal terms and reshape them toward antiliberal aims. In doing so, the new right pursues a distinct political objective: to capture the cultural terrain by transforming liberal languages of citizenship. For instance, Alain de Benoist argues:

> The ENR [European New Right] has always denounced what I call the ideology of Sameness, i.e., the universalist ideology that, in its religious or secular forms, seeks to reduce the diversity of the world—i.e., the diversity of cultures, value systems, and rooted ways of life—to one uniform model. . . . Insofar as it seeks to reduce diversity, which is the only true wealth of humankind, the ideology of Sameness is itself a caricature of equality. In fact it creates inequalities of the most unbearable kind. By contrast, equality—which must be defended whenever it is necessary—is quite another matter.[45]

This line of argument highlights a more nuanced role for liberal categories within the cultural politics of the new right. It sidesteps an unreserved critique of equality and instead claims a saving project—a reformed vision of equality that would not override cultural difference. This vision finds expression within what some segments of the new right have come to term (with some degree of internal controversy) the "right to difference."[46] That is, a more normatively defensible form of equality would be founded in the commitment that every people (construed as a bounded cultural totality) has an equal right to secure its existence against competing cultures or the spread of a global monoculture.[47]

As the formula—"the right to difference"—suggests, this version of equality is rooted within an adjacent political vocabulary: the diversity discourse that is regularly derided across the far right.[48] The critique typically runs as follows: once diversity is accepted as a basic social good, it helps to undermine the integrity of a host culture through its drive toward racial and ethnic integration.[49] This claim is given voice by a meme that is prominent within the far right media ecology, appearing regularly on banners, websites, bumper stickers, and billboards: "'Diversity' is a code word for white genocide." What defines new right metapolitics, however, is a reappropriation of this vocabulary to furnish a defense of ethnonationalism. De Benoist, for instance, depicts diversity as the most fundamental value that animates ethnonationalist projects of cultural defense:

> Diversity is inherent in the very movement of life, which flourishes as it becomes more complex. The plurality and variety of races, ethnic groups, languages, customs, even religions has characterised the development of humanity since the very beginning. Consequently, two attitudes are possible. For one, this biocultural diversity is a burden. . . . For the other, this diversity is to be welcomed, and should be maintained and cultivated. . . . The true wealth of the world is first and foremost the diversity of its cultures and peoples.[50]

Such appeals to diversity are now a staple of the new right—particularly among those who invoke a language of "biocultural diversity" to argue that racial groups differ in natural capacities.[51] As the phrase suggests, the new right uses "human biodiversity" to fold an argument for cultural defense into the established language of ecological protectionism. Just as ecosystems are held together by functionally differentiated systems of life, the diversity of cultures is said to reflect an analogous system of difference and hierarchy between peoples and races.[52] From this appeal to natural diversity, a broad set of political conclusions follow. Cultural and racial differences are not simply read back into the basic structures of nature. Instead, new right figures lean on the language of ecological conservationism in order to demand the preservation of these differences. In making such arguments, the new right draws from a long nativist history of using conservationist frameworks to foment anti-immigration sentiment—figuring immigrants as "invasive species" that pose a distinct danger to the cultural ecosystem.

For current purposes, what is most significant is how the new right employs the language of diversity to exploit its normative capital, while presenting ethnonationalist movements as its true heirs. To put their argument in short form: because cultures make possible varied forms of human life, any meaningful human diversity requires the preservation of cultural difference.[53] It is for this reason that ethnonationalist movements have increasingly rebranded their projects to halt population mixture as the sole path toward "true" difference (a stance they characteristically rebrand as "ethnopluralism"). For example, the United Kingdom chapter of Generation Identity, a pan-European identitarian organization, states as one of its core tenets, "We believe in true diversity in which all people have a right to preserve and promote their group identity in their homelands."[54] The American alt-right figure Richard Spencer goes further, describing white homeland projects as the safeguard of "true diversity and multiculturalism."[55] Some on the far right defend this "right to difference" on the grounds of cultural autonomy—that all bounded cultural groups are owed a right to preserve their own way of life.[56] Others push beyond a language of survival to present this right as a universal good through the role that cultural difference has played in the unfolding of human history.[57] If each culture represents the outcome of historical experiments, innovations, and biological capacities, then each represents a unique contribution to human life that would be lost within a global "monoculture." This intuition is reflected in far right memes that promote fears about racial and ethnic mixture. One oft-circulated meme pictures a set of vessels containing liquids of various colors. When poured together, all lose their distinct hues and instead blend into an undifferentiated brown—a visual analogy for the loss of cultural distinction that is supposedly unfolding through globalization and heightened migration.[58]

This project of "cultural protection" is troubled at a number of levels. Although a broad commitment to difference is often invoked by the ethnonationalist literature, the pursuit of this ideal has come to divide segments of the new right. As noted, Alain de Benoist has recently depicted the "right to difference" in a manner that resonates with some central commitments of liberal multiculturalism—where this right is extended to groups attempting to preserve their way of life, no matter where they find themselves (e.g., Muslims in France who wish to veil in secular spaces).[59] For the more radical segments of the new right, however, such a stance proves insufficiently attentive to the demographic and cultural crisis they associate with immigration in a so-called global age. Accordingly, a wide variety of figures and organizations take the more radical path of describing themselves as "identitarians," dedicated to one mission above all: preserving the identities of nations (and the unified cultures that ostensibly define them) against the varied forces of cosmopolitanism, globalization, and multiculturalism.[60] Among those who identify as identitarians across Europe and North America, the right to difference is conceived in more militant terms. Guillaume Faye, for instance, broke from the European New Right to argue that any effort to pursue this right of defense in a multicultural direction fails to address the depth of the threats faced by Europe in a global age. In Faye's terms, such a project "threatens to degenerate into a doctrine—an ethnic communitarianism—sanctioning the existence of non-European enclaves in our lands." The pluralist approach is ultimately a "Disneyland dream" that will erode both the ethnic and cultural identity of European nations.[61] This diagnosis of crisis yields a more extreme set of solutions for both European and North American identitarians: no remedy short of removing these cultural newcomers will prove sufficient to defend the nation's integrity or enable it to continue into the future. Accordingly, for much of the identitarian far right the perceived threat demands a different response: a "Great Return," "remigration," or "racial divorce," in which immigrants deemed incompatible with the host culture would be repatriated to their lands of origin.[62]

Before pursuing the full costs of these proposals, it is necessary to note the core strategies that define new right efforts to retake the cultural terrain. New right figures do not simply indict egalitarian commitments as threats to cultural difference.[63] Instead, they persistently lay claim to the *true* legacy of equality and difference in order to transform public debates on immigration and national identity. This metapolitical strategy rests on the tactic of rhetorical reversal—for example, although mainstream, liberal culture invokes values such as equality and diversity, only *we* (on the right) truly honor these values by working to preserve the cultural integrity of nations.[64] This rhetorical approach is intended to increase the mainstream appeal of new right commitments. But in doing so, this project raises significant normative

A French far right anti-immigration sticker campaign asserts that remigration is the solution to the population changes associated with the "Great Replacement."

concerns—perhaps most clearly through the resources it has contributed to aggressive movements for racial and cultural defense.

Metapolitics to What End? The Civic Costs

It is now possible to assess the political ambitions of this metapolitical project: how new right figures denounce central liberal ideals while, at the same time, restaging those ideals to inaugurate a new horizon for political thought and action. This project represents the offensive thrust of metapolitics, where symbols, values, and vocabularies are used as tactics to win public sentiment and reconfigure the cultural landscape. In the context of new right demographic fears, the central issue is how the specific values of equality and difference are transformed in order to shift civil society toward illiberal projects.

To begin, where many identitarian figures enlist diversity discourse toward a project of "cultural defense," this rhetoric conceals a more virulent set of commitments. As intellectual historians have demonstrated, at least one of the new right's goals in adopting this culturalist language is to extricate itself from the discredited tradition of fascism—particularly the fascist fixation on race as the source of national purity or pollution.[65] This effort to sanitize the image of the movement has been considerably troubled, however, by those who preserve a significant role for biology in their definition of nationhood and culture. In North American discussions, the racial dimension of these arguments tends to be foregrounded. White identitarians such as Richard Spencer, Greg Johnson, and Jared Taylor have explicitly argued that national identity is fundamentally rooted in race. And their political vision asserts the need for a racially defined homeland (i.e., an ethnostate) in which a white population would be able to "reproduce and fulfill our destiny, free from the interference of others."[66] Where the classic literature of the European New Right tends to be more rhetorically cautious, leading European identitarians routinely negotiate arguments for cultural defense through an explicitly racial lens.[67] Pierre Krebs, for instance, makes the link explicit: "Peoples, unlike man, who is made up of an intangible humanity, exist: they are biologically definable, sociologically identifiable and geographically localisable. . . . When a people . . . submerge their biological identity . . . they sign their death sentence for all eternity."[68] What is most significant in these positions is the abiding presence of biological themes, where culture is presented as an expression of genetic and racial potentials, shaped by social and geographic factors.[69] The significance of these biological commitments is reflected in the cited passage's outspoken fears over national degeneration: to deny or stray from this biological foundation is to court the "death sentence" of a given culture.

Some classic new right figures have attempted to contest these biological commitments, along with the fascist residues they carry.[70] Alain de Benoist, for instance, has argued that the sole official position of the European New Right is a defense of cultural difference, indifferent to race, that applies to cultural totalities no matter where they reside.[71] Even this rejoinder, however, has been targeted by critics. The philosophers Pierre-André Taguieff and Etienne Balibar contend that this reformed stance offers a "neo-racism" or "differentialist racism" that attempts to sanitize its invidious commitments through rhetorical means.[72] Where a classic racism commits to a table of racial hierarchy (where one race is placed at the top, and all others are measured as comparatively lacking or deficient), the culturalist wing of the new right pursues a different tack: the insistence on stark differences between cultural totalities and the related demand to eliminate any mixture of these groups.[73] As Taguieff argues, even while the new right commits itself to a public language of diversity, the "obsession of contact and the phobia of mixing" continue to define the privilege granted to the (homogeneous, bounded, fixed) *ethnos* over the (plural, contested) *demos*.[74] To be pure and remain the same, a culture must prevent or undo any mixture. It is for this reason that the anthropologist Verena Stolcke charges the new right with a xenophobic "cultural fundamentalism" that uses a sanitized language of culture to pursue a community "purified" of demographically inharmonious racial or ethnic groups.[75]

Such charges reveal how new right projects evoke some traditional fascist commitments—particularly in light of how their arguments for cultural "defense" have been adopted by ethnonationalist movements seeking to bring about ethnically and racially homogeneous homelands. That said, this chapter closes with attention to a different set of difficulties: the displacement that the values of equality and difference undergo when they are enlisted in the metapolitics examined to this point. To ask this question, it is useful to consider a point made by the French critical theorist Michel Foucault: value languages do not rest on a unitary, ahistorical bedrock of meaning; rather, they are contested objects of power. Value terms are a fundamental site of political struggle. They are taken up by parties in the civic arena, and in the process they undergo "substitutions, displacements, disguised conquests, and systematic reversals."[76] This insight is well illustrated by new right metapolitics, where political and moral values are reinvested with alternative meanings designed to reorient the landscape of civil society. A detailed look at how these commitments play out yields a more pointed conclusion: new right efforts to forge an alternative political imaginary threaten to damage the democratic public sphere.

One way to pursue this verdict rests in the programmatic phrase that new right figures use to defend against population change: the "right to difference." Within this formulation, each of the core terms is fundamentally altered. What is to be preserved is not the dignity or integrity of persons; rather, it is the historical and social conditions that are thought to lend meaning to human life. It is not individuals who can claim the right to difference; only cultural or racial totalities merit this status and the protections that follow.[77] Jared Taylor, the self-styled "white advocate" who heads the New Century Foundation, argues, for instance, that white separation movements claim "the right to pursue their destinies free from the unwanted embrace of others, to seek a future that is uniquely theirs within neighborhoods, institutions, regions, and ultimately nations in which they are the permanent and undisputed majority."[78] In such formulations, the rhetoric of rights is refashioned and absorbed into a narrative where bounded "biocultural" groups are the prime movers of history and sites of protection.[79] To flesh out this shift, it is useful to recall the language of biodiversity employed by major strains of the far right in defense of homogeneous cultural groups. Where the "right to difference" evokes a moral framework, with moral grounds, the biodiversity ideal draws from a naturalist framework that has no such moral resonance. Instead, diversity is defended on organic grounds of life or vitality, and the implications for failure are functionalist ones, such as system collapse or species extinction (reflected in this literature's pervasive recourse to metaphors of death and degeneration).[80]

These shifts in meaning make it possible to highlight a broader cost of new right metapolitics. To recall, the official project of the new right is not simply to challenge established narratives in academic seminars and professional journals, but ultimately to inaugurate social change by transforming the thoughts, sentiments, values, and images that bind civil society. A primary strategy for achieving this aim is to reengineer the civic languages that shape public debate and thought. This tactic is lauded by the alt-right author George Shaw, for whom "a concept captured in a term becomes a tool (or weapon) which can shape our thoughts and perceptions."[81] This effort to transform civic vocabularies can be put in more troubled terms, given the interests of this chapter. The new right overhaul of equality has been used to justify aims that are difficult to reconcile with even the most aggressive reconstitutions of the value within the liberal democratic tradition. This elasticity is perhaps clearest in those identitarians who invoke an "equal" right to cultural difference in order to justify what the political scientist Alberto Spektorowski has termed a "hierarchical multiculturalism" (i.e., the rank ordering of human cultures and races in terms of their putative values), as well as homogeneous ethnic groupings that demand the removal of ethnic others.[82] Memorably, this "right to difference" was featured in the nativist politics of Jean-Marie Le Pen, the former head of the French far right Front National, as he pursued a "France for the French." Or, to return to the thought leaders of the far right, Guillaume Faye employs this supposed right to endorse the forcible remigration of those immigrants who (in his terms) effect an "invasion" of European nations. As he argues: "De-migration . . . is both necessary and vital. It is humanly, politically, and historically necessary for us, the white men and women of Europe, to have these people return home. Let me state things clearly: whether willingly or by force, they shall indeed leave."[83] This proposal has been broadly echoed by identitarians in both Europe and North America who advocate for "remigration," "reconquest," or a "Great Return"—a large-scale process of repatriation that would remove "nonconforming" population groups.[84]

Those eager to defend the historic legacy of the European New Right have argued that these mandates for expulsion represent what happens when the ideal of cultural preservation is radicalized in the unruly spaces of civil society.[85] As the foregoing has detailed, however, these xenophobic proposals ultimately reflect the project that has defined the new right from its inception: to disrupt public discourse and to seed civil society with ideas designed to produce a different, antiliberal political imaginary. One essential avenue for this metapolitics is a polemical reconstitution of the liberal normative vocabulary—a project that takes exemplary form in the rise of the conservative media ecosphere and the meme warfare that characterizes alt-right Internet activism.[86] Indeed, perhaps the most obvious form of far right metapolitics is found in these bite-size visuals that can be immediately shared, liked, and revised according the controversy of the moment. From this vantage point, the exclusionary repackaging of core liberal values represents not a departure from the new right project but rather an outgrowth of its governing strategy. Accordingly, the discursive world of the new right often turns on formulas that invert the moral intuitions of liberal democracies. When President Barack Obama routinely argued that the nation's "diversity is our strength," the new right thought ecology responded with a popular counterformula: "Diversity is a weakness and homogeneity is strength."[87] Such jarring reversals reflect how the new right approaches normative terms, emptying them of their meaning and investing them with new content to reshape civic dialogues. It is for this reason that Pierre-André Taguieff describes new right metapolitics as a "demagogic operation" that aims to destabilize the civic vocabulary—where liberal policies are passed off as "authoritarian" and "neo-racism is passed as the 'right to be different.'"[88]

Minimally, then, the new right has provided intellectual grist for the resurgence of xenophobic, ethnopopulist, and nationalist projects throughout Europe and North America. And these outcomes are facilitated by the animating impulse of metapolitics, where the moral categories of liberal democracies are hollowed out, transformed, and recirculated to gain currency for antiliberal commitments.[89] Though this strategy gained prominence with the European New Right, it has expanded through what has come to be loosely known as the "new right" in North America and its alt-right offshoots (now often rebranded the "dissident right"). These metapolitical initiatives enter political discourse more broadly through mass-media figures who amplify narratives of decline, invasion, and replacement, thus engineering the perception of demographic threat that has fueled the rise of nativist and ethnopopulist movements on the recent electoral stage (e.g., Donald Trump, Viktor Orbán, Giorgia Meloni). Indeed, even the briefest tour through the right-wing media ecosystem will find efforts to depict migrant movements as "caravans," "invasions," "waves," or "floods"—conveying the sense of hostile, unstoppable forces that will yield nothing less than the destruction of the host nation.

The question that remains is the cost of this "language war" that defines broad sectors of the new right (and is now widely adopted across the far right). At one level, this cultural politics threatens the store of values and discourses on which democratic polities rely. To invoke the tradition of democratic thought, citizen rule hinges on public things—not simply common goods from which all civic participants might draw, but also a common stock of meanings that render possible civic conversations about a world that can be recognized as common.[90] In any truly pluralist society, these values are contested, though these negotiations take place against background understandings without which any meaningful exchange would be impossible. From this vantage point, new right metapolitics threatens the health of the democratic public sphere by stretching its orienting categories (in this case, equality) so far that they may no longer provide a meaningfully *common* civic vocabulary. The deformation of these resources is particularly prominent under conditions of heightened polarization, where citizens increasingly cannot agree on common authorities, common media worlds, or common futures. Under these conditions, it is not only that civic adversaries cannot agree on common truths; more radically, they cannot agree even on the epistemic standards through which contests over truth could be settled.

The more urgent implications, however, come clear through a consideration of the policies, dreams, and visions to which this cultural politics has been pressed. Where the new right persistently claims the true mantle of equality and diversity, one of its deepest underlying commitments is to a staunch antiegalitarianism. Indeed, its hostility toward an egalitarian politics is not limited to condemning equality as a value that facilitates widespread demographic change. Rather, new right and far right figures persistently maintain that egalitarian ideals commit a fundamental error in their estimation of the worth of human lives, cultures, and races.[91] This normative universe is founded in a commitment to ranks and hierarchies between both individuals and cultures. By extension, a politics of cultural or racial defense would preserve not only the differences among peoples in abstract terms but also what the new right views as their different ranks. This commitment is well captured by the alt-right poster and meme campaign that asserts, "Equality Is a False God."[92] At the movement level, there is perhaps no better illustration than the American far right militant organization the Proud Boys, who define themselves through a core commitment to Western chauvinism, exemplified by their motto, repeated at the outset of every meeting: "West Is Best."

These antiegalitarian commitments do significant work on the cultural battlefield of new right activism. For instance, the right-wing provocateur Christopher Rufo goes beyond advocating "discourse engineering" as a tool to secure political gains for the right.[93] In a more pointed sense, he enjoins conservative culture warriors to wage political battle using what he calls "linguistic weapons"—terms and categories that have been reconfigured to defame progressive movements, discredit their commitments in the public eye, and retrench existing hierarchies of power.[94] To promote this tactic, Rufo regularly distributes pamphlets filled with scripts of preformulated phrases and talking points to be taken up by far right activists as they wage campaigns against movements for civic equality. In Rufo's discursive world, pedagogies for racial equity are framed as "race-based Marxism" or "state-sanctioned racism," and movements for LGBTQ+ equality are tarred as supporting "groomers" (a term drawn from classic moral panics over child predators).[95] These linguistic weapons are not only used to guide public opinion toward or against certain policies; as political tools, they are designed to degrade political opponents by associating them with a variety of moral stains. From this perspective, the challenge posed by the new right metapolitical project goes beyond the fact that it destabilizes civic terms to suit the aims of an ascendant right; more important, it hollows out values, stripping them of their substantive meanings, so that they can be used as cudgels to seed public debates with antiegalitarian commitments.

The most troubling legacy of new right metapolitics, then, reflects the projects to which these tools have been set. The new right uses "linguistic weapons" not simply to influence public debate but also to preserve established hierarchies and patterns of dominance. To assess the ultimate implications of this cultural politics, it is necessary to go beyond new right efforts to pursue a "language war" conducted through terms, images, and symbols. More broadly, a meaningful evaluation must attend to the concrete projects that are promoted through these cultural interventions, particularly as these tactics are taken up by far right movements, actors, and organizations. Where hierarchy has long organized the far right imagination, this commitment becomes more ominous yet when negotiated through the racial fears and resentments that define the politics of demographic fear. Exploring these visions is the project of this book's remaining chapters.

CHAPTER 4

VISIONS OF ESCAPE

The Ethnostate and the Secessionist Dream of the Far Right

Our nation is of blood, not of paper. We need to wake up to our own dispossession, and the forces that made it possible. And we need to create a homeland in order to take back our own souls from a culture that has become a poison.

— *Gregory Hood, "An American Son," December 31, 2015*

Much recent political commentary is haunted by the specter of civic breakup. For instance, many scholars describe the rise of exclusive, gated communities as a form of secession for the affluent, who choose to live in such communities to insulate themselves from social inequality and unrest.[1] Within these enclaves, residents are sequestered behind gated walls and guard towers—measures that do not only control who can enter these spaces, but also provide a range of private substitutes for public goods (e.g., security, sanitation, recreation, public spaces). This diagnosis goes well beyond gated communities, as demonstrated by a wide literature that explores a gilded world for elites who live, learn, and travel differently from everyday citizens. These affluent global citizens no longer demonstrate a connection to any given nation, as their resources allow them to detach their interests from local communities.[2] The power of this diagnosis is confirmed by its popularity across the ideological spectrum. In a column for *American Conservative,* Mike Lofgren argues that this "secession is a withdrawal into enclaves, an internal immigration, whereby the rich disconnect themselves from the civic life of the nation and from any concern about its well being except as a place to extract loot."[3]

The literature on a class-based withdrawal from public goods reflects widespread concerns over the rise of a "new gilded age." A significant feature of the contemporary political scene, however, is a resurgence of the idea of secession—not as a metaphor for growing class divides but as a positive political ideal. Recent years, for instance, have seen movements for "Brexit" (the British secession from the European Union) and "Calexit" (an appeal for California to secede from the United States). And the quickest scan of popular political media finds commentators breathlessly asking whether it may be better to partition the nation, given the ideological divides that have led to increasing polarization.[4] For instance, Marjorie Taylor Greene, the far right U.S. congressional representative from Georgia, recently made news by proposing a "national divorce," where "red and blue states" would separate from one another and go their separate ways.[5] Secession, we are often told, may be preferable to a second civil war in a nation that can no longer find compromise.

Though the idea of "civic divorce" has become a thriving topic in newspapers and magazines, this chapter pursues a more specific question: how a neosecessionist vision has become a driving force in far right thought. Proponents differ in their details and reasoning, but the core logic remains consistent: secession is seen not simply as a last-case option but as the optimal solution to the deepest pathologies that nations suffer under conditions of globalization. In contrast to the "cultural secession" (i.e., withdrawal from dominant culture, music, television, and education) proposed by earlier generations of right-wing culture warriors, the recent push for secession takes strongly geopolitical form.[6] The extremist literature is filled with visions of homelands that could arise from the ruins of a divided nation—with names such as the Pacific Northwest Territorial Imperative, Ozarkia, and New Albion. In Europe, far right figures have endorsed the formation of Eurosiberia, an entirely new region stretching from Ireland across Russia, where the "traditional cultures" of Europe would be united.[7] And those strains of the far right that seek to "reclaim masculinity" against a "feminized society" have advocated for withdrawal into something approximating a pagan warrior culture, in which "men could be men" again (in some parodic version of hypermasculinity, performed for and with other men).[8]

A range of these visions will be treated in detail over the course of this chapter. In the United States, for instance, many secessionist dreams are grafted onto the separatist commitments that have long defined neo-Confederate and white power movements. Rather than offer a historical compendium of secessionist projects, however, the chapter will pursue two major aims. First, it will disentangle the multiple threads that inform the secessionist commitments of the recent far right. Though it is tempting to speak of a secessionist ideal, the singular case hardly captures the various influences and histories that run through these projects. As these strains are differentiated, what will come to the fore is the distinct vision that guides the far right politics of demographic fear: the ideal of an ethnically or racially homogeneous homeland—whether pitched specifically as a "white homeland" or presented in the more sanitized form of the "ethnostate" (itself typically a proxy phrase for a white racial nation). Although the political landscape contains various appeals to secession, the politics of demographic panic converges on a distinctively racialized vision of secession and a racialized vision of the world that would result. The pseudonymous far right author Michael O'Meara, for instance, hails the "movement to found a Whites-only nation-state somewhere in North America, once the poorly managed enterprise known as the United States collapses in a centrifugal dispersion of its decaying and perverted powers."[9] The core aim of this chapter is thus to step beyond far right criticisms of a multicultural society in order to explore the world they wish to build in its place. Detailing this social vision will expose some of the deepest pathologies of the far right's racial dreams.

The Secessionist Dreams of the Far Right: Precedents and Influences

To gain a sense of how deeply secessionist ideals are rooted in the far right imagination, it will be useful to begin with some concrete instances. Consider the following. In 2013, a planned community in Benawah County, Idaho, created a good deal of popular buzz.

The community, named the Citadel, would not be satisfied with mere gates; the plan was to construct a fortified wall along the full perimeter of the development. There would be no ordinance enforcement and no homeowners association. That said, to ensure some measure of communal security, every member over the age of thirteen would be mandated to carry a firearm, and the main industry of the complex would be a firearms factory.[10] This was hardly an isolated case. In 2008, followers of the right-libertarian U.S. congressional representative Ron Paul announced the purchase of one hundred acres of land in Texas, west of El Paso. The community they intended to found was to be named Paulville (after its ideological inspiration) and was to be dedicated to his archlibertarian vision. Although each member of the community was required to buy a plot at least an acre in size, all were left free to decide how to develop their own property. Even common utilities were to be distributed on a voluntary basis, leaving members the freedom to homestead within the space of the community.[11]

Neither of these projects came to fruition, but they are hardly alone. Indeed, one of the deepest dreams of the libertarian right is to find a geographic space in which a community of "true" liberty could take shape. Some particularly rich examples stem from the libertarian strains of Silicon Valley. Tech futurists often condemn the state of liberal democracies, but their utopian visions do not typically promote a more robust role for public goods or grassroots participation; rather, they seek what the tech entrepreneur and conservative political financier Peter Thiel has termed "an escape from politics in all its forms."[12] The most evocative instance along these lines is the Seasteading Institute, which is dedicated to the project of building an island nation beyond the jurisdiction of any standing governments. Here, the dream of sovereignty is mapped onto a familiar utopian geography: the *nonplace* that exists outside the bounds of the nation-state.[13] In this extranational space, entrepreneurs would be able to operate free of the regulations that are believed to quash innovation (a particularly fetishized good in the tech imagination). As the official statements of the Seasteading Institute propose, the optimal location for these experiments would be outer space, but given the prohibitive cost involved, the oceans offer the last viable sites where communities of radical freedom could be established. In these experimental communities, the ocean setting would permit governance to be conducted along market lines, with island colonies competing with one another for share of subjects. According to the seasteading advocates Patri Friedman and Brad Taylor, "If a family owns its own floating structure and becomes dissatisfied with the government it belongs to, it can simply sail away to another jurisdiction: with dynamic geography, people can vote with their houses."[14]

Such cases become easy headline fodder. They are not, however, utopian fantasies, wholly disconnected from the movement literature of the far right. Instead, they speak to a broader spirit of secession that has come to organize increasing sectors of the far right imagination.

To unpack these dreams, it will be useful to disentangle some of their major theoretical sources. As hinted by the seasteading literature, one of the most familiar wellsprings of secessionist thought is the hard-line tradition of right-libertarianism (and its paleolibertarian offshoot) that views community as a voluntary association between autonomous individuals and casts the state as an agent of violence. Because this tradition takes the autonomy of the individual as a baseline natural right, right-libertarians often place consent at the core of their secessionist dreams. Specifically, if the consent of the governed is required to ensure the legitimacy of governing bodies, citizens may withdraw their consent to signal their desire to reassociate in a different manner, under different institutions.[15] It is this vision that leads the right-libertarian economist Ludwig von Mises to argue that the voluntary nature of civic association retains absolute moral priority vis-à-vis the state. In his terms:

> The right of self-determination in regard to the question of membership in a state thus means: whenever the inhabitants of a particular territory, whether it be a single village, a whole district, or a series of adjacent districts, make it known, by a freely conducted plebiscite, that they no longer wish to remain united to the state to which they belong at the time, but wish either to form an independent state or to attach themselves to some other state, their wishes are to be respected and complied with.[16]

Although this libertarian lineage has long informed conservative debates over a political "right of exit," the contemporary secessionist imagination draws significantly from a competing ideological strain, the rights of cultural or ethnic groups to preserve their identities against what is depicted as an all-encompassing "monoculture."[17] At one level, this tradition targets what it depicts as the "gigantism" of the contemporary nation-state. The increasing size of this administrative apparatus means that it simply cannot do justice to the commitments or values of its various regions and localities.[18] Instead, the state imposes the will of distant bureaucrats on local communities, each of which possesses its own values, preferences, and needs. For those of a communitarian bent, then, the right of secession is founded in the right to withdraw from a broader association in order to preserve the values of a smaller community. In the United States, these arguments are often filtered through neo-Confederate terms of the "Lost Cause," a position that idealizes the traditions of the white American South, elides their violent racial history, and bemoans their supposed loss. These commitments are given voice in the work of the conservative philosopher Donald Livingston. According to Livingston, perhaps the most fundamental American contribution to political thought is a presumed right to secession, founded in the claim to regional and cultural sovereignty. He states: "A seceding people may even think that the government is not especially unjust. What they seek, however, is to be left alone to govern themselves as they see fit."[19] On this argument, the abiding political legacy of the United States is not the revolutionary impulse to overturn a given order, but rather the right to withdraw from the jurisdiction of the state in order to preserve a specific form of life.

As this brief primer reveals, the far right vision of secession has historically drawn from a number of ideological sources. Where libertarian ideals have long informed neo-secessionist dreams, growing segments of the far right distance themselves from the typically individualist commitments of libertarianism (including many individuals and organizations that previously avowed a libertarian identity). Though both ideological streams appeal to a sovereignty that is supposedly threatened by political institutions, far right secession advocates increasingly highlight the identity of groups, regions, or cultures as the good to be defended against the state or an all-encompassing monoculture. And these appeals to community take a strongly racialized direction within the far right politics of demographic fear. For much of the far right, the culture under attack (and the culture to be preserved) is not simply a set of practices, values, and traditions passed down through history—it is a specifically white racial inheritance. As a considerable extremist literature maintains, whiteness is the genetic foundation for the "true nation," and it is whiteness that has ostensibly been attacked through generations of government policies, ranging from integration to multiculturalism to affirmative action.[20] It is this moment of perceived crisis that gives shape to the separatist dreams of the far right. The guiding idea behind these projects of white separation is that "whites have legitimate group interests," and these interests can be realized only within a territory dedicated to "white culture" (itself presented as something that is both coherent and identifiable).[21]

This appeal to white interests means that one goal now rests at the forefront of the far right secessionist imagination: the establishment of a white racial homeland, typically referred to as the ethnostate. To actualize this vision, far right figures urge white subjects to define themselves through their ethnoracial core of whiteness (i.e., to develop "racial consciousness"), to purify this inheritance by protecting it from other cultural and racial influences, and to build political institutions dedicated to its preservation. As the alt-right author Gregory Hood puts this commitment: "The great imperative of our time is for the white European population within the United States to secure its existence by creating a homeland independent of the present American system. All other platforms, programs, and issues are distractions or deceptions."[22]

The Ethnostate Dream: Arguments and Essentials

Because the ethnostate has become one of the most notorious elements of the far right imagination, it is worthwhile to examine some of its core features. Put broadly, the ethnostate is not simply a secessionist proposal, indifferent to the type of community that will result; it is a substantive ideal for what secession should accomplish in light of the far right's demographic fears. For some, the ethnostate would follow the classic pattern of a *Herrenvolk* democracy—where one race reserves to itself political, social, and cultural dominance over other groups within a racially mixed polity.[23] For others, the ideal of the ethnostate is more radical, involving a nation forged around a monoethnic or monoracial constituency (or, in looser interpretations, a community in which the percentage of the nonwhite population would be kept below a specified level, and white majorities would possess exclusive rights to political sovereignty).[24] For the alt-right figurehead Richard Spencer, a white homeland is precisely the sort of ideal that could focus the diffuse anger of disaffected white majorities and consolidate them toward a single goal: "We need a *telos,* an outcome or end goal—something that we are working towards, that channels our energies. . . . The ideal I advocate is the creation of a White Ethno-State on the North American continent."[25] This dream of a white homeland acts as a lodestar for the white extremist imaginary. Just as the specter of racial displacement haunts white replacement narratives, so too does much of the far right tilt toward a positive ideal of white nationhood. The National Socialist Movement, a neo-Nazi organization that grew out of the American Nazi Party, states this point in blunt terms: "We demand our own territory for the sustenance of our people."[26]

Much white homeland activism draws from the unreconstructed dreams of the white power tradition. Take, for instance, the writings of David Lane, a white supremacist who provided ideological support for the violent extremist organization known as the Order (a militant group, active in the 1980s, that plotted armed insurrection against the U.S. government toward the goal of a white homeland).[27] According to Lane's infamous formula for white power movements ("the fourteen words"), a white homeland would be designed to "secure the existence of our people and a future for White children."[28] For the unvarnished white supremacist camps of the far right, then, the aim of the ethnostate can be put simply: if something recognizable as "the white race" is to survive, it requires a geopolitical space in which interracial reproduction is impossible and white people can reproduce their culture without the influence of other cultures, genetic potentials,

A promotional sign advertises the Northwest Front white ethnostate.

integration mandates, or what are decried as "antiwhite" educational platforms. In broad terms, Lane asserts that "no race of People can indefinitely continue their existence without territorial imperatives in which to propagate, protect, and promote their own kind."[29] These gestures are developed throughout the literature of white power movements. Harold Covington, a neo-Nazi figure associated with the white supremacist Northwest Front organization, proposed a symptomatic version of an ethnostate to be located in the Pacific Northwest region of the United States; named the Northwest Territorial Imperative, it would be a "safe and racially homogenous haven in that our people may rest, regroup, and replenish our numbers." Without such a preserve, "the Aryan race will perish from the North American continent and most likely from the rest of the earth as well."[30]

Much white homeland advocacy thus presents the vision in terms of racial defense. As ethnostate advocates argue, a geopolitical space of racial or ethnic purity is necessary if embattled whites are to contest their defeats and losses and "white culture" is to be preserved. For instance, the National Alliance, at one time a major neo-Nazi organization in the United States, holds that "after the sickness of 'multiculturalism,' . . . we must again have a racially clean area of the earth for the further development of our people. We must have White schools, White residential neighborhoods and recreation areas. . . . We must have no non-Whites in our living space, and we must have open space around us for expansion."[31] The language of this passage is instructive. Minimally, the reference to "white living space" self-consciously evokes classic Nazi appeals to *Lebensraum*—a trope that pervades much of the white supremacist literature on ethnic homelands.[32] Nazi formulas are ubiquitous in white homeland activism, as evinced by the "blood and soil" chants at the 2017 "Unite the Right" rally in Charlottesville. Furthermore, the rhetoric of expansion in the cited passage reflects how the defensive vision of "white survival" often gives way to a triumphalist dream of a resurgent white nation. The aim expressed in much ethnostate literature is not simply to survive within a white racial enclave, but to expand, grow, and retake the imagined territories of whiteness. For Billy Roper, who spearheads the white supremacist Shield Wall Network, this project of resurgence would be served by the white homeland of Ozarkia—a geographic expanse in the United States where the current racial concentrations are presented as ripe for attaining the ethnic homogeneity desired for white nationhood.[33] While Roper portrays the Ozark region as a de facto refuge from the demographic changes reshaping the United States, the ultimate aim for the ethnostate is not to operate as a defensive retreat but rather to furnish the base from which a white nation will be reborn. As he figures this expansionist vision: "Our new ethnostates will not be small. They will not be isolated. . . . They will grow to be a superpower. After a relatively short period of establishment and coalescence while our multiracial and nonWhite neighbors regress and collapse, New America will expand again, like a nuclear explosion pushing outwards once the atoms are bound together and compressed, their energy collected, and then released. Boom, baby. We will take it all back."[34]

This triumphal vision of white nationhood channels the classic themes of white power literature. As the scholar Alexandra Minna Stern has detailed, however, recent decades have seen efforts to make this vision palatable to a broader audience.[35] In this sanitized version, the ethnostate is described not as a means to secure white power, an Aryan stronghold, or racial supremacy, but rather as a solution to the problems unleashed by global modernity. Specifically, advocates typically present a white homeland as a means for cultural preservation in a time of global "panmixia."[36] Where all the trends of globalization are driving toward a homogeneous culture—with a McDonald's on every corner, the same fast fashion on style-conscious bodies, and Hollywood films in every cinema—monoethnic societies are presented as the means to preserve distinct cultures, races, and ethnicities. The core logic can be put simply: because groups stay separate in an ethnostate system, they will remain *different*. These nods to pluralist values are typically pushed further, to propose that ethnically homogeneous states should be allotted to other cultures and races, so that they can also preserve their difference against the "monoculture" of global modernity. The more elaborate ethnostate proposals thus often come equipped with detailed geographic maps that carve up the space of the United States into autonomous zones allotted for both white and nonwhite collectives.[37] For instance, the public literature for the New Albion ethnostate proposes parallel spaces with names such as Aztlan and the Free Black State, where nonwhite populations would pursue their own racially defined communities.[38] In the terms of Jared Taylor, head of the New Century Foundation, "What we ask for ourselves is nothing more nor less than what we want for people of all races: the right to pursue their destinies free from the unwanted embrace of others, to seek a future that is uniquely theirs within neighborhoods, institutions, regions, and ultimately nations in which they are the permanent and undisputed majority."[39]

Within much white separatist literature, then, the ethnostate is glossed in terms designed to increase its mainstream appeal. It is presented as the last stand of "diversity" in a world that is being homogenized through the ongoing mixture of populations.[40] This rhetorical strategy is given greater normative depth by those who promote ethnic enclaves as a cure for cultural crisis. For these advocates, the demand for a white homeland begins with the ostensible pathologies of a nation that has lost its way or squandered its future—typically as a result of multiculturalist commitments. This equation of pathology and diversity is particularly strong for those figures who (like Taylor) base their arguments in the tenets of "race realism." For these segments of the far right, multicultural commitments overlook the "real" differences between races that are purportedly written into their natural affinities, talents, and capacities. "Race realists" accordingly tend to commit themselves to brutely naturalistic renderings of social health, asserting that there simply *are* natural affinities for clustering with members of one's own ethnic or racial group, and to violate these affinities is to violate the mandates of nature.[41] Multicultural experiments therefore yield violence, conflict, and aggression between populations that are brought into "unnatural" social intimacy.[42] To push this claim further, racial integration is identified as the cause of a range of social pathologies: increases in crime, the degradation of neighborhoods, declines in educational outcomes, and widespread cultural tensions.[43] For "race realists," these social ills are all connected in that they represent the inevitable outcomes of policies that violate the deepest mandates of human identity. In the formula that haunts much race realist literature, "Racial diversity is a source of conflict, not strength."[44]

Though daunting at face value, these social ills are often presented as signs of the deeper civic cost that supposedly attends racial and ethnic integration: the loss of any coherent community. In a "functioning" society, members are meant to share significant common ground, but in a multiracial society, commonality and trust are corroded, producing a nation of strangers.[45] This is the basis for the fable that appears regularly in the literature of the far right—a tale of a bygone past in which a single culture reigned, neighbors knew one another, people left their doors unlocked, people of both genders (two in number, fixed by nature) knew their proper roles, and children played unsupervised in the streets. According to many ethnostate advocates, this golden age of civic solidarity can be salvaged only by restoring ethnoracial homogeneity. The white nationalist Greg Johnson, for instance, argues that "white nationalism is simply the idea of a society where everybody around you is kin. It is a society where you can understand and trust your fellow citizens. Where you can cooperate to pursue the common good . . . most importantly, it is a society in which you can feel at home. That's what White Nationalism is about: securing homelands for all white people."[46] This vision of civic renewal cuts a distinct figure in the right-wing literature of decline. Where lamentations over civic erosion are now familiar in conservative literature, the racialist vision of civic regeneration sidesteps the solutions that are often proposed (e.g., commitments to strengthening the institutions of civil society).[47] Instead, the ethnostate is presented as the ethnic and racial foundation for a community that could be whole and trusting again. Civic community, in this vision, is not a social accomplishment, sustained by a rich web of values or institutions, but the outgrowth of drives for racial affinity, inscribed within the ostensible "facts" of biology. Rather than shared civic histories or visions of a civic future, it is bonds of genetic commonality, hardwired into the biological foundations of race, that supposedly make kin.

Though the arguments for an ethnostate differ in detail across the far right, they typically rely on the same core commitment: the primary basis for human solidarity rests in biology (typically figured as race).[48] This premise leads to the corollary that appears throughout the ethnostate advocacy literature: to confound lines of racial affinity is to court civic conflict and dissolution. No amount of civic engineering can overcome these tendencies, which are supposedly hardwired into the basics of human biology. To heal the body politic and foster civic renewal, far right figures argue, it is necessary to eliminate racial mixture in favor of ethnically homogeneous communities, territories, and nations. The ethnostate, in this sense, represents a brutely naturalized vision of civic redemption, where politics can only bow to the obscure mandates of nature.

From Separatism to Supremacy: Tensions of the Ethnostate

Upon exploring the ethnostate debates, one trend has come to the fore. Though arguments for white homelands draw freely from the history of white supremacy, ethnostate advocates have increasingly attempted to obscure this patrimony.[49] For instance, many have sought to diminish the racist associations of the ethnostate by presenting it as a community dedicated to "traditional European values." Such appeals to shared values or traditions feature prominently in the promotional materials for the New Albion ethnostate, a racialized, white community that was envisioned as stretching across the northern half of the United States and up through Canada.[50] Rather than advertising a geography of racial victory, the New Albion literature frames its racial vision as "living in harmony with nature" according to the guiding traditions of "folkism" (a coded term meant to conjure the ideological wellsprings of Nazism).[51] This mission statement is reinforced by the visual culture of this ethnostate project. The New Albion brochures are peppered with photos of nature, colonial barns, and white families in pastoral settings. The official New Albion flag veers away from the usual image repertoire of white power movements to instead place a pine tree at its center. This presentation reflects a broader shift in the public face of white separation movements, as they seek purchase beyond the world of patent racial supremacists. The ethnostate is now often portrayed as a way for white populations to "go their own way" and preserve "European civilization" rather than as a means to secure white racial supremacy.

Although the sanitized presentation of the ethnostate stresses themes of community, culture, nature, and diversity, these appeals quickly take on a more ominous tone when they are mapped onto the language of racial destiny familiar from fascist narratives of nationhood. This overlap is well conveyed in the following passage from Richard Spencer, which slides uneasily from one register to the other:

> We need an ethno-state so that our people can "come home again," can live amongst family, and feel safe and secure. But we also need an Ethno-state so that Whites can again reach the stars. Before the onset of the "equality" sclerosis, Europeans had a unique ability to risk everything for ends that are super-human. We must give up the false dreams of equality and democracy . . . so that we can take up the new

> dreams of channelling our energies and labor towards the exploration of our universe, towards the fostering of a new people, who are healthier, stronger, more intelligent, more beautiful, more athletic. We need an ethno-state so that we could rival the ancients.[52]

In such renderings, the ethnostate is not simply a tool to secure an imagined era of social harmony. Rather, the argument channels those philosophical critics of modernity who have a particular appeal for the far right (e.g., Friedrich Nietzsche, Oswald Spengler).[53] These borrowings typically emphasize a core theme: modernity as a time of cultural decline, signaled by what Spencer describes as the "false dreams of equality and democracy."[54] Where modernity is condemned for "leveling down" humankind toward sameness and mediocrity, the possibility of cultural excellence hinges on the cultivation of great, singular human types, capable of tearing down life-denying values and creating new exemplars for life and culture.[55] Much far right literature, for instance, lionizes the "natural elite" or the "strong man" as the sole human type able to reclaim the nation from the masses of "last men" who are anaesthetized by consumerism and mass entertainment.[56] And, for ethnostate advocates, these themes of overcoming often take communal shape. As Spencer conveys in the cited passage, the ethnostate is presented not only as a place where a lost racial community can be recaptured for its own sake but ultimately as a site where the white race can actualize its unique racial destiny: to lead the nations of the world beyond the dead end of modernity.

The connections drawn between a white homeland and cultural advancement are not limited, however, to rarefied philosophical arguments over values or modernity. Similar claims are made by those who promote a white ethnostate in evolutionary terms, presenting genetic collectives as the movers of human progress. Within this racialized narrative of human development, a homogeneous white collective is granted the strongest potential for cultural advancement, owing to its ostensible genetic capacities. As Wilmot Robertson, the American far right author who popularized the term in his 1992 book *The Ethnostate,* argues:

"Whites should be saved, not for their own sake but because of their special place in the order of things. In all the innumerable galaxies out there, none may have any life form as advanced as *Homo sapiens*. Because they are that division of *Homo sapiens* most capable of carrying on the Faustian adventure, whites are precious commodities."[57] For those drawn to evolutionary narratives of history, a white ethnostate is necessary not only to preserve the white race but also to protect the ostensible white capacity to make irreplaceable contributions to human advancement.[58] For Robertson, only a state where white populations can maintain their genetic inheritance will allow them to "recover their spirits and morale and again take their place in the vanguard of the Great Evolutionary Trek."[59] The argument for racial separation thus gestures beyond interests specific to white constituencies to advertise gains for humankind more broadly. In doing so, it grafts the ethnostate onto the deepest fantasies of white supremacy, where the white race acts as a beacon to other races and cultures in order to pull the human condition forward.[60]

The above is hardly an exhaustive rendering of the various strains that coalesce in the far right dream of the ethnostate, and a broader account would need to explore how major European schools of the far right tend to organize their political dreams around what they instead term a "carnal homeland" (a vision where "indigenous Europeans" would forge a community that reflects only their own cultural commitments).[61] That said, the preceding discussion captures many of the far right's investments in an ethnically homogeneous homeland where white populations would be able to fulfill their unique "destiny."[62] In this sense, the ethnostate represents what the scholar of the far right Cynthia Miller-Idriss terms an effort to map utopian ideals onto a spatial setting.[63] For those who dream of white homelands, space is the setting in which fantasies of a glorious future or restored past are staged. Time is grafted onto territory, a spatial setting where change can be halted, a golden age restored, and an alternative future imagined. These dreams of a racial homeland thus go beyond ideals of racial preservation or political supremacy. This mythic geography promises something deeper: a state of racial wholeness to compensate for the grief, loss, and betrayal of the present. Simply put, the white ethnostate stakes its appeal on a rich emotional promise: this is a land where a forgotten, humiliated people can get what they deserve. It is a land where they can be "at home" again, surrounded by only their own practices, languages, and traditions.[64]

As the foregoing reveals, however, this racialized vision of community is riddled with tensions in both presentation and substance. Though much public literature of the ethnostate pitches a vision of difference, where racial or cultural groups follow their particular values or traditions, the far right persistently commits to a supremacist table of racial hierarchy. White separatist movements, for instance, typically argue that white populations should be granted the right to "go their own way." To this end, they often frame their commitment to white separation as part of a broader principle of ethnic autonomy—that all racial groups should be able "to pursue their unique destiny free from the embrace of large numbers of people unlike themselves."[65] Don Black, the former Ku Klux Klan leader who founded Stormfront.org, one of the most influential online platforms for white extremists, makes this point bluntly: "We believe that we as white people, as European Americans, have the right to pursue our destiny without interference from other races. And we feel that other races have that right as well."[66] And yet this asserted right to autonomy (one ostensibly owed to all peoples) is inflected by commitments to white racial superiority. The ominous language of a white racial destiny encountered throughout this chapter presses a vision of racial difference that assigns to the white race a higher capacity to contribute to human progress. Likewise, this claim of white racial supremacy persistently asserts the inferiority or relative incapacity of competing races. Greg Johnson puts this logic of racial hierarchy in brute terms when he argues that "not all peoples have an equal capacity for self-government" within his vision of ethnic homelands. For those ethnic and racial groups that cannot meaningfully exercise their collective autonomy, an ethnostate is neither appropriate nor possible. Instead, such peoples (all rendered by Johnson in exclusively nonwhite terms) "require benevolent paternalism and ethnic reservations."[67]

The Violent Sovereignty of the Ethnostate: The Question of Fascism

It is now possible to pry apart some of the pathologies that run through the white homeland debates. Perhaps most obviously, the justifications offered by ethnostate advocates often cycle between bad faith and significant tensions. While white separatism is often presented as a commitment to group autonomy, such appeals are frequently underpinned by assertions of white racial or cultural superiority. And this tension gives way to others when read against a longer, historical background. Once approached in this light, recent calls for the ethnostate stand in tension with the libertarian sources that have long stoked secessionist energies on the far right. Indeed, figures of the far right often identify the strong libertarian commitment to individual autonomy as a significant obstacle to the formation of racial solidarities and thus an enabling factor in the decline of white racial fortunes.[68] This increasing embrace of a racialized community (even within long-standing libertarian organizations, such as the Alabama-based Mises Institute) has fueled what one commentator has memorably described as the "insidious libertarian to alt-right pipeline" that defines recent migration to the far right.[69] John Bruce Leonard, chief editor of the far right publishing house Arktos, goes further, arguing that a "new ethnic unity" is required "if we are to neutralize the poison of so-called individualism."[70] This critique of individualism dovetails with many far right critiques of market society, in which individual consumption is seen as blinding white subjects to their ongoing dispossession.[71] In these critiques, market rewards are presented as an anesthetic or distraction that prevents white subjects from recognizing the collective attacks and losses they have suffered in an ostensibly "antiwhite" world.

Anxieties over consumerism and market rewards are not new in the far right political imagination. A long line of conservative figures have lamented how market values can corrode and colonize nonmarket spheres of life and values.[72] What brings the racialist right into stronger tension with libertarian strains of secessionist thought are the two groups' competing views of the state and their divergent stances toward its practical possibilities.

According to a robust tradition of right-libertarianism, the state represents one of the primary enemies of human freedom, an ever-expansive leviathan that must be carefully monitored and limited in the exercise of its coercive powers.[73] This antipathy toward the state does not just exist in the theoretical ether, as it plays a significant role in much far right activism. A major spur to the contemporary militia movement, for instance, is a deep mistrust of an expansive federal government—particularly its increasing militarized relationship to its own citizens. These anxieties were given exemplary form in the cases that have entered into the far right antistate mythology: the 1992 raid on the white separatist Randy Weaver at Ruby Ridge, Idaho, and the 1993 siege of the Branch Davidian compound in Waco, Texas. In both cases, federal law enforcement officers brought the coercive powers of the state to bear on private individuals.[74] Indeed, much of the militia movement (now rebranding itself as the "patriot movement") regards an expansive central government as little more than an enemy of individual or regional autonomy. This hostility toward centralized authority is magnified by a central trope of the far right forums: the claim that the state has been captured by global interests, so that it represents a kind of enemy to the "true nation."[75] Such charges take particularly virulent form in the anti-Semitic conspiracy theory that international Jewish interests have infiltrated the state, creating what is often termed the Zionist Occupation Government, or ZOG. This fantasy of an international Jewish cabal that seeks to undermine competing nations or races links much antistate fulmination to the anti-Semitic currents that run through the politics of demographic fear.[76] In a characteristic rendering, the National Alliance claims: "Since the end of the Second World War, no White government has been under the control of White men with our values and our ideology. White governments everywhere are terminally corrupt, led by collaborators with the Jews." This "collaboration" has ultimately led the state to become "the malignant monster it is today: the single most dangerous and destructive enemy our race has ever known."[77]

One distinguishing feature of the ethnostate vision, then, is its distance from the anarchist and libertarian strains that long informed far right secessionist dreams.[78] Where secessionist movements often take a strongly antigovernment stance, much ethnostate advocacy instead details an expansive role for state planning, ranging from education to culture to immigration control. As Greg Johnson proposes:

> All White Nationalist policies require government action. They are not going to happen simply by leaving people alone. . . . White Nationalism by its very nature is statist rather than libertarian, collectivist rather than individualist, illiberal rather than liberal. We believe that there is a common good—the survival and flourishing of our people—which can only be promoted by government policy, and we believe that whenever private interests conflict with the common good, the common good must win out.[79]

Those who promote the ethnostate thus occupy a distinctive place on the far right landscape. Where libertarian figures seek to shrink the state to a minimalist form, ethnostate advocates view the state in more instrumental terms, as a tool that could be used to bring about substantive policy goals. In the case of the ethnostate, the core aim of government would be to secure and preserve a white nation.[80] The public platform of the National Alliance expresses these statist tendencies in clear terms: "Perhaps the time will come when we can afford to have minimal government once again, but that time lies in the remote future. The fact is that we need a strong, centralized government spanning several continents to coordinate many important tasks during the first few decades of a White world: the establishment of White living space, the rooting out of racially destructive institutions, and the reorganization of society on a new basis."[81]

These commitments highlight an important ambivalence in the ethnostate debates. Although the far right literature routinely celebrates the work of "strong men" and "born leaders"—in the classic cult of the hero—the actions of such individuals alone are not sufficient for establishing the white nation to come. Instead, for major segments of the far right, a white homeland can only be secured if the coercive powers of the state are placed in the hands of these new elites. This project is typically envisioned through a number of distinct stages. First, in a process of "recapture," the state will be taken back from the adversaries of the "real" nation (typically rendered as "globalists" of some stripe).[82] Only after the state is secured for its "true heirs" can its institutions be turned to the task of creating a white homeland, by distilling a predominantly (or exclusively) white racial concentration from the present state of ethnic and cultural mixture.

This mission typically revolves around halting nonwhite immigration and removing members of ethnic and racial groups deemed incompatible with the desired ethnic composition—though proposals for accomplishing these goals take on a variety of casts. Those ethnostate advocates who seek to appeal beyond an audience of unrepentant white extremists present the imperative for removal in terms designed to obscure the violence of expulsion. Greg Johnson, for instance, persistently stresses a "nonviolent" process of removal, which he euphemistically terms a "slow cleanse."[83] In this vision, a wide variety of economic incentives and civil sanctions would be marshaled against nonwhite residents to ensure their departure. For those nonwhite individuals who have sufficiently long standing in the community and are past the age of reproduction, Johnson proposes a system of "reservations" or resettlement within the white homeland.[84] The more militant identitarian strains present the imperative in more uncompromising terms: removal by any means possible. As the French identitarian Guillaume Faye argues, the imperative for territorial control demands "a clear policy of *de-migration*, i.e., those people's voluntary or forced departures, in parallel to a complete suspension of further arrivals."[85] Here, the degree of perceived cultural threat justifies an equally radical response, reflected in the calls across the European identitarian literature for a "reconquest" of the nations of Europe (a project defined by strongly Islamophobic currents).[86] And, as the next chapter will explore, state-led efforts to secure a desired racial concentration typically grapple with another central question: What policies or incentives would promote the reproductive practices necessary for the future of a majority-white nation? In this connection, at least one of the tasks envisioned by the National Alliance is the prevention of interracial marriage and reproduction: "The central task of a new government will be to reverse the racially devolutionary course of the last few millennia and keep it reversed: a long-term eugenics program involving at least the entire populations of Europe and America. Such a task is necessarily intrusive, and it will require large-scale organization."[87]

Even this limited engagement helps to highlight one of the defining features of ethnostate projects. For a wide variety of white secessionists, the task is not to withdraw from the state in order to secure a life of individual autonomy. Indeed, a culture of individualism is often described as one of the factors that helped to generate the perceived state of crisis by permitting the neglect of collective white interests. According to Patriot Front, an American white nationalist organization known for its street demonstrations, "Individualism, while originally good in concept and proposition, has been allowed to run rampant in our modern society, where it has become a plague in its amplification."[88] The central path toward an ethnostate instead demands the formation of white racial consciousness, founded on the collective interests of white subjects; and to serve these interests, a sovereign government must be placed under the exclusive direction of white citizens. In pursuing these goals, movements for white homelands forge a pathological form of racial populism. Where the characteristic trope of populism is to "take back" the nation for the "true" or "genuine" people, the vision of the ethnostate takes a more muscular stance, in which the apparatus of the state (and its monopoly on coercive force) is turned toward the ideal of racial separation.[89] Ethnostate advocates do not simply insist that the state should be used for the substantive policy interests of a resurgent right. Rather, their vision of social engineering reflects a classic commitment of fascist experiments—to establish a state apparatus that reflects the interests of an organic, racially defined "people" and enforces a hierarchical vision of human difference.

This appeal to a muscular state helps flesh out the fascist residues that litter the far right landscape.[90] Much far right literature of recent decades has attempted to reclaim or revive the classic literature, iconography, and themes of fascism. And many of these borrowings have tracked the ideal of an "organic" community, bound by race and committed to human hierarchy.[91] The

Vanguard America organization, which played a major role in the 2017 "Unite the Right" rally, straightforwardly embraced the fascist ideal and placed it at the heart of its vision for the future. As one Vanguard screed portrayed the battle for a white ethnic future: "Just being White will not be enough to earn protection; everyone will have to live up to the standards of this budding ultranationalist form of Fascism that has sprung up. Everyone will be bound around that axe, in unity. . . . American Fascism will once again make this nation a bastion of hope for all of Western Civilization and will pave the way to secure the existence of our people and a future for White children."[92] As the ethnostate literature reveals, the nods to fascism that pervade the movement literature of the far right are not solely cosmetic—as might be suggested by alt-right commitments to a "fashy" personal aesthetic or "fashwave" music and visual culture. Nor do these allusions simply reflect a nostalgic desire for national unity against the dispersion of modernity. At bottom, these visions of political redemption are firmly rooted within the long tradition of a fascist politics—appealing to strong state measures to bring about the rebirth of an organic, racial people.[93]

This dream of radical rebirth ties the ethnostate to the heart of the fascist ideal: a new age for the chosen racial people that will revive and actualize the destiny embedded within their ancient, organic roots. And the affinity with fascism is rooted more deeply than a dream of rebirth or a vague language of racial destiny. To render the links more clearly, the fascist ideal rests on the use of political mobilization to bring about this age of glory and wholeness. It is here that the ethnostate takes on a particularly troubling resonance. If a white nation is to be secured—if embattled whites are to find a land where they can be "at home" again—the ethnostate literature arrives at a single conclusion: this destiny will be delivered only through a state apparatus equipped with coercive powers to break the claim of the old, eliminate the ostensible threats to an integrated white people, and give birth to a redeemed white nation.

CHAPTER 5

THE REPRODUCTIVE POLITICS OF A "NICE, WHITE NATION"

The Biopolitics of the Far Right

Having a lot of White babies is a great way to fight genocide.

— *"WhiteMan," user comment on whitedate.net forum, posted August 14, 2021*

In March 2019, a white extremist, Brenton Tarrant, entered two different mosques in Christchurch, New Zealand, and opened fire with a weapon covered in white supremacist slogans. He killed fifty-one Muslims at their places of worship and wounded forty others, and was arrested while driving to a third location, where he planned to carry out further violence. In the aftermath of the murders, police found that Tarrant had posted a manifesto online, titled simply "The Great Replacement." After some preliminary remarks, the opening lines of the manifesto state: "It's the birthrates. It's the birthrates. It's the birthrates. If there is one thing I want you to remember from these writings, it's that the birthrates must change. Even if we were to deport all non-Europeans from our lands tomorrow, the European people would still be spiraling into decay and eventual death."[1]

Though it would be easy to dismiss this screed as little more than a murderous race fantasy, concerns over birthrates have long played a central role in the far right politics of demographic fear. Armed with demographic data, figures of the far right argue that nation after nation is experiencing a process of "reverse colonization" in which native populations are being "replaced" by cultural newcomers (particularly Muslims and immigrants from the global South). At one level, they assert that this "demographic swamping" has been facilitated by permissive immigration policies. At another level, much far right literature argues that this ongoing "invasion" is magnified by another trend within the nations of the West: the decline in native birthrates. Greg Johnson, who heads the white nationalist media organization Counter-Currents, concludes that "white birthrates are below replacement levels in every country around the globe. If this trend continues, white countries will cease to exist."[2]

Far right figures claim that these overlapping factors lead toward one outcome: the nations of the West are facing a process of "white erasure" that is unfolding with quasi-arithmetic certainty.[3] Given the rise in immigration levels and the decline in reproductive rates, white majorities are fated to come to an end. In terms that reflect the dire character of this analysis, the American alt-right figure Richard Spencer argues that "any future immigration-restriction efforts are meaningless. Even if *all* immigration, legal and illegal, were miraculously halted tomorrow morning, our country's demographic destiny would merely be delayed by a decade or two."[4] This fatalism is well represented by the home page of the white extremist website the Daily Stormer, which features a graphic charting the current white percentage of the population (both in the United States and across the globe) and mapping its decline in real time, like a stock report tracking the ongoing fortunes of the white race.[5] Unlike a stock report, however, the graphic offers no hope of a market rebound. Instead, the trajectory leads inevitably downward, toward the point when white subjects will be a minority in their own lands and their cultures effaced.

As noted in earlier chapters, such demographic fears have spawned a number of countermeasures. Much of the critical attention has focused on the far right's proposals to halt the influx of migrants—typically through some combination of immigration controls, deportations, and incentives for relocation. A flyer distributed by the National Alliance, a neo-Nazi organiza-

Promotional flyer from the National Alliance promotes the deportation of immigrants.

tion in the United States, captures that position in brute terms: against a graphic of immigrants running (presumably to cross a border), the caption reads, "SEND THEM BACK. They can't make White babies."[6] Some of the proposed anti-immigration measures are intended to be enacted by the state after it has been purged of "globalist" elements and reclaimed by the "true" nation. Others have already been put into practice by identitarian groups who have taken matters into their own hands to make up for the perceived failures of the state. At the southern border of the United States, a number of paramilitary groups have elected to take on tasks of border control, patrolling the border area to identify and intercept migrants attempting to enter the nation.[7] Armed groups such as the Minuteman Project routinely detain migrants, report their movements to Border Patrol offices, and destroy supplies left to aid those who cross the arid borderlands.

Parallel movements in Europe have seen identitarian groups patrolling the Mediterranean Sea and mountain passes of the Alps in an effort to intercept migrants (and secure footage to be used in their online media campaigns).[8] What has received comparatively fewer headlines, however, is the other "natalist" objective pursued by the far right: the stimulation of white birthrates as a counteroffensive in the perceived "demographic war" taking place across Europe and North America.

The most notorious expressions of this imperative appear in the manifestos written by recent perpetrators of white extremist violence. The manifesto written by Tarrant, for instance, repeatedly returns to this point: "Whilst we are facing birth rates at subreplacement levels, then our people are dying."[9] Concentrating solely on these extremist screeds, however, would miss how far this imperative extends across the far right, as well as how deeply this demographic fear is rooted in a long history of natalist politics that views reproduction as a site of struggle for national identity. As this chapter will explore, nativists concerned with demographic change have long feared the reproductive tendencies of competing population groups. And just as often, they have turned this anxiety within, to indict the white population's flagging or undisciplined reproductive habits. To understand the fixation on birthrates, however, it is necessary to account for how the far right ultimately views reproduction as a battlefield—a site where the nation is under assault but might yet be defended and potentially won. Exploring this vision of natal warfare will highlight the closure of the far right political imagination, where the future of the white nation is possible only through a violent constellation surrounding gender, sexuality, and masculinity.

Far Right Reproductive Fears: The Biopolitical Impulse

The far right investment in reproduction as a site of power ultimately reflects a biopolitical impulse.[10] This concept is typically associated with the French critical theorist Michel Foucault, who describes biopolitics as a form of power that goes beyond the regulation of action and attempts to manage "life itself."[11] The classic biopolitical projects were conducted toward a certain aim: to ensure the health and size of the nation in an age when economic and military strength depended on a vital, growing population. These campaigns operated through a broad range of strategies: vaccines, physical education, dietary information, sanitation infrastructure, regulation of the food supply, epidemiological research, and so forth. Within this cluster of issues, sexuality took on particular importance. As Foucault details, sexuality is not a brute biological force that exists outside history or social practice; instead, it came to be scrutinized and managed to serve the imperatives of nationhood. It was through sexuality that nations moved from an obsession with "bloodlines" (a backward-looking lens, designed to track lines of noble descent) toward a focus on "sex"—the range of behaviors through which the future of a people, class, or nation is secured through reproduction.[12]

Reproduction and sexuality play a significant role in the demographic concerns of the far right. On one side, the literature of white reaction persistently figures the reproductive habits of nonwhite immigrants as a primary weapon in the process of "demographic replacement." To illustrate this threat, far right authors often quote the following remarks reputedly made in 1974 by Algerian leader Houari Boumediene, speaking before the General Assembly of the United Nations: "One day millions of men will leave the southern hemisphere of this planet to burst into the northern one. But not as friends. Because they will burst in to conquer, and they will conquer by populating it with their children. Victory will come to us from the wombs of our women."[13] Though the passage is wholly apocryphal, its popularity with far right figures reflects how they consistently frame reproduction in militarized terms, as a potential "weapon of war." On the other side, the far right's fixation on "competitive breeding" is matched by a critical turn inward, to scrutinize the reproductive habits of white populations.[14] This scrutiny leads the literature of demographic fear to a recurring set of questions: Are white populations reproducing enough to keep up with ethnic competitors? Are the lines between races and ethnicities being maintained, or are reproductive practices mixing these groups? Does our prevailing culture of sexuality promote reproduction, or does it idealize "perverse" or nonreproductive sexual behaviors?

To explore these concerns, it will be helpful to begin with the concept of "demographic winter," which casts a long shadow across the racialist right. In simplest terms, this phrase refers to trends in the global North, where reproductive rates have dropped below replacement level. This diagnosis presents a stark contrast to the "population explosion" predicted by the biologist Paul Ehrlich in his influential 1968 book *The Population Bomb,* which raised fears of overpopulation, mass starvation, and environmental despoliation on a planet with too much life to support.[15] Instead of overpopulation, the specter that haunts much recent literature is a "depopulation bomb" or "demographic desertification."[16] The formulas may vary, but the central concern is clear: nation after nation has seen death rates eclipse birthrates—a trend that will eventually lead (we are told) to widespread economic collapse. Critics lament that if this "baby bust" continues, there will not be enough people to fill jobs, supply the tax base needed to sustain social services, or perform socially necessary labor.[17] And yet the ethnonationalist imagination has quickly translated these economic concerns into racially fraught terms. Patrick Buchanan, the paleoconservative who twice ran for the Republican presidential nomination, bluntly asserts: "Peoples of European descent are . . . aging, dying, disappearing. This is the existential crisis of the West. And among the peoples of color who will replace them, the poorest in the least developed nations are reproducing fastest."[18] It is not, then, just that nations with decreased fertility will require population infusions in order to provide necessary economic goods—it is *who* is being introduced to these nations that raises hackles across the far right. Their racialist fears follow directly from what is presented as the iron law of demographic change. Because fertility rates have dropped below replacement levels across Europe and North America, the resulting population deficits must be made up by immigration from the global South and Muslim nations. And to push the lament to its conclusions, it is not simply that white populations will eventually find themselves outnumbered by nonwhite populations across the global North; the ultimate fear is that the historic cultures associated with these white majorities will also die out in the process.[19] In the oft-cited formula that circulates through the far right: "Demography is destiny."

Although this diagnosis is rooted in the unique dynamics of the globalized present, it channels long-standing anxieties over nationhood, immigration, and reproduction. The early decades of the twentieth century, for instance, were defined by a similar demographic panic in the United States that was pitched as a problem of "race suicide." As the American conservationist Madison Grant argued in the influential *Passing of the Great Race* (1916), heightened immigration from southern Europe posed a threat that went well beyond the tensions of cultural mixture. According to Grant, such an influx would yield a more significant shift, as the new immigrants, with their high reproductive rates, threatened to displace the so-called Nordic race from its historic preeminence at the heart of the nation. This situation, if left to continue, would end in exactly the same sort of "replacement" feared by the far right today: "The result is that one class or type in a population expands more rapidly than another and ultimately replaces it. This process of replacement of one type by another does not mean that the race changes or is transformed into another. It is a replacement pure and simple."[20] Though Grant's book was widely influential, he was hardly alone in offering this eulogy for a white nation.[21] In his 1920 book *The Rising Tide of Color against White World-Supremacy,* the economist Lothrop Stoddard raised similar fears regarding the potential eclipse of the white race on the world stage—fears that were founded in what he termed "a tremendous and steadily augmenting outward thrust of surplus colored men from overcrowded colored homelands."[22]

These historic fears over the changing composition of the nation were underpinned by anxieties that racial mixture would exact its greatest cost on future generations. Here, panic over the decline of white, Nordic majorities was coupled with a racialized verdict on the quality of the populations that were coming into ascendancy. Stoddard offered a particularly clear rendering of these concerns: "Wherever one looked in the white world, it was precisely those peoples of highest genetic worth whose birthrate fell off most sharply. . . . Everywhere the better types (on which the future of the race depends) were numerically stationary or dwindling, while conversely, the lower types were gaining ground."[23] Such fears over social decline helped inspire a wide range of efforts to manage the size and composition of the U.S. population. The race suicide panic fueled protracted experiments in both immigration and reproductive control, led by an alliance of nativists and progressives who advocated for eugenics policies designed to ensure the "racial quality" of the nation.[24]

Though it is unwise to draw too neat a parallel, the discourse surrounding this historical controversy anticipated central themes of ongoing far right "replacement" debates. The arguments of both periods hew to a familiar narrative thread: "racial substitution" is unfolding through the overlapping currents of immigration and reproduction. Furthermore, this process has not happened by accident, but is driven (at least partially) by self-destructive tendencies of the host nation, which opened its borders to seek the economic benefits of immigration.[25] As a result, the process of "ethnosuicide" can be halted only through a heroic act from within. For example, the "race suicide" panic inspired efforts to resist the perceived threat by curbing immigration and limiting the reproduction of perceived "defectives" through eugenics laws, which proliferated throughout the nation.[26] Madison Grant endorsed these measures in glowing terms: "The most practical and hopeful method of race improvement is through the elimination of the least desirable elements in the nation by depriving them of the power to contribute to future generations."[27] Although today's far right cannot rely on an existing state apparatus to carry out such extended reproductive controls, its aspirations take a clear biopolitical path, designed to turn the tide when "population replacement" is believed to have reached terminal velocity. As the following sections will explore, these biological imperatives are aimed at one objective above all: to secure a future for a race that is feared to have none.

Reproduction as Racial Combat: The Path to White Futurity

In light of these concerns, the politics of demographic fear pushes a broad imperative: that ethnic or racial substitution can be held off only by committed efforts to reverse decades of white population decline. This biopolitical project typically follows two distinct trajectories. On the one hand, many figures call for a halt to immigration and the removal of ethnic or racial groups deemed incompatible with white majorities. On the other hand, major strains of the far right pursue a pronatalist approach, hoping to secure the future of a reinvigorated white nation by increasing the production of "authentic" white children.[28]

As a result, fertility and reproduction play significant roles in the politics of demographic fear, reaching well beyond the debates of professional demographers. The white supremacist Internet forum Stormfront (where "every month is white history month") features a characteristic thread titled "How would we bring about a White Baby Boom?," which is dedicated to how white fertility rates could be stimulated at the grassroots level.[29] And the manifesto of Payton Gendron, the white extremist who killed ten Black people in a Buffalo supermarket in 2022, conspicuously appeals to an increase in white birthrates as the path to saving a white nation: "To maintain a population the people must achieve a birth rate that reaches replacement fertility levels. . . . White people are failing to reproduce, failing to create families, failing to have children."[30] Such commentary is not limited to scattered extremists posting in the dark corners of the Internet. Elected officials at the highest levels have expressed similar views, thus mainstreaming and institutionalizing these natalist arguments. Viktor Orbán, the ethnonationalist prime minister of Hungary, has pursued a campaign promoting "procreation, not immigration" to stimulate Hungarian population growth; this project seeks to induce "native" reproduction through financial incentives, free fertility treatments, tax breaks, and the like.[31] And during his tenure as a U.S. congressional representative from Iowa, Steve King notoriously promoted white reproduction over immigration by asserting that "we can't restore our civilization with somebody else's babies."[32] Such assertions reflect the ambivalence about fertility among those gripped by immigration-based replacement fears. Where reproduction is routinely indicted as the path to nonwhite ascendancy, it doubles as an avenue through which a majority-white nation might be salvaged.

As scholars have demonstrated, this investment in reproduction is defined by an intense concern for the bodies and sexuality of ethnically desirable (typically white) women.[33] Women have played a variety of roles in the racialist literature. At one end of the spectrum, white women have long been depicted as targets of sexual predation, in need of saving from the lusts and appetites of nonwhite males. These anxieties over white womanhood and racial vulnerability are well captured in D. W. Griffith's notorious 1915 film *The Birth of a Nation,* often dubbed the cinematic masterpiece of white supremacy. The film centers on the grievances and racial tensions of the American South in the years surrounding the Civil War. In one infamous scene, a white woman leaps from a cliff rather than suffer sexual violation at the hands of a Black man (played by a white actor in blackface).[34] Here, the body of the white woman stages a variety of raciopolitical fears that plagued the South during the Reconstruction era. The white woman is rendered an object of Black lust (a metaphor for the "rape of the South"), a figure in need of male protection, and the battleground for a nation undergoing shifting racial hierarchies. These fears are replicated in recent far right literature that bolsters its narrative of immigrant "invasion" through a daily litany of sexual assaults committed by nonwhite immigrants (often simply termed "rapefugees") against white women. Here sexual violence serves as a metaphor for the nation's perceived vulnerability and penetrability by dark-skinned others. At the other end of the spectrum, recent white supremacist literature emphasizes more active roles for women, drawn from the artificial mythology crafted by many far right organizations.[35] References to "Valkyries" and "shield maidens" signal a form of participation in which women take on the role of race warriors, spreading the word, performing logistics work, and advocating for white interests within the extremist media ecology.[36] These appeals to Germanic, Celtic, and Norse mythology are mirrored by the visual iconography of much white supremacist literature, which often depicts women in the mold of Aryan goddesses, with blond hair, blue eyes, Norse or Germanic hair stylings, and flowing robes drawn from the mythic imaginary.[37]

The journalist Seyward Darby argues that the increasing media profile of women is viewed as particularly significant in order to soften the "hard messages" that define the far right.[38] Within the politics of demographic fear, however, women's highest value lies in the reproductive contribution they can make to the nation. Because white decline is ultimately tracked back to low birthrates, female reproductive capacity takes on a hyperbolic importance. As the historian Kathleen Belew has detailed, white power movements often frame reproduction in distinctly militarized terms. In a situation of perceived demographic "war," bearing white babies is presented as participating in a form of "racial combat"; every contribution of a "pure white baby" represents a blow against the population decline of the white race.[39] This sentiment is exemplified by the flyer campaign of the National Alliance that features photographs of white families and children with a single formula superimposed on scenes of white domesticity: "Commit a revolutionary act. Have a White child."

This reproductive imperative shapes the gender imaginary of white reaction movements, where the genders are persistently divided along essentialist lines. Men are defined through their active, dynamic tendencies, while women are defined through their reproductive and nurturing characters.[40] This taxonomy is well expressed by Vanguard America—an avowedly fascist white supremacist group that played a major role in the 2017 Charlottesville "Unite the Right" rally. In an essay that refuses any presumption of gender equality, a writer for the organization staunchly asserts that a future white nation hinges on recognizing the "separate purposes" of the genders: "The man's duty is to fight and die for his people, to serve his race and family until he draws his last breath. A woman's duty is to continue the race and her people, to serve as the caretakers and sculptors of the next generation of men and women."[41] This essentialized reduction of women to their reproductive and nurturing capacities is not just a staple of the movement literature; women of the far right themselves often

Promotional flyer from the National Alliance enjoins white families to reproduce as a form of demographic battle.

express the same views. For instance, Ayla Stewart, the far right social media personality who goes by the moniker "Wife with a Purpose," famously pitched a "white baby challenge," using her own six children as an aspirational model for other women.[42] As she hailed fellow white women, "I've made six, match or beat me!" This challenge clearly illustrates the central imperative of far right natalist politics. In a situation of perceived demographic eclipse, the most significant counteroffensive available to members of a threatened racial majority is to reproduce at a rate that will make up for the perceived dereliction of other white families. The more "authentically white" babies that can be produced by a single "racially pure" womb, the better. One participant on a white nationalist social media channel made this logic clear: "Three children is said to be replacement rates, personally I want six. If all white nationalists have six, I think we can make a real difference."[43]

The emphasis on reproduction places women in a unique position in the far right imagination: those who safeguard the possibility of white futurity. For instance, one white nationalist dating site, WhiteDate.net, advertises its services with glossy ads of happy white couples and families accompanied by the tagline "Men create our present. Women create our future."[44] The service even comes with a promise of quality control—that site members are "white verified" to ensure that the genetic future they create will be authentically white.[45] This formula is echoed by the slogan of the Women for Aryan Unity, an American white supremacist group: "Securing our future one child at a time."[46] In the European context, the identitarian Daniel Friberg, head of a major far right publishing house, offers the following guidance to women who want to ensure the survival of European cultures: "The plummeting birth rates of Europe must be reversed. Be sure to have at least three children, and raise them well. In this regard, the future of Europe rests squarely in your hands."[47]

The natalist emphasis on the future reflects a tension that runs through the racial politics of the far right. As argued in earlier chapters, white reaction politics is essentially melancholic. Its political imagination refuses the futurity essential to politics under conditions of change. Instead, the politics of white reaction is oriented by rage toward a present in which white populations are ostensibly dispossessed and humiliated. This anger is stoked by a narrative in which their nations are being handed over to others, and their culture, history, and achievements are denigrated. Because the future of the nation is considered to be under siege, the politics of white melancholia is defined by a desire to recapture a fictive past—an idealized time when the nation was trusting and whole, whiteness was the unquestioned cultural medium, and white racial identity sat atop the social hierarchy.[48] This revanchist politics is well illustrated by Donald Trump's presidential campaign slogan, "Make America Great Again," a motto that wears its nostalgia on its sleeve, substituting an idealized golden age of the nation for any capacity to imagine new, common futures.[49]

Against this background, far right figures often render women as the "gatekeepers" to racial futurity. For instance, the official publication of the neo-Nazi National Vanguard organization announces: "Women are the gatekeepers of life. . . . If we don't have proud White women, who love their people, and pass this love onto their children, then our people have no future."[50] By placing women (specifically, women's bodies) at the axis of racial futurity, white reaction politics taps currents that have long defined white supremacist movements. For David Lane, the influential American white supremacist, this reproductive imperative rests at the heart of the white power mission. In his notorious formula for white supremacy ("the fourteen words"), Lane asserts, "We must secure the existence of our people and a future for white children."[51] As a program for the future, the formula plays out in multiple directions. On the one hand, it appeals to the core promise of the ethnostate detailed in the previous chapter. The "future for white children" is to be secured through a racially homogeneous space dedicated to the traditions, customs, and culture that define what is presented as an "authentically white" lifestyle. This ideal is clearly avowed by the public literature of the National Alliance: "We must once again provide the sort of social and spiritual environment in which our own [white] nature can express itself in music, in art and architecture, in literature, in philosophy and scholarship, in the mass media, and in the lifestyles of the people."[52]

On the other hand, white children are presented *as* the future for a white nation—a future that is biologically possible only through the reproductive capacity of women. David Lane boils this intuition down to a lapidary formula: "The life of a race springs from the wombs of its women."[53] The significance of white reproduction to the far right is not untroubled, however. Just as the white womb carries a supercharged capacity to restore the future of the race, so too is it persistently threatened by subversion and corruption. The literature of demographic fear routinely presents interracial reproduction as perhaps the greatest reproductive sin that white subjects can commit—an act that blurs racial lines at the deep, biological level.[54] It is for this reason that interracial reproduction is pitched as a more significant threat than the hybridization of culture, because it supposedly adulterates the deepest biological essences that are believed to underpin white culture and identity.[55] Far right literature thus often frames interracial reproduction not simply as an act that results in the "mongrelization" of genetic identity but as a type of racial crime. Indeed, throughout the literature, mixed-race unions are treated as particularly heinous offenses.[56] Kevin Alfred Strom, the American white supremacist who led the National Vanguard organization, describes "racemixing" as a "crime worse than murder." He elaborates: "By their actions they are killing us. They kill not an individual. They kill the infinite generations of our future. Their crime—the crime of racial mixture—is far, far worse than mere murder."[57]

The intense anxieties surrounding interracial reproduction speak to how deeply the racialist right invests in reproduction as the path to racial futurity. White women who bear nonwhite children do not simply shirk the reproductive duty they ostensibly owe to their race; they effectively "pollute" their wombs, depriving their race of the offspring required for racial survival. In the white power movement literature, miscegenation is thus frequently presented as a co-optation of a white future—an active decision to dedicate white reproductive capacities to a nonwhite world. It is for this reason that far right figures consistently describe interracial relationships as "race treason" or a "bedroom genocide" of the white race.[58] The rage surrounding this perception of racial betrayal is well captured in the iconic 1978 white supremacist novel *The Turner Diaries*.[59] Written pseudonymously by the white supremacist William Pierce, the novel offers a violent fantasy of a white power movement (the Organization) that rises against the government (the System) in order to destroy racial competitors and subject the globe to white rule. The book has achieved legendary status among white extremist movements, which rely on it for both tactical and ideological inspiration. What is relevant for present concerns is an episode in the novel that has passed into the mythology of white power activism: the Day of the Rope. This event is a day of vengeance against all the perceived enemies of the white race, culminating in the public hanging of all "race traitors"—a group that explicitly includes women who reproduce with nonwhite men. The victims' bodies are left in the streets, marked by signs to identify their supposed crimes. Where individuals who have committed other offenses receive signs that read "I betrayed my race," women who have produced mixed-race offspring are instead marked with a different judgment: "I defiled my race." This verdict brings to a head the fears that surround female sexual autonomy on the racialized far right. While other acts can offend against racial interests in material or cultural terms, women commit a far greater offense through their wayward sexual choices: they can degrade the race itself.

Reproductive Threats: The Antifeminism of the Far Right

As the foregoing highlights, the troubled politics of demographic anxiety commits itself to a far-reaching natalist vision. If the "native" white race is being swamped by a "demographic flood," then enhanced reproduction is the site where a white nation will yet be won. This defensive vision of reproduction has cast a long spell in the far right tradition of racial nationhood, including the infamous fascist experiments of twentieth-century Spain, Italy, and Germany.[60] And yet these aspirations are troubled by a range of anxieties over how white reproduction has supposedly been undermined. To grasp the depth of investment in this biopolitical project, then, it is necessary to take a more expansive approach to what far right figures view as the "concerted attack on the [white] victim group's ability to procreate, to form families and have children."[61]

Though interracial reproduction is treated with particular venom, it is hardly the only fear that haunts far right reproductive politics. Within this natalist ideal, any sexual forms that diverge from reproductive imperatives are cast as a dereliction of duty. Homosexuality, for instance, is typically condemned for cheating the race out of the "natural" reproductive outcomes of sexual activity.[62] The Women for Aryan Unity, a white supremacist organization, indicts same-sex attachments as a form of treason to the race: "Two women cannot produce Aryan children any faster than two men can. . . . It does not matter if you are two men or two women together. It is still a crime against nature and treason against the movement."[63] The homophobia that defines many far right forums is hardly unique. Gender-affirming care has likewise become a primary object of condemnation—"transgenderism" is depicted as an effort to distort embodied nature, where there are "only two genders," designed to meet in reproductive outcomes. And those motivated by panic over birthrates have long targeted the practice of abortion.[64] Where moralized opposition to abortion typically turns on the sources or origins of life, major strains of the far right oppose the practice on different grounds: its impact on specifically white or European reproductive outcomes. The perceived sin is not simply the failure to procreate for the good of the nation but how women *decide* to refuse reproductive duty, enabled by technologies of reproductive choice. Patrick Buchanan expresses these misgivings in characteristically hyperbolic terms: "Western women are terminating their pregnancies at a rate that represents autogenocide for peoples of European ancestry and an end of their nations."[65]

Though disparate, what binds this group of fears in the far right imagination is how they are all believed to reflect a design with one intended outcome: the diminishment of white reproduction. The ongoing decline in white birthrates is thus removed from natural ebbs and flows and is viewed instead as part of a targeted campaign against the viability of white nations. It is for this reason that figures of the far right have long railed against a "depopulation agenda" pushed by the "enemies of whiteness" (usually some combination of medical and media elites, drawn from the reservoir of anti-Semitic conspiracy theory).[66] Greg Johnson emphasizes these social dynamics, arguing that "the causes of white extinction are not blind forces of nature, like an asteroid colliding with the Earth. They were all created by human beings. Some of them are quite recent, like feminism encouraging young women to prefer careers over motherhood, birth control pills, legalized abortion—and overturning racial segregation, immigration restrictions, and bans on miscegenation."[67] The issues cited here range widely: interracial reproduction, technologies of reproductive autonomy, and increased participation of women in the formal workforce. One supposed "cause" of reproductive decline calls for particular attention, however, due to its significance within the politics of demographic panic: feminism.

Feminist commitments occupy a uniquely troubled place in the gender imaginary of the far right. The far right literature routinely pitches feminism as "a ploy, a trick . . . aimed at the destruction of the White race."[68] In concrete terms, feminism is indicted for distorting gender roles and eroding the family, the building block of a racially unified society.[69] This charge is typically accompanied by some standard laments. Because feminism promises women that they will find fulfillment through individual careers, they pursue their individual ambitions over their reproductive duty to their nation or race. Furthermore, the increasing independence of women in a "feminist society" means that the domestic sphere has supposedly been upended. Not only are children diminished in number, but their care, upbringing, and education are outsourced to people outside the family (public school teachers, day-care workers, and so on)—a situation that permits the spread of "antiwhite" ideologies and diminishes the stability of the family unit. Within the family itself, feminism leads women to seize increasing autonomy, inverting the proper gender hierarchy based in the "natural" ordering tendency of men. This cascading series of fears is captured by the Women for Aryan Unity, who argue that feminism yields a state where "many women have lost touch with their natural loving instincts. Consequently, the family is in disarray, sexual depravity is rampant and birth rates have plummeted."[70]

The far right hostility toward feminism is thus linked to anxieties over birthrates, though it encompasses broader concerns about the destabilization of gender roles and hierarchies. By encouraging fulfillment in the workplace, the feminist movement unleashes far-reaching disruptions in the social and economic order, leaving men incapable of fulfilling their "natural" provider role and contributing to the epidemic of "surplus white men"—those who are humiliated and angry because of their inability to perform their perceived duty.[71] Here, fears of "population replacement" overlap with currents of gender rage that fuel the explicit antifeminism of the far right media ecology. Where women are valued primarily for their reproductive capacity (if dedicated to appropriately race-conscious aims), feminist commitments are regularly condemned and derided.[72] Far right forums distribute caricatures of feminist women that depict them either as alone and childless, having squandered their reproductive prime (i.e., "cat ladies" or "wine aunts"), or as engaged in a "cock carousel" of promiscuity, hopping between sexual partners without committing to their reproductive duty for the good of the racial nation.[73] These are women, in the words of the alt-right author Wolfie James, who "drivel about fair pay, consequence-free sex, or growing out all their body hair while demanding government-subsidized birth control and abortions."[74] What unites these caricatures is how they are meant to reflect the outcomes of feminist values. A society founded on these ideals not only deprives men of their vocation to protect and provide but also sends women down a path that eliminates possibilities for a genuinely fulfilled, female life.[75] This essentialized equation of women and mothering lies behind the alt-right online harassment campaign in which women (particularly those without children) are bombarded with photos of empty egg boxes, intended to signify their diminishing (or exhausted) fertility and thus their diminishing (or exhausted) capacity to fulfill their utility for the natalist vision of the far right.[76]

Broadly put, far right forums and literature consistently deride feminist movements, depicting them as a "spiritual poison that turned a lot of White women into the repulsive, shrieking, anti-White genocidal harridans that they are today."[77] These antifeminist commitments are particularly prominent within what is often termed the "manosphere"—an Internet subculture dedicated to male victimhood narratives and virulent ideals of male supremacy. As scholars have demonstrated, a number of subgroups make up the broader world of the manosphere (e.g., "gamers," "men's rights activists," "pickup artists," "men going their own way"), but these groups tend to converge on a common set of grievances: that a world of unbound feminism has upset the proper gender hierarchy and deprived men of what is rightfully theirs.[78] In the familiar terms of online male activism, this reversal of social hierarchies has led to a "gynocracy" or "matriarchal society," where men are disenfranchised, displaced, and disrespected. They are subjected to a world structured around women's impulses, powers, and needs. Even their "natural male instincts" are derided as "toxic masculinity"—something for which they are made to apologize.

For major segments of the manosphere, the costs of a "feminized" society are considerable. Not only does this society unsettle the proper gender order, but it also strips from men the benefits they have been led to expect as their entitlement—what they are *owed* by virtue of playing their traditional masculine role. As they see it, the political movement for women's equality has betrayed its originally sympathetic aims and increasingly tipped over into something more destructive: a "war against men." These resentments take a particularly virulent shape in response to the anxieties over sexuality and reproduction explored throughout this chapter. Here, the rage of the manosphere sets itself against a distinct target: a "feminized" culture that deprives men of the sexual satisfaction they are due.

The most notorious instances of this rage are associated with members of what is termed the "incel" (short for "involuntarily celibate") community—an Internet subculture of largely male makeup that defines itself in terms of its sexual deprivation and relational loneliness.[79] According to the typology that makes up the incel imaginary, a sexually permissive society divides humans into a variety of types. Those who are conventionally attractive (what incel lexicon terms "Chads" and "Stacys") are the beneficiaries of the majority of sexual relationships. The alpha male "Chads" secure the great majority of sexual activity and the great majority of women looking for sexual partners. This dynamic is magnified by what the manosphere typically refers to as female "hypergamy." According to this pseudoscientific belief, women are driven (on evolutionary grounds) to flock to the most desirable available partner, no matter their own relationship status.[80] Within this typology, incels are those who were born with a lesser "sexual market value" (whether because of appearance, height, intelligence, income, sociability, or some other characteristic). This natural assignment means that incels are locked out of the sexual activity they view as their birthright. The rage of this subculture has entered public consciousness through headline cases of misogynistic violence enacted by aggrieved incels who, radicalized by online forums of male anger, have conducted mass attacks against women—and, ultimately, against the wider "feminized" world that deprives them of the pleasure to which they believe they are entitled.[81] A particularly infamous case is Elliot Rodger, an incel who went on a shooting rampage in 2014 near the University of California, Santa Barbara, killing six and injuring fourteen as he sought to exact "retribution" on the women of that community. In 2018, Alek Minassian rented a motor vehicle to conduct mass violence in Toronto, Canada, where he killed eleven and injured fifteen in an effort to follow Rodger's lead and "overthrow all the Chads and Stacys." These doers of violence are regularly lauded in the more patently misogynistic incel forums, where the moniker of "Saint" is appended to their names—the same "honor" that white extremists extend to xenophobic mass shooters.

Male supremacist movements both crystallize and amplify far right anxieties over gender and sexuality. They channel the fears that surround the perceived displacement of men in a "feminized" society, and they focus these currents of rage through the reproductive imperatives that define white reaction politics. To recall this natalist vision, the female body is more than a potential source of male pleasure; instead, the white woman's reproductive capacity is the gateway to a possible white future, so long as it is not waylaid by nonwhite reproduction or abortion. The former is framed as a perversion of this natal power, and the latter represents an autotermination of the white nation's future (even while many segments of the far right endorse expanded abortion access for nonwhite groups).[82]

It is from this perspective that women's sexual autonomy (itself viewed as a hallmark of a "feminist society") is particularly reviled. A central far right trope holds that feminism has long undermined reproduction by leading women to "prefer careers to families" and to pursue "abortion on demand." For the natalist politics of the far right, it is not simply a refusal of male pleasure that is at stake, but a refusal to contribute to the (already imperiled) future of the racial nation. Accordingly, the male supremacist forums often turn toward a single imperative: to reign in female sexual freedom so that reproduction can be brought under male dominion. Andrew Anglin, the editor of the antifeminist, white supremacist website the Daily Stormer, puts the sentiment in particularly misogynistic terms: "These wombs belong to us, not the idiot creatures that they are attached to. They were given to us by God to reproduce ourselves within. The dumb animals they are attached to were supposed to serve us, but they have gotten out of control. We always need to be looking for new ways to get these stupid animals to give us back the wombs they have stolen from us."[83] This statement of reproductive ownership is a culmination of the antifeminist currents that characterize the male supremacist strains of the far right. It is not simply that women's sexual autonomy might lead them to "betray" their race through interracial relationships. This outrage is redoubled by the insistence that women who exercise sexual autonomy effectively withhold something from its rightful male possessors. The womb that can open a path to a white future is figured as *our* womb, one that belongs to its racial people, to be dedicated (under male stewardship) to aims of racial preservation.[84] And yet, at present, this womb is viewed as unruly and unwilling. It is in need of male mastery if the race is to have a future.

Time Is a Flat Circle: The Return to Tradition

Overall, then, the biopolitical project of the far right takes one characteristic shape: enhanced reproduction toward the aim of racial renewal. In the more forward-looking visions, the flagging reproductive rates of white nations would be boosted by reproductive technologies and pregnancy surrogates.[85] In practical terms, this project is well illustrated by the Internet-based surrogacy service that announces its mission bluntly in its name: WhiteChild .net. This site, which is the fertility wing of the white nationalist dating site WhiteDate.net, announces its core mission as "part of the pro-white movement that gathers awakened White People who are race-conscious and willing to support each other to fight our people's extinction."[86] The platform offers a variety of services, ranging from matching couples with sperm or egg donors (limited to donors who have not been vaccinated against Covid-19) to facilitating searches for "authentically white" surrogates who can bear children for white families. The home page of the site is festooned with images of white children and families, coupled with natalist mottos. For instance, a closeup of a white baby, cradled in white hands, is accompanied by the slogan, "Today, we [white people] need to act, to create our future, exploiting all possibilities to continue our lines."[87]

More common are proposals to enhance reproduction through behavioral and institutional shifts. Within these natalist debates, one argument persistently comes to the fore: if the future of the white nation is to be salvaged, the present culture of sexual freedom must be rejected. And, since white women are central to this vision of a white future, this imperative lays particular weight on reorienting female sexuality toward the needs of white nationhood.

The proposed approaches toward this objective run along a spectrum. In the more extreme versions, women would be compelled to contribute their reproductive labor to a resurgent white nation. Such commitments were on display at the 2017 "Unite the Right" march in Charlottesville, where the infamous "You will not replace us" chant was periodically interrupted by a more esoteric cry: "White sharia now!" The call for "white sharia" reflects an Islamophobic caricature of a theocratic ideal, in which female sexual autonomy would be curbed in favor of patriarchal control over women's bodies.[88] The vision of "white sharia," which is associated with the alt-right blogger Sacco Vandal, spread quickly through the more extreme segments of the manosphere. Though the meme is almost certainly a parodic effort to shock liberal sensibilities (in the vein of alt-right hyperbole), it crystallizes some of the core beliefs of the far right thought ecology. At the heart of the meme is the insistence that the decline in white reproduction (and thus the declining fortunes of the white nation) can be reversed only through "a radical, rigid form of extreme, regimented patriarchy" that would entail control over women's bodies and freedoms. The central intuition of "white sharia" follows directly from the demographic panic detailed throughout this chapter. As Vandal explains: "White babies, White babies, and—again—White babies! Members of our race are not having enough children. And one, or two, or three, or four simply aren't going to cut it. Our men need harems, and the members of those harems need to be baby factories. . . . These are cold, calculated plans to save our dying race."[89]

The less outwardly extreme camps of the far right tamp down such appeals to coerced reproduction and instead glorify the family as the site of national (and white) regeneration. These gestures are reflected in the movement literature, where white families with multiple children take on a nearly mythical stature, presented as the nucleus through which a white homeland will be rebuilt. White nationalist memes regularly employ one repeated image to figure the future of a reconstituted white nation: an all-white family, with multiple children, set in bucolic natural surroundings, with text overlay such as "This is the future we fight for." In the stark formulation of the National Socialist Movement (a neo-Nazi organization in the United States that grew out of the American Nazi Party): "The future of our race extends from our White family and we will protect our family from any behaviors which may corrupt it. Our children are our strength and our future."[90]

This political investment in the family is radicalized by those who idealize what they present as the "traditional" family—particularly the "tradwife" movement, which has built a significant social media presence in recent years. This movement is characterized by an emphasis on essentialized gender distinctions, a commitment for wives to submit to their husbands, and—what is particularly relevant for current interests—an emphasis on families as the wellspring of reproduction. The family is presented not only as the proper domain for female agency but also as the site where women find fulfillment by gaining proficiency in the full range of homemaking activities.[91] To this end, the social media presence of tradwife culture is filled with all manner of advice on the household skills women must master to play their role in a "traditional" family—from sewing to canning to homeschooling to budgeting to hostessing to cooking. One of the most significant domestic arts hallowed by the tradwife movement is the woman's imperative to provide sexual fulfillment for the male head of the household and to discipline her body in order to remain sexually attractive to the male (an imperative that is persistently inflected by the demand for modest, "feminine" fashion choices).[92]

The tradwife movement continues the antifeminism that defines the gender imaginary of the far right, as announced by the ubiquitous hashtag that accompanies tradwife culture on social media platforms: #femininenotfeminist.[93] This antifeminist performance comes with a wrinkle, however, as figures within the movement routinely conscript the language of feminism in order to depict their participation in a "tradfamily" as an act of choice, and thus a moment of the autonomy that is typically celebrated by feminist movements.[94] What is most interesting about the tradwife movement for current purposes is how it reflects the temporality of far right biopolitics as tracked through this chapter. Where the wombs of women are figured as the site of white futurity, and their nurturing activity shelters the germinating white nation, this futurity is secured through a conscious effort to embody and live an imagined past.[95] In the past invoked by tradwives, men and women knew their "proper places" within relationships of dominion and submission, support and provision. The nation was at its greatest during this mythic time, rooted in the health of its family structure. This imagined golden age (a period that can vary for different "tradfamilies") was not simply a time of white majorities, cashed out in brute demographic terms, but a time when an all-encompassing style of life was guided by the values of a "traditional" social order.[96] To restage this ideal, tradwife culture often embraces the aesthetics of a mythicized golden age—through home furnishings, dress, and personal style. In terms of labor divisions, the "tradfamily" typically commits to a gendered breakdown, with a commitment to a male economic breadwinner. As the communication scholar Ashley Mattheis has demonstrated, even when tradwife influencers do not outwardly avow commitments to racial nationalism, this effort to live an ahistorical domestic scene is suffused with the historic commitments of upper-middle-class whiteness—where the economic guarantees of whiteness enabled women to stay at home, protected from public exposure, while white men left the home to perform the labor that was presented as their birthright.[97]

The tradwife movement is hardly alone in its efforts to resurrect a lost golden age. Indeed, the movement symptomatizes a broader trend within much of the far right that is more broadly termed "retroculture"—an effort to resist the supposed pathologies of modernity by consciously assuming the rhythms, styles, and values of an idealized historical stage.[98] Tradlife social media entrepreneurs glorify the cultural achievements of the past in order to deride what they take to be the cheapness, soullessness, and ugliness of contemporary culture. Though the most obvious manifestations of retroculture stem from the aesthetics of bygone eras, the deeper political currents demand a turn away from the individualism of "modern life" and toward more communal values and behaviors.[99] Central to this "communal" turn is one imperative above all others: to bear the children and form the families that can furnish a future for an ostensibly endangered white nation.

The natalist vision of white nationhood tracked in this chapter thus employs and yet goes well beyond the naturalist commitments that grip the far right imagination. Far right actors persistently view nature as the basis for a redeemed nation, arguing that race and ethnicity furnish the deepest, biological grounds for identity, community, and hierarchy.[100] The reproductive project of white nationhood represents the final step of this naturalized antipolitics, where the path to futurity is reduced to the biological function of reproduction. And pursuing this path requires resurrecting the practices of an imagined historical time when gender roles were ostensibly their most natural. One way to read this reduction of politics is as a symptom of the far right's exhausted political imagination. As previous chapters have detailed, a staple of far right thought is its melancholic character, its incapacity to imagine new futures or to make new common worlds. That said, these efforts to graft a natal politics onto the supposed lead strings of nature carry troubling implications that exceed a failure of political imagination. As exhibited by the outspoken role for patriarchal ideals, this political vision does not simply misrecognize culturally and historically specific domestic arrangements for the putatively natural order of gender. And it does not simply petrify idealized snapshots from the nation's history to represent the sole face of tradition.[101] In a more troubling sense, the biopolitics of the far right naturalizes currents of gender hierarchy that have long defined the far right imagination. If biological reproduction will be the saving power of the white nation, it is a saving power in which the "natural tendencies" of women (particularly their sexuality) must be carefully domesticated and enlisted in reproductive combat—what the journalist Katherine Joyce terms "the maternity ward as battleground."[102] Or, put more broadly, if the far right seeks to gain the future through a form of natal warfare, at least one of the casualties of this warfare is sexual self-determination as a core ideal for women's lives.[103]

CODA

THE SPREAD OF THE NARRATIVE AND ITS CIVIC COSTS

On October 19, 2022, the television journalist Lara Logan was interviewed on the ultraconservative Newsmax television network. She began the segment with a set of warnings about immigration and the state of U.S. border politics. Then, as she picked up steam, Logan lurched into a more hectoring line of thought, asserting that the current "flood" of immigrants over the nation's borders is evidence of something far more sinister than simple migration. Instead, it reflects a plan by global organizations to erode the nation. For those familiar with Great Replacement theory, the move was not surprising, particularly given the venue. What was noteworthy was Logan's insistence that she had access to evidence confirming that this plan was hatched at the highest levels:

> I spoke to a man who was actually holding the documents in his hand. . . . He said he infiltrated the global cabal at the UN level. . . . What he witnessed himself was these documents that show that the plan—there is a plan—and this was several years ago, right, the plan was to infiltrate a hundred million illegal immigrants . . . and these people would dilute what they called the pool of Patriots. . . . It's right out of the playbook, right out of the socialist playbook. You divide and conquer.
>
> The open border is Satan's way of taking control of the world through all of these people who are his stooges and his servants. . . . You all know [Yuval] Harari and all the rest of

> them at the World Economic Forum. You know, the ones who want us eating insects, cockroaches, and that while they dine on the blood of children? Those are the people, right?[1]

The segment offered a master class in the central tropes of the Great Replacement narrative. The essentials were all present: mass immigration, engineered by a global cabal, is corroding the nation. And the account dipped into particularly extreme territory when Logan referenced a set of satanic powers operating through the global cabal—culminating in the conspiracy fable of blood libel (a classic anti-Semitic trope involving elites who consume the blood of children for occult purposes).[2]

This rant proved to be of questionable utility for both network and correspondent. The public outcry and ridicule over the performance led the network to break public ties with Logan and disavow her contributions. The episode did, however, reveal the ongoing vitality of Great Replacement theory, even after a series of xenophobic mass shootings had been explicitly linked to the replacement narrative. The far right television personality Tucker Carlson, for instance, frequently employed the language and terms of replacement thought in his nightly broadcast on Fox News.[3] And themes of replacement continue to play a role in the public statements of right-wing elected officials. For example, in March 2023, the far right congressional representative Marjorie Taylor Greene tweeted: "We have no idea who or what is coming across our Southern border. But we do know that we're being systematically and intentionally replaced by Joe Biden and the Democrats' open border policies."[4] In the European context, the recently elected prime minister of Italy, Giorgia Meloni, spoke repeatedly about the "ethnic substitution" of Italians throughout the campaign leading to her 2022 election. In terms that hew closely to the established lines of the replacement narrative, Meloni described the changes unfolding across Italy not simply as immigration that might tip the balance away from "native" Italians but rather as part of a plan hatched by "financial speculators"—explicitly evoking the anti-Semitic specter of "globalist" elites engineering these changes behind the scenes.[5]

To assess the ongoing impact of replacement thought, it is

necessary to push further. What defines the current moment is not only the abiding presence of the replacement narrative on the political stage but also how the narrative continues to evolve as it travels into new contexts and settings. In February 2023, Kais Saied, the president of Tunisia, drew from the repertoire of replacement ideology to portray his nation as the victim of an immigration-based siege conducted by migrants from sub-Saharan African nations. Where appeals to the Great Replacement are typically rooted in the demographic fears of the global North (and suffused with a language of whiteness), Saied instead accented the characteristic anti-Blackness of the narrative. He depicted the recent surge in immigration as an effort to erase the Arabic and Islamic roots of Tunisian identity, a plan to transform Tunisia into a "purely African" nation. In an address to the Tunisian National Security Council, Saied pushed further into the core mythology of the replacement narrative, claiming that increased sub-Saharan migration ultimately reflects a "criminal arrangement" intentionally designed "to change the demographic composition of Tunisia."[6] These assertions did not fall on deaf ears. Soon after this speech, Tunisia experienced waves of violence against immigrants, conducted by both state and nonstate actors.[7]

This episode illustrates the core features of the narrative, even as it moves into new geographic and cultural terrain. Anxieties over traditional roles, hierarchies, and economies of power are reduced to the singular axis of immigration. The dark-skinned immigrant serves as a totem for the otherwise unmanageable fears that attend social changes. It is on this figure that the blame for these changes can be placed. And the innumerable causal powers behind such changes can be reduced in complexity, ascribed to the shadowy figure of the global elite. The supposed threat of this enemy is well reflected in an image of "globalism" that has become ubiquitous in far right visual culture: elite hands float above a globe, connected to the world by the marionette strings they manipulate to direct the course of events in nation after nation.

The elasticity of the replacement narrative is not, however, confined to how the narrative travels across the globe. Where replacement fears are most familiar in debates over immigration, its language of "erasure," "replacement," and "substitution" is now invoked far beyond the context of demographic change. As a result, the far right landscape has seen a contagion effect, where tropes of replacement are used more widely to galvanize fear and outrage in traditionally dominant groups that are facing challenges to their social, cultural, or political power.

To understand this contagion, it is useful to consider one of the threads that runs through the preceding chapters: far right anxieties over gender and sexuality. Recent years have seen widespread attacks on the visibility, integrity, and safety of LGBTQ+ groups, ranging from physical violence to policy initiatives to legislative assaults on LGBTQ+ visibility, rights, and access to medical care. Drag shows and Pride festivals are increasingly targeted by far right actors, driven by imagined threats to children or vague harms to moral propriety. These attacks have reached particularly virulent form in the ongoing campaign waged against transgender individuals. This transphobic campaign reflects deep strains of the far right thought ecology, particularly the insistence on natural distinctions between groups, genders, and individuals. Where the far right has long drawn from nature to justify its beliefs in human hierarchy, technologies of gender flexibility are thought to reflect the unmooring of gender from natural assignment and, more broadly, the denial of any natural categories or differences. For this reason, a popular far right meme (appearing frequently on T-shirts and bumper stickers) insists that "there are only two genders"—a strategy that attempts to reroot social roles and relationships within a nature that provides an authoritative, eternal scaffolding for human differences.

What is most relevant at present is how this surge of transphobic politics increasingly draws from the reservoir of replacement theory, negotiated through the traditional language of women's movements. This brand of anti-trans activism (typically termed "gender-critical feminism" or "trans-exclusionary radical feminism," often shortened to TERF) bases its arguments in one core fear: that the inclusion of transgender individuals within the (legal, institutional, and cultural) ambit of "women" will effectively "erase" the biological meanings of female life, along with the powers, capabilities, and values that are regarded as distinctively female. These arguments span a wide variety of cases and contexts—from the gendered capacity to bear life to gendered sporting achievement. In all these instances, the lability of gender is presented as a threat to replace "biological" womanhood. As Pamela Paul, an American newspaper columnist, has notoriously argued in an opinion piece for the *New York Times*, "In a world of chosen gender identities, women as a biological category don't exist. Some might even call this kind of thing erasure."[8] Such charges of erasure are not limited to the op-ed pages of major newspapers. Instead, these fears have spawned a variety of countermeasures, designed to neutralize this supposed threat to biological womanhood. For instance, they have mobilized campaigns to set definitive standards for who counts as an "authentic" woman—standards that would call for a variety of invasive measures to determine who qualifies. And these efforts to establish binding criteria for womanhood are matched by ongoing legislative campaigns to restrict the benefits, protections, access, and supports that would ordinarily be extended to those who qualify as female.

The terms and categories of replacement ideology thus reverberate well beyond the issues typically associated with replacement theory. At one level, this metastasis is reflected in the narrative's spread through civil society—beyond the forums of dedicated extremists, into legacy media and into the conversations of those who would otherwise be unwilling to avow an identity as white supremacists or white nationalists. At another level, however, the elasticity of the narrative is reflected in how activists promote fears of "erasure" in new contexts, debates, and settings. The far right media ecology is filled with laments over the supposed erasure of men (in a "feminist" society) and of women (through "transgenderism" or "gender ideology"). And, increasingly, the burgeoning Christian nationalist movement claims that Christianity is being erased from the cultural life of the nation.[9] In all of these cases, the language of replacement and erasure is used to engineer the perception of an existential threat in situations where traditional norms, identities, and hierarchies are challenged or unsettled.[10]

This expansion permits a more pointed approach to the dangers of the replacement narrative. Perhaps the greatest threats of replacement thought stem from how it fuels the victimhood that defines far right political culture. What distinguishes much far right literature is its distinct vision of social change, where movements for civic equality are framed as attacks on historically dominant groups. When viewed through this lens of persecution, an increasing public role for nonwhite, nonmale histories or values cannot appear as a process of greater pluralism; it is instead depicted as a "war against white people" or a "war against men." Or the supposed war is framed in more specific terms, as an attack on "straight white men" or "white Christian men."[11] These various "wars" are often folded into one another, in the model of nesting dolls. As the infamous manosphere blogger Daryush Valizadeh (who writes under the pseudonym "Roosh") has stated, "What I thought was a war against men is really a battle within a bigger war against white people."[12] This language of aggression is often repurposed by the right-wing thought ecology to assert a more granular series of wars waged by cultural minorities on cherished majority cultures or traditions. This is the basis for the repeated appeals in the conservative media ecosphere to a "war on the family," a "war on history," a "war on the West," a "war on parents," a "war on Christmas," a "war on Christianity," or a "war on Confederate monuments" (a list that is hardly exhaustive).[13] Each of these formulations reflects a single essential grievance: those who represent the proper core of the nation are currently under an unjust attack that seeks to strip them of the status and goods that are rightfully theirs.

It is now possible to tease out the civic costs of this discourse of replacement, erasure, and victimhood. This narrative does not simply assert a position of victimhood in the abstract. In doing so, it masks existing structures of power. Traditionally dominant groups, despite their disproportionate access to material and cultural power, are portrayed as the victims in an ongoing campaign to strip them of their birthrights.[14] Conversely, movements for social and racial equality are figured as aggressors, conducting a vindictive "war" to tear down the histories and accomplishments of others. As a result, the framework of victimhood inverts the moral coordinates of civic life. By placing historically dominant groups in the position of victimhood, the narrative of replacement ultimately effaces those hierarchies that have granted them unequal access to social goods. And by figuring historically marginalized groups as aggressors, this inverted logic of victimhood seeks to undercut movements for civic equality.[15]

The dangers of this inversion do not stop with masking relationships of social power. There is also a more practical upshot to the far right's politics of victimhood: it is through this narrative of persecution that the far right claims legitimacy for its violent dreams. More specifically, the stance of victimhood permits the unfettered assertion of supposed rights—and justifies extreme measures on the part of those who are ostensibly under attack. In a situation of victimhood, hard words and actions are not only permissible, they are demanded on grounds of self-preservation.[16] The narrative construction of victimhood thus grants to white reaction movements the classic appeal of extremist organizations—the claim to righteousness. The severity of the threat (cultural or ethnic elimination) and the justice of the cause (cultural or racial preservation) mean that even the most extreme reactions can be construed as moves within a war of defense. To paraphrase a sentiment that runs throughout the forums of the far right: they have not chosen this war; it has, instead, been thrust upon them. This logic extends well beyond questions of justification to enter into the motivational resources of white reaction politics. In the inverted world of far right victimhood, it is the "founding stock" citizen, fighting to preserve an order of privilege, who is the hero of history. This deformed grammar of justification is reflected in recent episodes of white extremist violence, where aggrieved white men have taken up arms to commit racial violence against those they perceived as invaders. In the manifestos that have come to be a staple of this xenophobic violence, one theme comes to the fore: it is the embattled white native who is the true victim of social and demographic change. And in the face of this victimhood, the use of violence is both just and necessary, to strike a righteous blow against an unjust aggressor.[17]

The costs of replacement theory thus go beyond a fashionable coinage. The discourse of replacement, displacement, and erasure has spread through the far right ecosphere, creating an aggressive community of victimhood. This narrative does not simply tell a story about social change; it also constructs a world where righteous figures are under attack by a broad set of enemies. These are enemies that have set their sights on the most precious goods of all: the nation, its traditions, its resources, and its culture. The expanding ideology of replacement thus helps to crystallize the various frustrations surrounding globalization and social change into a single thread of persecution and dispossession that yields one persistent outcome: the rage of grievance.

The contemporary political landscape is shaped by a dizzying array of changes. If there is one staple of the contemporary far right, it is that the movement is fundamentally defined in reaction to a world in which "all that is solid melts into air." The far right literature persistently bemoans change: changes to culture, to populations, to gender roles, to language, to families (among other things). And its laments are accompanied by a consistent narrative about the status of traditional majorities: "We are the ones who are left behind by these changes. We are the ones who are unheard, who are losing everything. Not only is the civic terrain fundamentally reconfigured, but *we* no longer have a say in these changes. They are forced upon us by corrupt or wicked others who gain through our loss. We are forgotten, ignored, and humiliated." Increasingly, these claims of persecution and displacement take one characteristic form: "We are being replaced."

The costs of this far-reaching narrative have been detailed throughout this book. In the face of this violent political imagination, one question rises to the fore: How might narratives of change be fashioned so that they do not end in revanchist efforts to recapture an idealized "golden age"? This question can be put in more specific terms, given this book's overriding concern with the politics of fear that surrounds demographic change: Is the violent political imagination of the far right reducible to its fixation on loss? Must demographic change be met with a defensive, paranoiac vision that hardens the grievance of loss into a desire to restore the claims of whiteness? Or are there narratives of change that could yield greater possibilities for civic solidarity?

These questions are given useful focus by the political theorist Simon Stow, who draws from the disparate politics of mourning that run through American civic history. As Stow argues, polities are characteristically shaped by the stories they tell about their dead and their experiences of grieving cherished practices, traditions, territories, or persons that have been lost. Accordingly, the most significant political question is not whether losses should or should not structure the body politic, as all communities are shaped, to some degree, by this experience. Battles are lost, disasters strike, and heroes die or betray their causes. Rather, the operative question is which approaches to loss are most "conducive to the political well-being" of a given polity in the face of loss.[18] As detailed throughout this book, significant strains of the far right demonstrate a temptation toward nostalgia that seeks to "return" to a mythic past of wholeness, harmony, and greatness.[19] And this desire for return is coupled with a rage toward the present, along with all those agents who supposedly helped to bring this state about. Stow notes, however, an alternative, "tragic" type of mourning with greater democratic resources—an approach to loss that does not seek an imagined moment of wholeness but instead marks the violence by which civic "togetherness" has historically been forged and maintained.[20] Where a melancholic politics seeks to restore a lost age—to make the nation "great again" (or at least "great again" for its historically dominant groups)—a tragic sensibility approaches even these idealized moments with an eye toward the possibilities they squandered, the voices they silenced, and the futures they closed off.

These gestures are obviously rendered with the broadest of strokes. They are intended to raise questions rather than to offer airtight answers or detailed action plans. For example, in the face of loss, what narratives of nationhood would permit a democratic people to go on in a less violent fashion, with greater concern for its pluralist fabric? What forms of civic memory would best acknowledge the violence embedded within even the most idealized moments of the nation? And these questions could be tailored more closely to the central concerns of this book: What narratives would be best equipped to process experiences of deep, demographic change without encouraging aggressive, rearguard efforts to reclaim an imagined, idealized past?

When set against the destructive far right politics of loss, these broad gestures take on greater substance. Where the far right seeks to recapture an idealized national community, forged in the bonds of whiteness, a chastened memory of loss would mark how the bonds of the national "we" were historically forged by the suppression of other possibilities and consider those political capabilities that were lost by this suppression. A civic memory dedicated to greater democratic capacity would, for instance, dwell upon a different site of foundational loss: how the powers of whiteness have historically forestalled a politics of material equality or class alliance by securing social, political, and material benefit along possessive, racialized lines. This path of civic reckoning would avoid the fuzzy calls for civic "togetherness" that are so often voiced by centrist political figures. And it would likewise resist the melancholic turn of the far right, which seeks a return to some mythicized golden age when groups all knew their "proper" places and the community was bound by an untroubled reverence for the same traditions. A more democratically generative politics of loss would thematize the solidarities suppressed by the racial polity and thus highlight its abiding democratic costs. Minimally, the possessive logic of whiteness has undercut the capacity of diverse constituencies to mobilize toward more equitable futures—a cost that is particularly damaging in a time defined by growing material insecurities. And, in doing so, this invidious racial practice has yielded a loss of democratic potency, reflected by widespread grievances over powerlessness, de-democratization, and class predation in neoliberal times.

Memorializing these solidarities, then, would not only mark their suppression in a documentary sense but also broaden and reinvigorate the civic imagination. A racially chastened form of civic memory would aim to sketch possibilities for combinations, mobilizations, and constituencies that have historically been foreclosed by the cleavages of whiteness. It would, in the terms raised earlier, *mourn* these solidarities as something squandered by the violence of the white racial order, so that new investments could be enabled. The resulting expanded narrative of civic loss would resonate with the central grievances raised by the populist surge of recent years—namely, the felt lack of democratic access to institutions now turned over to distant elites, antidemocratic judicial bodies, or market metrics. Amid the resentments and grievances that define civic narratives of dispossession, the theme of powerlessness looms large (i.e., *they* are doing it to us behind closed doors; *we* have no say in what these elites do). But where these populist energies have been persistently hijacked by the far right and set to work for a rearguard politics of racial grievance, a democratically informed narrative of civic loss would fasten upon racial cleavage as itself an obstacle to the democratic energies desired by so many across the raciopolitical spectrum.

Given the depth of white resentment, it is unwise to expect that a simple change in civic stories could uproot the malice that fuels the politics of racial reaction. And the work of narrative can hardly substitute for the patient work of movement building and organization required to contest these reactionary powers or the material violence they enable in civic life. The violence that far right movements enact against vulnerable populations demands equally muscular responses of protection and support. And yet, the far right has invested so deeply in the world of symbol, language, and narrative that this terrain remains essential for contesting its malignant vision toward a less violent, more pluralist civic imagination.

ACKNOWLEDGMENTS

Writing a book is an odd thing. In the process, a writer incurs many debts for many things. There are small kindnesses along the way. The offhand remarks that germinate and bloom. The studied critiques that might reorient or deepen the project. The scholars who precede you and forge a path. And, of course, the encouragement and guidance expressed in ways both large and small.

Over the course of writing this book, I accumulated many such debts. At Lafayette College, I am lucky to be surrounded by a supportive department. The PQ Crew has been a constant source of fellowship. And I have benefited greatly from the research support offered by the EXCEL Scholars program at the college, particularly the work of Jacob Moldover and Katelin Seber.

I thank Daniel O'Neill, Matt Stein, Lawrie Balfour, Katie Helke, John Hultgren, and Ronald Beiner for their many contributions to the project. At the University of Minnesota Press, I thank my editor, Pieter Martin, who has been supportive and enthusiastic from the beginning. I also thank a number of anonymous reviewers who took the time to slog through earlier, clunkier versions of the manuscript; they opened my eyes to many things and saved me from unpromising paths.

Most important, I bear an immeasurable debt to my family. The writing of a book strains even the most generous of family units. So much time dedicated to a screen that could have been spent on play or cuddles or laughter or care. I offer my gratitude, debt, and apologies to the two child miracles who changed my life immeasurably for the better: Billie and Hawthorne. They teach me every day why the future matters so very much (and why it must be salvaged from the malignant visions of the far right). The greatest debt of gratitude goes to my wife, Joelle, who made this book possible. She easily put more work into this project than I did. She makes every day better.

My mother, Patricia O'Leary, died in the early days of this project. There is a reason this book so frequently dwells on questions of loss, mourning, and a melancholic grasping after the past. Her passing taught me more about grief than any library of books ever could. I owe her so much. And I miss her every damn day.

NOTES

Introduction

1. The literature on rage and civic unrest is considerable. See, for instance, Mustafa Dikeç, *Urban Rage: The Revolt of the Excluded* (New Haven, Conn.: Yale University Press, 2017); Bernard Stiegler, *Uncontrollable Societies of Disaffected Individuals: Disbelief and Discredit,* vol. 2, trans. David Ross (Malden, Mass.: Polity Press, 2013).
2. For a historic exploration of the connection between right-wing movements and the politics of rage, see Carol Anderson, *White Rage: The Unspoken Truth of Our Racial Divide* (New York: Bloomsbury, 2017); Dan Carter, *The Politics of Rage: George Wallace, the Origins of the New Conservatism, and the Transformation of American Politics* (Baton Rouge: Louisiana State University Press, 2000); Martin Durham, *White Rage: The Extreme Right and American Politics* (New York: Routledge, 2007); D. J. Mulloy, *Years of Rage: From the Klan to the Alt-Right* (Lanham, Md.: Rowman & Littlefield, 2021).
3. See, for instance, Jennifer Silva, *We're Still Here: Pain and Politics in the Heart of America* (New York: Oxford University Press, 2019); Robert Wuthnow, *The Left Behind: Decline and Rage in Rural America* (Princeton, N.J.: Princeton University Press, 2018).
4. Peter Sloterdijk, *Rage and Time: A Psychopolitical Investigation* (New York: Columbia University Press, 2010).
5. Douglas Mercer, "After the Awakening," *National Vanguard,* February 22, 2022, https://nationalvanguard.org.
6. Guillaume Faye, *The Colonisation of Europe,* trans. Roger Adwan (London: Arktos, 2016), 23.
7. Renaud Camus, *Le Grand Remplacement* (Sablons, France: Chez l'auteur, 2011); Renaud Camus, *You Will Not Replace Us!* (Sablons, France: Chez l'auteur, 2018).
8. A number of candidates for major public office have recently referred to population replacement as an accomplished fact. For a clear instance in the European context, see Eric Zemmour's speech to announce his candidacy for the French presidency, in Rod Dreher, "Eric Zemmour's Blockbuster Speech," *American Conservative,* October 3, 2019, https://www.theamericanconservative.com. Such appeals have flourished in the United States among Republican candidates for office. For instance, one candidate for national office, Neil Kumar, made "Stop the Great Replacement" the very first item in his 2022 platform for political office. See "Neil for Arkansas 2022 Platform," available on the Internet Archive, accessed August 17, 2023, https://

web.archive.org/web/20210909045224/https://neilforarkansas.com/platform.

9. For a symptomatic discussion of "demographic winter" from within the racialist right, see Patrick J. Buchanan, *Suicide of a Superpower: Will America Survive to 2025?* (New York: St. Martin's Press, 2011), 162–89.
10. This demographic literature is considerable. For example, see Darrell Bricker and John Ibbitson, *Empty Planet: The Shock of Global Population Decline* (New York: Crown, 2019); Phillip Longman, *The Empty Cradle: How Falling Birthrates Threaten World Prosperity and What to Do about It* (New York: Basic Books, 2004).
11. Daily Stormer, accessed August 24, 2023, https://dailystormer.in.
12. Jean Raspail, *The Camp of the Saints,* trans. Norman Shapiro (New York: Charles Scribner & Sons, 1975).
13. Richard Coudenhove-Kalergi, *Praktischer Idealismus* (Vienna: Paneuropa Verlag, 1925), 22–23.
14. Mick Greenhough, *Brave New Europe* (Aylesbury, England: Shield-Crest, 2017), 3. Much recent ethnonationalist and white extremist interest in the Kalergi Plan conspiracy theory was stoked by the publication of Gerd Honsik, *Rassismus Legal? Der Juden drittes Reich? Halt dem Kalergi-Plan!* (La Mancha: Bright-Rainbow Verlag, 2005).
15. Madison Grant, *The Passing of the Great Race: Or, The Racial Basis of European History* (1916; repr., New York: Charles Scribner, 1936), 91.
16. Quoted in Jonathan Peter Spiro, *Defending the Master Race: Conservation, Eugenics, and the Legacy of Madison Grant* (Lebanon, N.H.: University of Vermont Press, 2009), 98.
17. See, for instance, Camus, *You Will Not Replace Us!,* 60–64. See also Guillaume Faye, *Ethnic Apocalypse: The Coming European Civil War,* trans. Roger Adwan (London: Arktos, 2019), 10–14. In a symptomatic denunciation, Alex Kurtagic asserts that "this [replacement] process enjoys the ongoing complicity of the indigenous' ruling elites, who, wittingly or unwittingly, instigated it in the first place out of a perceived economic need, and have since institutionalized it out of political opportunism, greed, a sense of historical guilt, or befuddlement with an ideology of human universalism." Alex Kurtagic, "The Great Erasure," in *The Great Erasure: The Reconstruction of White Identity,* ed. Richard Spencer (Whitefish, Mont.: Washington Summit, 2012), 24.
18. See, for instance, Brett Stevens, "Are 'the Great Replacement' and 'White Genocide' Conspiracy Theories?," Amerika, March 30, 2019, https://www.amerika.org. A particularly clear performance is offered by the far right video personality Lana Lokteff; see Lana Lokteff, "The Truth about the Great Replacement," Red Ice TV, May 21, 2022, https://redice.tv/red-ice-tv.
19. Patrick J. Buchanan, *The Death of the West: How Dying Populations*

and Immigrant Invasions Imperil Our Country and Civilization (New York: St. Martin's Press, 2002), 209.

20. Richard Hofstadter, "The Paranoid Style in American Politics," in *The Paranoid Style in American Politics, and Other Essays* (New York: Vintage Books, 2008), 29. The far right recourse to a paranoid politics has been noted by others. See, for instance, Michael Kimmel, *Angry White Men: American Masculinity at the End of an Era* (New York: Nation Books, 2013), 21–25, 229–37; Russell Muirhead and Nancy Rosenblum, *A Lot of People Are Saying: The New Conspiracism and the Assault on Democracy* (Princeton, N.J.: Princeton University Press, 2019), 43–49.
21. As Hofstadter notes, "The modern right wing . . . feels dispossessed: America has largely been taken away from them and their kind, though they are determined to try to repossess it and to prevent the final destructive act of subversion. . . . Their predecessors discovered foreign conspiracies; the modern radical right finds that conspiracy also embraces betrayal at home." Hofstadter, "Paranoid Style," 23–24.
22. For instance, the conservative media personality Tucker Carlson used his platform on Fox News to assert that the Democratic Party in the United States has crafted immigration policy to bring about "the replacement of legacy Americans with more obedient people from far-away countries." Quoted in Dominick Mastrangelo, "Critics Blast Tucker Carlson's Immigration Remarks amid Border Surge," *The Hill*, September 23, 2021, https://thehill.com. Likewise, J. D. Vance, a far right U.S. senator from Ohio, proposed in 2022 that the Democratic Party "decided that they can't win reelection in 2022 unless they bring in a large number of new voters to replace the voters that are already here." Quoted in Susan Milligan, "From Embrace to 'Replace,'" *U.S. News & World Report*, May 20, 2022, https://www.usnews.com.
23. For a clear instance, see Patrick J. Buchanan, *State of Emergency: The Third-World Invasion and Conquest of America* (New York: Thomas Dunne Books, 2006).
24. These existential tropes of white extermination figure prominently in the far right's literature and advocacy. For a symptomatic case, see Greg Johnson, *The White Nationalist Manifesto* (San Francisco: Counter-Currents Publishing, 2019), 9–22.
25. Jared Taylor, "If We Do Nothing" (June 1996), *American Renaissance*, January 7, 2011, https://www.amren.com.
26. Buchanan, *Suicide of a Superpower*, 174.
27. Quoted in Pablo Gorondi, "Hungary's Orban: Western Europe Is under Migrant Invasion," AP News, March 15, 2018, https://apnews.com. See also Camus, *You Will Not Replace Us!*, 32–34.
28. There is a significant demographic panic literature that pushes this

Islamophobic threat narrative. See, for instance, Bruce Bawer, *While Europe Slept: How Radical Islam Is Destroying the West from Within* (New York: Broadway Books, 2006); Melanie Phillips, *Londonistan* (New York: Encounter Books, 2006); Bat Ye'or, *EurAbia: The Euro-Arab Axis* (Madison, N.J.: Fairleigh Dickinson University Press, 2006).

29. For an in-depth discussion of this effort to secure white solidarity through xenophobic cruelty, see Cristina Beltrán, *Citizenship as Cruelty: How Migrant Suffering Sustains White Democracy* (Minneapolis: University of Minnesota Press, 2020).
30. For a useful discussion of how antistate anger mobilized the Tea Party movement, see Theda Skocpol and Vanessa Williamson, *The Tea Party and the Remaking of Republican Conservatism* (New York: Oxford University Press, 2013). On right-wing animus toward entitlement programs (particularly as it takes racialized shape), see Ange-Marie Hancock, *The Politics of Disgust: The Public Identity of the Welfare Queen* (New York: New York University Press, 2004); Daniel Martinez HoSang and Joseph E. Lowndes, *Producers, Parasites, Patriots: Race and the New Right-Wing Politics of Precarity* (Minneapolis: University of Minnesota Press, 2019).
31. For an insightful discussion of these themes, see Myesha Cherry, *The Case for Rage: Why Anger Is Essential for Anti-racist Struggle* (New York: Oxford University Press, 2021).
32. For reflections on how anger can serve justice, see Martha Nussbaum, *Anger and Forgiveness: Resentment, Generosity, Justice* (New York: Oxford University Press, 2016).
33. For an excellent account of how affect (and rage, more narrowly) can inform a movement politics, see Deborah Gould, *Moving Politics: Emotion and ACT-UP's Fight against AIDS* (Chicago: University of Chicago Press, 2009).
34. Audre Lorde, *Sister Outsider* (New York: Penguin Books, 2020), 118. See also Brittney Cooper's account of the emancipatory work of rage from a raced and gendered position in *Eloquent Rage: A Black Feminist Discovers Her Superpower* (New York: St. Martin's Press, 2008). Soraya Chemaly specifically examines the gendered power of rage in *Rage Becomes Her: The Power of Women's Anger* (New York: Atria, 2018).
35. Michael Kimmel addresses this rage of "aggrieved entitlement" throughout his book *Angry White Men.*
36. Rage against "dethronement" or "lost entitlement" is at the heart of Wendy Brown's diagnosis of white reaction politics in *In the Ruins of Neoliberalism: The Rise of Antidemocratic Politics in the West* (New York: Columbia University Press, 2019), 161–88.
37. A symptomatic lament in this vein is found in Gregory Hood, "A White Nationalist Memo to White Male Republicans," Counter-

Currents, August 31, 2016, https://counter-currents.com. This essay has been reprinted in Gregory Hood, *Waking Up from the American Dream* (San Francisco: Counter-Currents Publishing, 2016).

38. An example is the well-known case of Dylann Roof, who killed nine Black parishioners at a historically Black church in Charleston, South Carolina, in a professed effort to spark a race war. For an overview, see Rachel Kaadzi Ghansah, "A Most American Terrorist: The Making of Dylann Roof," *GQ,* August 21, 2017, https://www.gq.com.
39. This argument is detailed in Kathleen Belew, "There Are No Lone Wolves: The White Power Movement at War," in *A Field Guide to White Supremacy,* ed. Kathleen Belew and Ramón A. Gutiérrez (Oakland: University of California Press, 2021), 312–23. See also Daniel Byman, *Spreading Hate: The Global Rise of White Supremacist Terrorism* (New York: Oxford University Press, 2022); Sara Kamali, *Homegrown Hate: Why White Nationalists and Militant Islamists Are Waging War against the United States* (Oakland: University of California Press, 2021), 219–46.
40. In this sense, those extremists who emerge from the far right media ecology represent an aberrant version of the "networks of outrage" that Manuel Castells associates with social movements in a networked era. See Manuel Castells, *Networks of Outrage and Hope: Social Movements in the Internet Age* (Malden, Mass.: Polity Press, 2012).
41. For reflections on the role of narrative in extremist cultures, see J. M. Berger, *Extremism* (Cambridge: MIT Press, 2018); Kurt Braddock, *Weaponized Words: The Strategic Role of Persuasion in Violent Radicalization and Counter-radicalization* (New York: Cambridge University Press, 2020); Ruth Wodak, *The Politics of Fear: The Shameless Normalization of Far-Right Discourse,* 2nd ed. (London: SAGE, 2020).
42. See Cas Mudde, *The Far Right Today* (Medford, Mass.: Polity Press, 2019). Cynthia Miller-Idriss likewise notes some of the terminological difficulties involved in capturing the many faces of the far right. Cynthia Miller-Idriss, *Hate in the Homeland: The New Global Far Right* (Princeton, N.J.: Princeton University Press, 2020), 15–17.
43. For a more encyclopedic, comprehensive approach to the far right, see David Bennett, *The Party of Fear: From Nativist Movements to the New Right in American History* (New York: Vintage Books, 1995); Leonard Zeskind, *Blood and Politics: The History of the White Nationalist Movement from the Margins to the Mainstream* (New York: Farrar, Straus and Giroux, 2009).

1. "You Will Not Replace Us"

1. Camus, *You Will Not Replace Us!,* 11.
2. Eric Kaufmann, *Whiteshift: Populism, Immigration, and the Future of White Majorities* (New York: Penguin Books, 2019), 1–2.
3. Camus, *You Will Not Replace Us!,* 23.

4. For a trenchant discussion of these anxieties, see Wendy Brown, *Walled States, Waning Sovereignty* (New York: Zone Books, 2010).
5. On this appeal to an organic or "carnal" basis of the nation, see José Pedro Zúquete, *The Identitarians: The Movement against Globalism and Islam in Europe* (Notre Dame, Ind.: University of Notre Dame Press, 2018), 109–13.
6. Gregory Hood, "Race: The First Principle," Counter-Currents, May 14, 2013, https://counter-currents.com. This essay has been reprinted in Hood, *Waking Up from the American Dream.*
7. Guillaume Faye, *Why We Fight: Manifesto of the European Resistance,* trans. Michael O'Meara (London: Arktos, 2011), 35.
8. For a useful overview of populism, see Jan-Werner Müller, *What Is Populism?* (Philadelphia: University of Pennsylvania Press, 2016). For some recent accounts of the populist turn that highlight its racialized dimensions, see Aurelien Mondon and Aaron Winter, *Reactionary Democracy: How Racism and the Populist Far Right Became Mainstream* (New York: Verso, 2020); Marco Revelli, *The New Populism: Democracy Stares into the Abyss,* trans. David Broder (New York: Verso, 2019).
9. In this regard, the new ethnonationalism distinguishes itself from those strains of the far right that attempt to stress a more multicultural, multiracial formulation of their exclusionary ideals. See, for instance, HoSang and Lowndes, *Producers, Parasites, Patriots,* 103–28.
10. See Lindsey Bever, "'Make America White Again': A Politician's Billboard Ignites Uproar," *Washington Post,* June 23, 2016, https://www.washingtonpost.com. Tyler's official campaign website is now defunct, but it has been archived on the Internet Archive, accessed August 18, 2023, https://web.archive.org/web/20171201000000*/ricktylerforcongress.com. This candidate was not alone. As noted in the Introduction, Neil Kumar ran for the U.S. Congress in Arkansas in 2022 on a platform that included as its first policy proposal "Stop the Great Replacement." See "Neil for Arkansas 2022 Platform."
11. On this shifting relationship to whiteness, see Ashley Jardina, *White Identity Politics* (New York: Cambridge University Press, 2019), 6–7. There is a considerable literature on how whiteness is effectively the unmarked, invisible standard against which all variations are judged as deviations. See, for instance, Iris Young, *Justice and the Politics of Difference* (Princeton, N.J.: Princeton University Press, 1990), chap. 2.
12. See, for instance, Anderson, *White Rage.*
13. Juliet Hooker, "Black Protest/White Grievance: On the Problem of White Political Imaginations Not Shaped by Loss," *South Atlantic Quarterly* 116, no. 3 (July 2017): 484.
14. Wilmot Robertson, *The Ethnostate: An Unblinkered Prospectus for an Advanced Statecraft* (Cape Canaveral, Fla.: Howard Allen, 1992), 170. Camus describes ethnonationalist movements aimed at restoring

ethnic or racial cores to European nations as driven by "grief over the loss of one's country and one's people." Camus, *You Will Not Replace Us!,* 25. This judgment is reflected in Patrick Buchanan's references to "sadness" and "melancholy" as he analogizes the "loss" of the nation to the death of a parent. See Buchanan, *Death of the West,* 1.

15. Other scholars have addressed the notion of a melancholic nationalism, though in different contexts, with different meanings and different conclusions. See, for instance, Jocelyn Maclure, *Quebec Identity: The Challenge of Pluralism,* trans. Peter Feldstein (Montreal: McGill-Queen's University Press, 2003), 19–60; Ewa Plonowska Ziarek, "Melancholic Nationalism and the Pathologies of Commemorating the Holocaust in Poland," in *Imaginary Neighbors: Mediating Polish–Jewish Relations after the Holocaust,* ed. Dorota Glowacka and Joanna Zylinska (Lincoln: University of Nebraska Press, 2007), 301–26.
16. Aziz Rana, *The Two Faces of American Freedom* (Cambridge, Mass.: Harvard University Press, 2010). For productive reflections on this positional logic of race, see Ian Haney López, *White by Law: The Legal Construction of Race* (New York: New York University Press, 2006), chap. 6.
17. As Cheryl Harris has argued, for instance, to be white in a world forged by chattel slavery is to hold a distinct position in the landscape of power, as one who cannot become the property of another. See Cheryl Harris, "Whiteness as Property," *Harvard Law Review* 106, no. 8 (1993): 1707–91.
18. Race as a status of power (rather than nature) has become a staple of critical race studies. See, for instance, Karen Fields and Barbara Fields, *Racecraft: The Soul of Inequality in American Life* (New York: Verso, 2014); Joel Olson, *The Abolition of White Democracy* (Minneapolis: University of Minnesota Press, 2004); Charles W. Mills, *The Racial Contract* (Ithaca, N.Y.: Cornell University Press, 1997).
19. Olson, *Abolition of White Democracy,* 38–39.
20. The canonical articulation of this point appears in W. E. B. Du Bois, *Black Reconstruction in America* (1935; repr., New York: Free Press, 1998), 700. For a reading that brings out Du Bois's more substantive concerns about white domination, see Ella Myers, "Beyond the Psychological Wage: Du Bois on White Domination," *Political Theory* 47, no. 1 (2019): 6–31.
21. On this point, see Jardina, *White Identity Politics,* 160–61; Noel Ignatiev, *How the Irish Became White* (New York: Routledge, 1995); David Roediger, *Working toward Whiteness: How America's Immigrants Became White* (New York: Basic Books, 2006).
22. Here I mean to push against Judith Shklar's influential argument that the good of citizenship (specifically, racial citizenship) is ultimately

a matter of social standing that transcends material or participatory benefits. See Judith N. Shklar, *American Citizenship: The Quest for Inclusion* (Cambridge, Mass.: Harvard University Press, 1991). For helpful discussions of Shklar's analysis (both of which highlight how Shklar does not follow this racial logic of citizenship to its historical or normative conclusions), see Andrew Dilts, *Punishment and Inclusion: Race, Membership, and the Limits of American Liberalism* (New York: Fordham University Press, 2014), chap. 5; Olson, *Abolition of White Democracy*, 39–44.

23. For discussions of how these material guarantees were built into the basic provisions of New Deal politics, see Ira Katznelson, *When Affirmative Action Was White: An Untold History of Racial Inequality in Twentieth-Century America* (New York: W. W. Norton, 2005); Joseph E. Lowndes, *From the New Deal to the New Right: Race and the Southern Origins of Modern Conservatism* (New Haven, Conn.: Yale University Press, 2008).
24. See Harris, "Whiteness as Property." See also Minkah Makalani, "Black Lives Matter and the Limits of Formal Black Politics," *South Atlantic Quarterly* 116, no. 3 (July 2017): 529–52; Olson, *Abolition of White Democracy*, xviii–xxi.
25. Richard Spencer, "Spencer Speaks! (the Transcript)," *Radix Journal*, December 9, 2016, https://radixjournal.com.
26. Regarding this ambivalence, I draw from Ghassan Hage, *White Nation: Fantasies of White Supremacy in a Multicultural Society* (New York: Routledge, 2000), 42–46.
27. Hage, *White Nation*, 40.
28. Hage, *White Nation*, 46.
29. In Allen's terms, such losses reveal the torsions of democratic life: "Democracy puts its citizens under a strange form of psychological pressure by building them up as sovereigns and then regularly undermining each citizen's experience of sovereignty." Danielle Allen, *Talking to Strangers: Anxieties of Citizenship since* Brown v. Board of Education (Chicago: University of Chicago Press, 2004), 27.
30. See Allen, *Talking to Strangers*, 45–49. See also the discussion of Allen's work in Hooker, "Black Protest/White Grievance," 485–86.
31. See, for instance, Kimmel, *Angry White Men*, 1–27.
32. On this point, see Hooker, "Black Protest/White Grievance," 486; Jardina, *White Identity Politics*, 268. A symptomatic instance is offered by Richard Spencer, "Facing the Future as a Minority," *Radix Journal*, September 28, 2016, https://radixjournal.com.
33. Buchanan, *Suicide of a Superpower*, 134. The term "ethnomasochism" also appears throughout the work of European identitarian figures, such as Guillaume Faye, Daniel Friberg, and Pierre Krebs. See, for instance, Daniel Friberg, *The Real Right Returns: A Handbook for the True Opposition* (London: Arktos, 2015), 85–86. For a critical discus-

sion of this theme in the European context, see Zúquete, *The Identitarians,* 131–37.

34. Jared Taylor, for instance, argues: "What whites are expected to do is without precedent in human history. We have the power to keep our lands for ourselves, but we are throwing them open to aliens, aliens who despise us as they take what is ours. Many nations have been overrun by powerful invaders. Never has any people or nation let itself be pillaged by the weak. This is a mental sickness unique to whites and unique to our era." Jared Taylor, "What Is the Alt Right?," *American Renaissance,* October 11, 2016, https://www.amren.com.
35. The following passage from the American white nationalist Greg Johnson is instructive: "White genocide has not happened in a sudden burst of violence, and it will not be solved that way either. White genocide is a process unfolding over generations. Its architects knew very well that its ultimate end is the extinction of the white race. But they were not interested in a quick paroxysm of slaughter, as emotionally satisfying as that might have been. They knew that it is difficult to mobilize people to commit mass murder, and it is risky. . . . Therefore, they conceived a slower, safer process of genocide. They knew that if anti-white demographic trends were set in motion and sustained over time—i.e., lower birthrates, collapsing families, miscegenation, non-white immigration, non-white penetration of white living spaces, etc.—the long term result would be white extinction, and very few whites would become aware of it, much less fight back, until resistance was pretty much futile anyway." Greg Johnson, *The White Nationalist Manifesto,* 2nd ed. (San Francisco: Counter-Currents Publishing, 2019), 42.
36. In a symptomatic formulation, Camus claims, "Population swamping or 'demographic invasion' is a different matter entirely. It undermines the very identity of the nation or the people targeted by the swamping." Camus, *You Will Not Replace Us!,* 45.
37. See Jared Taylor, *White Identity: Racial Consciousness in the 21st Century* (Oakton, Va.: New Century Books, 2011), chap. 9.
38. See Samuel Huntington, *Who Are We? The Challenges to America's National Identity* (New York: Simon & Shuster, 2005), esp. chaps. 1 and 8. For specific references to "beachheads," see 63–64, 193, 226.
39. See Camus, *You Will Not Replace Us!,* 51–53; Faye, *Ethnic Apocalypse.*
40. This viewpoint is particularly prevalent among those invested in the pseudoscience of racial difference. In this connection, see Wilmot Robertson, *The Dispossessed Majority* (Cape Canaveral, Fla.: Howard Allen, 1973). Dorothy Roberts addresses parallel anxieties over Black reproduction in *Killing the Black Body: Race, Reproduction, and the Meaning of Liberty* (New York: Vintage Books, 1997). For a useful discussion of how these fears focus on Latinx reproduction specifically, see Leo R. Chavez, "Fear of White Replacement: Latina Fertility,

White Demographic Decline, and Immigration Reform," in Belew and Gutiérrez, *Field Guide to White Supremacy,* 177–202.

41. See Buchanan, *Death of the West,* 11–24; Johnson, *White Nationalist Manifesto.*
42. This argument is detailed throughout Arlie Russell Hochschild, *Strangers in Their Own Land: Anger and Mourning on the American Right* (New York: New Press, 2016). Jared Taylor sketches the ultimate conclusion of this "unwelcome, uncalled for, irreversible change": "Whites become refugees in their own land." Taylor, "If We Do Nothing."
43. Quoted in Alexandra Minna Stern, *Proud Boys and the White Ethnostate: How the Alt-Right Is Warping the American Imagination* (Boston: Beacon Press, 2019), 132.
44. As Jared Taylor renders this fantasy of attachment: "People have every right to expect their children and their children's children to be able to grow up and walk in the ways of their ancestors. They have a powerful, natural desire that their grandchildren be like them—that they speak the same language, sing the same songs, tell the same stories, pray to the same God, take pride in the same past, hope the same hopes, love the same nation, and honor the same traditions. The crucial elements of peoplehood cannot be preserved in the face of a flood of aliens, especially when the central institutions of the nation itself preach fashionable falsehoods about the equivalence of all races, cultures, and peoples." Taylor, "If We Do Nothing."
45. Generation Identity, recruitment video, available on the Internet Archive, accessed October 4, 2023, https://web.archive.org/web/20190829180214/http://generation-identity.org.uk/media.
46. Wendy Brown first articulated this argument in *States of Injury: Power and Freedom in Late Modernity* (Princeton, N.J.: Princeton University Press, 1995), 52–76. She revisits the core terms of this argument in diagnosing white masculinist nationalisms in her 2019 book *In the Ruins of Neoliberalism.* On this connection between ressentiment and reactive-melancholic politics, see Ceran Özselcuk, "Mourning, Melancholy, and the Politics of Class Transformation," *Rethinking Marxism* 18, no. 2 (April 2006): 225–40.
47. This is the standard far right narrative on the cultural work of "white guilt." A symptomatic articulation appears in Gregory Hood, "The New Kulaks: Whites as an Enemy Class," in *A Fair Hearing: The Alt-Right in the Words of Its Members and Leaders,* ed. George T. Shaw (London: Arktos, 2018), 3–14.
48. Hochschild, *Strangers in Their Own Land,* 135–51.
49. See Hooker, "Black Protest/White Grievance," 489–91; David Neiwert, *Alt-America: The Rise of the Radical Right in the Age of Trump* (New York: Verso, 2018), chap. 5.

50. The political theorist Wendy Brown observes that this resentment mobilizes "a permanent politics of revenge" that seeks to tear down and undo the work of all those forces and enemies (e.g., feminists, cosmopolitans, multiculturalists, globalists) that have ostensibly disenfranchised the white working male. She notes that this ethos of ressentiment helps to explain the popularity of "outsider" figures within the contemporary political scene—those who refuse the traditional languages of diplomacy, multilateralism, inclusion, and civic respect. Brown, *In the Ruins of Neoliberalism*, 177, 121.
51. Although Brown does not take this step, she hints at it when she identifies, in passing, an "aggrieved melancholy for a phantasmatic past." Brown, *In the Ruins of Neoliberalism*, 119.
52. The classic site of this diagnosis is, of course, Sigmund Freud's "Mourning and Melancholia," in *The Standard Edition of the Complete Psychological Works of Sigmund Freud*, vol. 14, trans. James Strachey (London: Hogarth Press, 1917), 243–58.
53. Seth Moglen, "On Mourning Social Injury," *Psychoanalysis, Culture & Society* 10, no. 2 (August 2005): 159, 161.
54. In the scholarly literature, this narrative runs throughout Hochschild's ethnographic work. In one rendering, she proposes: "You are a stranger in your own land. You do not recognize yourself in how others see you. It is a struggle to feel seen and honored. . . . Through no fault of your own, and in ways that are hidden, you are slipping backward." Hochschild, *Strangers in Their Own Land*, 144. Such images of estrangement appear consistently within the literature of the far right. See, for instance, Buchanan, *Death of the West*, 5.
55. Jeffrey Alexander, *Trauma: A Social Theory* (Malden, Mass.: Polity Press, 2012), 15. For discussion of how social narratives, more broadly, provide the framework for learning and performing racial identity, see Clarissa Rile Hayward, *How Americans Make Race: Stories, Institutions, Spaces* (New York: Cambridge University Press, 2013).
56. This point is supported by both ethnographic and survey evidence. See, for instance, Justin Gest, *The New Minority: White Working Class Politics in an Age of Immigration and Inequality* (New York: Oxford University Press, 2016); Jardina, *White Identity Politics*, 133–39.
57. The Vanguard America website is now defunct, but the poster may be viewed at the archived version of the site on the Internet Archive, accessed August 18, 2023, https://web.archive.org/web/20170720053910/https://bloodandsoil.org/posters.
58. For in-depth discussions of this explicitly male fantasy of racial control, see Susanne Kaiser, *Political Masculinity: How Incels, Fundamentalists and Authoritarians Mobilize for Patriarchy*, trans. Valentine A. Pakis (Medford, Mass.: Polity Press, 2022); Kimmel, *Angry White Men*.
59. Greg Johnson argues that "Jews are . . . among the principal promoters of trends conducive to white genocide, such as massive non-white

immigration, racial integration, miscegenation, feminism, and sexual liberation." See Johnson, *White Nationalist Manifesto,* 20.

60. This is particularly the case for those who espouse the fiction of the Zionist Occupational Government (ZOG)—a cabal that has ostensibly taken control of global organizations in order to impose a New World Order across the globe. Kathleen Belew examines the role of ZOG in the white nationalist imagination (particularly its paramilitary variants) in *Bring the War Home: The White Power Movement and Paramilitary America* (Cambridge, Mass.: Harvard University Press, 2018). More broadly, Greg Johnson describes the Jew as a "fundamental enemy" of the white race, owing to "the Jewish role in opening white nations to non-white immigration." Greg Johnson, *Truth, Justice, and a Nice White Country* (San Francisco: Counter-Currents Publishing, 2015), 92. On the pervasiveness of anti-Semitism within the alt-right, see Kimmel, *Angry White Men,* 12–24, 242–48.
61. The far right is defined by significant anti-Semitic currents. For symptomatic cases, see David Duke, *Jewish Supremacism: My Awakening on the Jewish Question* (Covington, La.: Free Speech Press, 2002); George Lincoln Rockwell, "In Hoc Signo Vinces," in *Encyclopedia of White Power: A Sourcebook on the Racist Radical Right,* ed. Jeffrey Kaplan (Walnut Creek, Calif.: AltaMira Press, 2000), 439–52. For a piece that specifically connects these anti-Semitic strains to the belief in "white replacement," see Douglas Mercer, "Until We Stop Them," *National Vanguard,* July 27, 2022, https://nationalvanguard.org.
62. In a characteristic rendering, Jared Taylor argues: "We are told over and over that it is the duty of all Americans to 'celebrate diversity.' . . . But to ask whites to 'celebrate diversity' means asking them to rejoice in their own declining numbers and dwindling influence." Taylor, "What Is the Alt Right?"
63. Judith Butler has enlisted melancholia as a structure for subjecthood more generally, as a marker of those attachments that individuals must forswear to achieve normalized patterns of identity. See Judith Butler, *Gender Trouble: Feminism and the Subversion of Identity* (New York: Routledge, 1990), 73–83. She expands this argument in *The Psychic Life of Power: Theories in Subjection* (Stanford, Calif.: Stanford University Press, 1997), 132–50, 167–98. Likewise, Anne Cheng has productively theorized the subjectivity of abject racial groups as distinctly melancholic in *The Melancholy of Race: Psychoanalysis, Assimilation, and Hidden Grief* (New York: Oxford University Press, 2000). Another noteworthy instance is Casey Ryan Kelly, whose excellent book on the topic came to my attention too late to grapple with in the writing process (as this chapter originally appeared in article form some years ago). Kelly also reads the state of white masculinity as a form of aggressive melancholy, driven by fantasies of victimhood. Though we overlap on key points, there are important

distinctions between our accounts. For instance, where Kelly emphasizes how melancholic loss is associated with the Freudian death drive (and thus, in his terms, spawns a distinctive thanatopolitics), in this book I am more interested in how *social* melancholia (bound up with melancholic social narratives) binds communities of rage and forecloses a meaningful political future. Likewise, where Kelly uses melancholia to analyze the aggressive politics of masculinity, my focus is on the politics of demographic fear, as structured by narratives of racial replacement. See Casey Ryan Kelly, *Apocalypse Man: The Death Drive and the Rhetoric of White Masculine Victimhood* (Columbus: Ohio State University Press, 2020). In a provocative article, Kate Manne also argues for a melancholic dimension of whiteness, though her account stresses an argument of moral loss, in dialogue with Judith Butler and Jean-Paul Sartre. See Kate Manne, "Melancholy Whiteness (or, Shame-Faced in Shadows)," *Philosophy and Phenomenological Research* 96, no. 1 (January 2018): 233–42.

64. Douglas Crimp, "Mourning and Militancy," *October* 51 (Winter 1989): 3–18. See also the helpful discussion of these themes in Ann Cvetkovich, *An Archive of Feelings: Trauma, Sexuality, and Lesbian Public Cultures* (Durham, N.C.: Duke University Press, 2003), 205–38.
65. Alexander Mitscherlich and Margarete Mitscherlich, *The Inability to Mourn: Principles of Collective Behavior,* trans. B. R. Placzek (New York: Grove Press, 1975).
66. Paul Gilroy, *Postcolonial Melancholia* (New York: Columbia University Press, 2005), 98–106. Judith Butler makes similar arguments on the inability to grieve the "foreign" targets of geopolitical violence in *Precarious Life: The Powers of Mourning and Violence* (New York: Verso, 2004), 36, 46. Anne Cheng details this simultaneous refusal and retention of the racialized other (as a structure of white identity formation) in *Melancholy of Race,* 3–30.
67. Carol Anderson details the animating impulses of white rage in specifically anti-Black terms. She argues that "the trigger for white rage, inevitably, is black advancement. It is not the mere presence of black people that is the problem; rather, it is blackness with ambition, with drive, with purpose, with aspirations, and with demands for full and equal citizenship." Anderson, *White Rage,* 3.
68. Kimmel, *Angry White Men,* 18.
69. See, for instance, George Lipsitz, *The Possessive Investment in Whiteness: How White People Benefit from Identity Politics* (Philadelphia: Temple University Press, 2006).
70. See Taylor, "If We Do Nothing." Taylor's argument made some public waves when he expressed his views in an online video. See Jared Taylor, "Immigration and the Old Indian Trick," *American Renaissance,* January 2, 2019, https://www.amren.com.
71. For an evocative account of the lived grief experienced by the Crow

tribe under conditions of settler colonialism, see Jonathan Lear, *Radical Hope: Ethics in the Face of Cultural Devastation* (Cambridge, Mass.: Harvard University Press, 2006).

72. There is a robust critical literature on trauma as a lens for unlocking social experience. See Cathy Caruth, *Unclaimed Experience: Trauma, Narrative, and History* (Baltimore: Johns Hopkins University Press, 1996); Dominic LaCapra, "Trauma, Absence, Loss," *Critical Inquiry* 25 (Summer 1999): 696–727. For a critical rejoinder to trauma discourse, see Didier Fassin and Richard Rechtman, *The Empire of Trauma: An Inquiry into the Condition of Victimhood,* trans. Rachel Gomme (Princeton, N.J.: Princeton University Press, 2009).
73. I owe this phrase to an anonymous reviewer for the journal *Political Theory.*
74. Here I follow Juliet Hooker, who helpfully notes the utility of Mills's argument for theorizing white grievance politics. See Hooker, "Black Protest/White Grievance," 487. On the connection between anti-Blackness and racialized "bad faith," see Lewis Gordon, *Bad Faith and Antiblack Racism* (Atlantic Highlands, N.J.: Humanities Press, 1995).
75. Mills, *Racial Contract,* 18.
76. Gilroy, *Postcolonial Melancholia,* 99.
77. Others may acknowledge the historic violence of a white nation with a caveat: the violence was necessary to birth a nation that now stands as a beacon to others—the benefits yielded by the violence have outweighed the costs.
78. This is the argument Johnson makes in his *White Nationalist Manifesto.* See also Buchanan, *Death of the West.*
79. Johnson, *White Nationalist Manifesto.* See also Robertson, *The Ethnostate.* As I will detail in later chapters, however, Robertson's argument is based less in the grief of loss than in a spuriously evolutionist insistence that racial separation is necessary for global cultural progress (itself premised on the superiority of white historical accomplishment).
80. For informative background on these separatist projects, see Stern, *Proud Boys and the White Ethnostate,* chap. 3.
81. See, for instance, Ziarek, "Melancholic Nationalism," 314–18.
82. As Seth Moglen notes: "To the degree that victims of social injuries seek only to retrieve what they have lost in the mode of rigid replication, the work of mourning remains unfinished and obstructed. In social as in private processes of grieving, the capacity to imagine only replication is a sign that the bereaved can gain access to libidinal energies only to the degree that they remain exclusively attached to something lost." Moglen, "On Mourning Social Injury," 163. In reference to Germany's refusal to come to terms with its past violence, Alexander and Margarete Mitscherlich observe that

"what is consumed in the defense of a self anxious to protect itself against bitter reproaches of conscience and doubts of its own worth is thus unavailable for mastering the present." Mitscherlich and Mitscherlich, *Inability to Mourn,* 16.

83. Jeffrey Prager, "Melancholic Identities: Post-traumatic Loss, Memory and Identity Formation," in *Identity in Question,* ed. Anthony Elliott and Paul du Gay (London: SAGE, 2009), 147. This is Prager's gloss on a point from Tzvetan Todorov.
84. Sara Ahmed offers a useful diagnosis of these appeals to love: "The white subjects claim the place of hosts ('our shores'), at the same time as they claim the position of the victim. . . . The narrative hence suggests that it is love for the nation that make the white Aryans feel hate toward others who, in 'taking away' the nation, are taking away their history, as well as their future." Sara Ahmed, *The Cultural Politics of Emotion* (New York: Routledge, 2004), 43.
85. The emphasis on futurity is, of course, a staple of Hannah Arendt's reading of politics. See Hannah Arendt, "Freedom and Politics," in *Thinking without a Banister: Essays in Understanding, 1953–1975* (New York: Schocken, 2018), 220–44. On the relationships among mourning, melancholia, and the politics of futurity, see also Wendy Brown, *Edgework: Critical Essays on Knowledge and Politics* (Princeton, N.J.: Princeton University Press, 2005), 98–115.
86. This reactionary impulse is noted in Kimmel, *Angry White Men,* 17–21; Stern, *Proud Boys and the White Ethnostate,* 33–49.
87. Hooker, "Black Protest/White Grievance," 488.
88. For the most prominent example, see Olson, *Abolition of White Democracy.* In more evocative terms, Noel Ignatiev proposes that "so-called whites must cease to exist as whites in order to realize themselves as something else; to put it another way: white people must commit suicide as whites in order to come alive as workers, or youth, or women, or whatever other identity can induce them to change from the miserable, petulant, subordinated creatures they are now into freely associated, fully developed human subjects." Noel Ignatiev, "The Point Is Not to Interpret Whiteness but to Abolish It" (talk given at the University of California, Berkeley, April 1997).
89. The white population is, in the galvanizing terms of Wilmot Robertson, a "dispossessed majority." See Robertson, *Dispossessed Majority.*
90. Bever, "'Make America White Again.'"
91. Kimmel details this economic framework for white reaction in *Angry White Men,* 1–30. See also Brown, *In the Ruins of Neoliberalism,* 174–81.
92. HoSang and Lowndes, *Producers, Parasites, Patriots,* 67.
93. As Pippa Norris and Ronald Inglehart argue, it is important not to oversell these material factors in accounting for the racial backlash of the far right. If economic dispossession and white precarity feature into far right mobilizing narratives, they are hardly the

sole factors contributing to this racialized politics of reaction. Pippa Norris and Ronald Inglehart, *Cultural Backlash: Trump, Brexit, and Authoritarian Populism* (New York: Cambridge University Press, 2019), 132–74.

94. The literature on racial capitalism is extensive. The canonical case is Cedric Robinson, *Black Marxism: The Making of the Black Radical Tradition* (Chapel Hill: University of North Carolina Press, 1983). And a much wider literature has arisen to explore the broader entanglements of race and capitalism. See, for instance, Destin Jenkins and Justin Leroy, *Histories of Racial Capitalism* (New York: Columbia University Press, 2021); Manning Marable, *How Capitalism Underdeveloped Black America: Problems in Race, Political Economy, and Society* (Cambridge, Mass.: South End Press, 2000); Jodi Melamed, "Racial Capitalism," *Critical Ethnic Studies* 1, no. 1 (2015): 76–85; Michael Ralph and Maya Sighal, "Racial Capitalism," *Theory and Society* 48, no. 6 (2019): 851–81.
95. For an informative ethnographic account of these economic grievances, see Silva, *We're Still Here.*
96. For some reflections on the contested politics of monuments, see Karen L Cox, *No Common Ground: Confederate Monuments and the Ongoing Fight for Racial Justice* (Chapel Hill: University of North Carolina Press, 2021); Sanford Levinson, *Written in Stone: Public Monuments in Changing Societies,* 20th anniversary ed. (Durham, N.C.: Duke University Press, 2018).
97. Max Greenwood, "Trump on Removing Confederate Statues: 'They're Trying to Take Away Our Culture,'" *The Hill,* August 22, 2017, https://thehill.com.
98. For a critical account of "Lost Cause" politics and its connection to traditions of white supremacy, see Adam Domby, *The False Cause: Fraud, Fabrication, and White Supremacy in Confederate Memory* (Charlottesville: University of Virginia Press, 2020).
99. For characteristic far right commentary on the value of memorializing the Confederacy, see Chad Crowley, "Why the Confederacy Matters," Counter-Currents, September 21, 2017, https://counter-currents.com; Veiko Hessler, "General Lee Rides Again," Counter-Currents, August 24, 2017, https://counter-currents.com.

2. The Catastrophist Vision of the Far Right

1. The popular media have produced a considerable number of think pieces on the possibility of a "second civil war" in the United States. For a quick sampling, see the December 2019 issue of *The Atlantic,* which is dedicated entirely to the question "How to Stop a Civil War?"; William G. Gale and Darrell M. West, "Is the US Headed for Another Civil War?," Brookings Institution, September 16, 2021, https://www.brookings.edu; Stephen Marche, "The Next US Civil

War Is Already Here—We Just Refuse to See It," *The Guardian,* January 4, 2022, https://www.theguardian.com; Robert Reich, "The Second American Civil War Is Already Happening," *The Guardian,* May 11, 2022, https://www.theguardian.com.

2. For an overview of how the new right theorizes the meaning and possibilities of this period, see Roger Griffin, "Between Metapolitics and *Apoliteia*: The Nouvelle Droite's Strategy for Conserving the Fascist Vision in the 'Interregnum,'" *Modern & Contemporary France* 8, no. 1 (2000): 35–53. A symptomatic expression of this vision of decline can be found in Joakim Andersen, *Rising from the Ruins: The Right of the 21st Century,* trans. Gustav Hörngren (London: Arktos, 2018).
3. Julius Evola, *Men among the Ruins: Post-war Reflections of a Radical Traditionalist,* trans. Guido Stucco (Rochester, Vt.: Inner Traditions, 2002).
4. Guillaume Faye, for instance, argues that the present state of Europe is ultimately a "convergence of catastrophes"—foremost of which is the catastrophe inaugurated by mass immigration. See Guillaume Faye, *Archeofuturism: European Visions of the Post-catastrophic Age,* trans. Sergio Knipe (London: Arktos, 2010).
5. On this point, see Buchanan, *Death of the West,* chap. 9; Samuel Francis, "Winning the Culture War," *Chronicles: A Magazine of American Culture,* December 1993, 12–15.
6. James Davis, "At War with the Future: Catastrophism and the Right," in *Catastrophism: The Apocalyptic Politics of Collapse and Rebirth,* ed. Sasha Lilley, David McNally, Eddie Yuen, and James Davis (Oakland, Calif.: PM Press, 2012), 78.
7. Corey Robin identifies the theme of loss or decline as central to the tradition of conservative thought. Corey Robin, *The Reactionary Mind: Conservatism from Edmund Burke to Donald Trump,* 2nd ed. (New York: Oxford University Press, 2017).
8. Buchanan, *Death of the West,* 23.
9. Faye, *Ethnic Apocalypse,* 49.
10. Camus, *You Will Not Replace Us!,* 21, 28.
11. See, for instance, Achille Mbembe, *Critique of Black Reason,* trans. Laurent Dubois (Durham, N.C.: Duke University Press, 2017).
12. On the fear of race war as an important element in the early American political imagination, see Kay Wright Lewis, *A Curse upon the Nation: Race, Freedom, and Extermination in America and the Atlantic World* (Athens: University of Georgia Press, 2017); Nikhil Pal Singh, *Race and America's Long War* (Oakland: University of California Press, 2017), 123–51; Joel Williamson, *The Crucible of Race: Black–White Relations in the American South since Emancipation* (New York: Oxford University Press, 1984).
13. Michel Foucault, *"Society Must Be Defended": Lectures at the Collège*

de France, 1975–76, trans. David Macey (New York: Picador Press, 2003), 50–51.

14. As Foucault elaborates: "The other race . . . is a race that is permanently, ceaselessly infiltrating the social body, or which is, rather, constantly being re-created in and by the social fabric. In other words, what we see as a polarity, as a binary rift within society, is not a clash between two distinct races. It is the splitting of a single race into a superrace and a subrace." Foucault, *"Society Must Be Defended,"* 61.
15. This metaphor of pruning is central to Zygmunt Bauman's reading of the Holocaust. See Zygmunt Bauman, *Modernity and the Holocaust* (Ithaca, N.Y.: Cornell University Press, 1991), 92–93. It also figures prominently in Roberto Esposito's account of thanatopolitics in *Bios: Biopolitics and Philosophy,* trans. Timothy Campbell (Minneapolis: University of Minnesota Press, 2008), chap. 4.
16. As Foucault describes the centrality of racism for fascist biopolitics: "What in fact is racism? It is primarily a way of introducing a break into the domain of life that is under power's control: the break between what must live and what must die." Foucault, *"Society Must Be Defended,"* 254.
17. Foucault, *"Society Must Be Defended,"* 61.
18. Faye, *Why We Fight,* 94. Renaud Camus likewise identifies a "colonization of Europe" that is currently unfolding through non-European mass immigration—one that reflects a "population swamping or 'demographic invasion.'" Camus, *You Will Not Replace Us!,* 45. Likewise, Pierre Vial has coined the pithy expression "immigration-invasion" to characterize the demographic shifts enacted by global migration (particularly Islamic and North African) into Europe. Cited in Zúquete, *The Identitarians,* 131.
19. Spencer, "Spencer Speaks!"
20. On these anxieties over nation-state sovereignty, see Brown, *Walled States, Waning Sovereignty.* The global character of this race war language is also helpfully treated in Alexander Barder, *Global Race War: International Politics and Racial Hierarchy* (New York: Oxford University Press, 2021), 211–36.
21. This theme of "collaboration" is a central trope to the literature on population 'replacement'—a complicity between political leaders and the invading forces that are ostensibly taking the nation from those natives to whom it rightfully belongs. See Camus, *You Will Not Replace Us!,* 59–64. Or, as Daniel Friberg argues, "Alien masses settle in our homelands, with the explicit support of the elites, and the peoples of our continent do nothing to protest it." Friberg, *The Real Right Returns,* 17. Guillaume Faye, in typically acerbic terms, argues, "For the first time in history, the invaded are assisting the invaders: in the Mediterranean, one proceeds to rescue illegal migrants

who know all too well that they will never be expelled should they manage to disembark on our soil. They depend on us and on our kindness for assistance. . . . Such behaviour is utter madness: it is a mixture of masochism and delusional humanitarianism on the part of our authorities, who are thus complicit in the destruction of their own people through populational flooding." Faye, *Ethnic Apocalypse,* 13–14.

22. Johnson, *White Nationalist Manifesto,* 12–13.
23. Pierre Krebs, *Fighting for the Essence: Western Ethnosuicide or European Renaissance?,* trans. Alexander Jacob (London: Arktos, 2012), 23.
24. This effort to tie cultural identity to genetic and biological factors is what Guillaume Faye terms "enrootedness." See Faye, *Why We Fight,* 133–34. For a critical discussion, see Chetan Bhatt, "White Extinction: Metaphysical Elements of Contemporary Western Fascism," *Theory, Culture & Society* 38, no. 1 (2021): 36–39.
25. Particularly virulent reactions to "miscegenation" can be found in the *White Man's Bible*—the founding document for the white supremacist Church of the Creator. In this work, Ben Klassen describes multiracial societies as a "slop pail, filled with garbage only fit for hogs." Ben Klassen, *White Man's Bible,* accessed May 3, 2021, https://creativitymovement.net.
26. Such themes help to explain the obsession with "miscegenation" for much of the far right. Guillaume Faye, for instance, derides the danger of *métissage* as follows: "With the replacement population that comes with Third World colonisation, miscegenation threatens to destroy our germen, i.e., the roots of European civilisation. Ethnoracially mixed populations, similarly, foster instability and rarely carry out great historical creations." Faye, *Why We Fight,* 194. In the American context, concerns over miscegenation figure prominently within the white supremacist literature. See, for instance, David Lane, *Deceived, Damned, and Defiant: The Revolutionary Writings of David Lane,* ed. Katja Lane (St. Maries, Idaho: 14 Word Press, 1999).
27. For overviews of the long historical relationship between the far right and ecological discourse, see John Hultgren, *Border Walls Gone Green: Nature and Anti-immigrant Politics in America* (Minneapolis: University of Minnesota Press, 2015), 33–54; Sam Moore and Alex Roberts, *The Rise of Ecofascism: Climate Change and the Far Right* (Malden, Mass.: Polity Press, 2022), 14–45.
28. For a discussion of this argument and the Carrying Capacity Network, see Hultgren, *Border Walls Gone Green,* 78–81.
29. See, for instance, Nikolas Rose, *The Politics of Life Itself: Biomedicine, Power, and Subjectivity in the Twenty-First Century* (Princeton, N.J.: Princeton University Press, 2007), chap. 2.
30. As Chetan Bhatt has argued, this concern with the "rootedness" of peoples (and the potential loss of this connection) motivates much

of the far right. See Bhatt, "White Extinction." For direct expressions of this concern for ethnocultural rootedness, see Faye, *Why We Fight,* 37–39, 148–49; Michael O'Meara, *New Culture, New Right: Anti-liberalism in Postmodern Europe* (London: Arktos, 2013), 65–72.

31. This formula paraphrases the following verdict from Pierre Krebs: "The society qualified wrongly as multiracial is no more tolerant of races or ethnic groups—on the contrary, it encourages their biological eradication, through panmixia—than it is respectful of the different cultural paradigms that it forces to disappear into the egalitarian and uniformising mould of identitarian deracination. This society is in reality *raciophobic* by nature and *culturicidal* by vocation." Krebs, *Fighting for the Essence,* 19.
32. For an in-depth discussion of the Islamophobia that runs through identitarian thought, see Zúquete, *The Identitarians,* 168–226.
33. In symptomatic terms, Jared Taylor argues that "the demographic forces we have set in motion have created conditions that are inherently unstable and potentially violent. All other groups are growing in numbers and have a vivid racial identity. Only whites have no racial identity, are constantly on the defensive, and constantly in retreat. They have a choice: regain a sense of identity and the resolve to maintain their numbers, their traditions, and their way of life—or face oblivion." Taylor, *White Identity,* 295.
34. The terms "ethnosuicide" and "ethnomasochism" are prominent in the far right literature of demographic anxiety. See, for instance, Faye, *Why We Fight,* 136; Friberg, *The Real Right Returns,* 85–86.
35. Jared Taylor, "Race Realism and the Alt-Right," in *The Alternative Right,* ed. Greg Johnson (San Francisco: Counter-Currents Publishing, 2018).
36. Krebs, *Fighting for the Essence,* 35
37. Kurtagic, "The Great Erasure," 29.
38. Johnson, *White Nationalist Manifesto,* 40–41. As Chetan Bhatt has argued, this focus on "white extinction" may ultimately be the uniting factor joining the disparate threads of the global far right. Bhatt, "White Extinction," 31.
39. See, for instance, Jardina, *White Identity Politics,* 136–38. For a discussion of this appeal to "antiwhite" discrimination in a European context, see Zúquete, *The Identitarians,* 282–89. For a representative presentation from within the far right, see Gregory Hood, "A White Nationalist Memo to White Male Republicans," Counter-Currents, November 9, 2012, https://counter-currents.com.
40. Neil Kumar, "White Identity Nationalism, Part 1," Counter-Currents, May 25, 2022, https://counter-currents.com.
41. On these claims of "reverse racism" or antiwhite discrimination, see Jardina, *White Identity Politics,* 144–45. For a direct expression of these charges, see Hood, "New Kulaks." Zúquete addresses charges

of antiwhite discrimination in the European context in *The Identitarians,* 282–89.

42. For an exploration of this topic, see Paul Jackson, "White Genocide: Postwar Fascism and the Ideological Value of Evoking Existential Conflicts," in *The Routledge History of Genocide,* ed. Cathie Carmichael and Richard C. Maguire (New York: Routledge, 2015), 207–26.
43. Quoted in Zúquete, *The Identitarians,* 333.
44. Greg Johnson, "Irreconcilable Differences: The Case for Racial Divorce," in *Truth, Justice, and a Nice White Country.*
45. Kurtagic, "The Great Erasure," 23.
46. Faye, *Colonisation of Europe,* xviii. Here, Faye channels the belief, widely shared across the racialist right, that this explicit stance of war represents a justified response to the tacit war that has long been unfolding in the form of the annexation of public space by migrant "invaders." For instance, the Christchurch shooter, Brenton Tarrant, channels this intuition when he insists that "the invaders must be removed from European soil, regardless from where they came or when they came. Roma, African, Indian, Turkish, Semitic or other. If they are not of our people, but live in our lands, they must be removed. Where they are removed to is not our concern, or responsibility. . . . How they are removed is irrelevant, peacefully, forcefully, happily, violently or diplomatically. They must be removed." Tarrant, "The Great Replacement," 7, accessed June 20, 2020, https://imgprod.ilfoglio.it/userUpload/The_Great_Replacementconvertito.pdf.
47. For an informative account of the Christchurch shootings that links the violence to the online technologies of white extremism, see Byman, *Spreading Hate,* 93–122.
48. Tarrant, "The Great Replacement," 7.
49. Tarrant, "The Great Replacement," 8.
50. Victoria Klesty, "Norwegian Killer Breivik Begins Parole Hearing with Nazi Salute," Reuters, January 18, 2022, https://www.reuters.com.
51. Patrick Crusius, "The Inconvenient Truth," accessed May 17, 2020, https://randallpacker.com.
52. This ideal is particularly clear in the manifesto of John Earnest, who attacked a synagogue in Poway, California, in April 2019. As the screed details, he conducted his attack to show that "there is at least one European man alive who is willing to take a stand against the injustice that the Jew has inflicted upon him. That my act will inspire others to take a stand as well. And when this revolution starts gaining traction (if I am not killed) I expect to be freed from prison and continue the fight. I do not seek fame. I do not seek power. I only wish to inspire others and be a soldier that has the honor and privilege of defending his race in its greatest hour of need." John Earnest, "An Open Letter," n.d., 2, accessed October 4,

2023, https://www.ideology.us. On the theme of "soft genocide" in the literature of demographic anxiety, see Friberg, *The Real Right Returns,* 102.

53. Kathleen Belew details how such seemingly "isolated" acts are linked, inspired, and prepared by organized networks of white extremist violence whose members pursue a strategy of "leaderless resistance." See Belew, "There Are No Lone Wolves."
54. Quoted in Zúquete, *The Identitarians,* 333.
55. The internet presence of the group is now defunct, though an archived version can be found on the Internet Archive, accessed August 21, 2023, https://web.archive.org/web/20230000000000*/http://europaeische-aktion.org/?v=7516fd43adaa.
56. For an excellent history of the Creativity movement, see Michael Barkun, *Religion and the Racist Right: The Origins of the Christian Identity Movement* (Chapel Hill: University of North Carolina Press, 1997).
57. For discussion of the call for RAHOWA, see Kamali, *Homegrown Hate,* 54–57, 161–80.
58. Ben Klassen, *Rahowa! This Planet Is All Ours* (Otto, N.C.: Creativity Alliance, 1987), 10. This belief that the races were created in separation, lending a divine mandate for racial segregation, is typically termed "polygenism." For a useful historical account of how this belief structured the politics of social Darwinism, see Barder, *Global Race War,* chap. 2.
59. The RAHOWA project is hardly the only vision that negotiates white supremacy through a theological mandate of racial separation. For instance, Martin H. Millard asserts that "God says Whites are different than all other races and that we must not blend in with them, but always remain separate in all ways possible." Martin H. Millard, "Whiteness over All," *National Vanguard,* October 31, 2021, https://nationalvanguard.org.
60. Faye, *Ethnic Apocalypse,* 16. Faye's turn toward an increasingly confrontational, militaristic stance is described in Jean-Yves Camus, "Guillaume Faye, from New Right Intellectual to Prophet of the Racial Civil War," in *Contemporary Far-Right Thinkers and the Future of Liberal Democracy,* ed. A. James McAdams and Alejandro Castrillon (New York: Routledge, 2022), 66–81.
61. Faye, *Ethnic Apocalypse,* 208. On Faye's appeals to race war and the demand for "reconquest," see Barder, *Global Race War,* 231–33.
62. There is a voluminous literature invoked by the radical right to support the contention that there are "real" differences between the races. A symptomatic instance is Edward Dutton, *Making Sense of Race* (Whitefish, Mont.: Washington Summit, 2020). See also Jared Taylor, "Race Realism," in Shaw, *A Fair Hearing,* 115–25.
63. See Markus Willinger, *Generation Identity: A Declaration of War*

against the '68ers (London: Arktos, 2013), 71–72. See also Taylor, "Race Realism and the Alt-Right"; Zúquete, *The Identitarians,* 270–78.

64. Krebs, *Fighting for the Essence,* 84. Greg Johnson offers a similar formulation in defending his vision of white separatism: "Racial divorce is not really about individuals at all. It is about the incompatibility of groups. . . . Thus my desire for racial divorce is based simply on the recognition that whites and blacks *as groups* have irreconcilable differences that make it impossible for them to be fully happy when forced to live in the same system." Johnson, *Truth, Justice, and a Nice White Country,* 49.
65. Taylor, "What Is the Alt Right?"
66. Charles Lindholm and José Pedro Zúquete, *The Struggle for the World: Liberation Movements for the 21st Century* (Stanford, Calif.: Stanford University Press, 2010), 50. For an account that stresses this theme of the present as an interregnum, see Andersen, *Rising from the Ruins.* See also Faye, *Why We Fight,* 178–79.
67. The standard point of intersection between this Hindu vision of history and fascist politics is the work of Savitra Devi. For an overview of her contributions to both classic and contemporary fascism, see Nicholas Goodrick-Clarke, *Black Sun: Aryan Cults, Esoteric Nazism and the Politics of Identity* (New York: New York University Press, 2002). See also Stern, *Proud Boys and the White Ethnostate,* 38–42.
68. See Julius Evola, *Revolt against the Modern World,* trans. Guido Stucco (Rochester, Vt.: Inner Traditions, 1995).
69. Griffin, "Between Metapolitics and *Apoliteia,*" 37. See also Roger Griffin, *The Nature of Fascism* (New York: Routledge, 2006), 26–38.
70. For discussion of the significance of conflict and threat narratives for extremist groups, see Berger, *Extremism,* chaps. 2–3.
71. Camus, *You Will Not Replace Us!,* 51–54.
72. On the role of "metapolitics" in the far right, see Friberg, *The Real Right Returns,* chap. 2; Pierre Krebs, "The Metapolitical Rebirth of Europe," in *Fascism,* ed. Roger Griffin (New York: Oxford University Press, 1995), 348–50; Tomislav Sunic, *Against Democracy and Equality: The European New Right* (London: Arktos, 2011), 69–74.
73. Jackson, "White Genocide," 224.
74. For an example of this sense of an unavowed, everyday aggression, see Camus, *You Will Not Replace Us!,* 52–53.
75. Tarrant, "The Great Replacement," 39.
76. See, for instance, Guillaume Faye's reflections on the "born leader" in *Why We Fight,* 86–88.
77. "Manifesto," Patriot Front, accessed July 5, 2022, https://patriotfront.us. This hortatory effort to inspire action from "brave white men" is echoed by the alt-right figure Gregory Hood: "Do you get it yet? America, your America, is finished. But you don't have to be. It's time to fight for what comes next. It's time to fight for a country of

our own. It's time to stop being Americans. It's time to start being White Men again." Hood, "White Nationalist Memo" (2012).

78. As numerous observers have noted, the formula is poached from a self-published novel by G. Michael Hopf, *Those Who Remain: A Postapocalyptic Novel* (2016). This theme of militant masculinity—the belief that white manhood must prevail in order to save the nation from catastrophe—is well treated in Kelly, *Apocalypse Man*.
79. See, for instance, Bernard Forchtner, "Nation, Nature, Purity: Extreme-Right Biodiversity in Germany," *Patterns of Prejudice* 53, no. 3 (2019): 285–301; Blair Taylor, "Alt-Right Ecology: Ecofascism and Far-Right Environmentalism in the United States," in *The Far Right and the Environment*, ed. Bernhard Forchtner (New York: Routledge, 2020).
80. Verena Stolcke, "New Boundaries, New Rhetorics of Exclusion in Europe," *Current Anthropology* 36, no. 1 (1995): 7.
81. In the classic terms of Hannah Arendt, the discursive world of the ethnonationalist right does not just tend to produce violent outcomes through a cognitive habituation to aggression; rather, it is a political imaginary that itself conveys violence. That is, it removes conflict from the realm of speech and negotiation (the sphere of politics) and relocates it within the domain of force. See Hannah Arendt, *The Human Condition*, 2nd ed. (Chicago: University of Chicago Press, 1998).
82. Tarrant, "The Great Replacement," 69.
83. Tarrant, "The Great Replacement," 28. For reflections on this closure of politics, see Matthew Kriner, Meghan Conroy, and Yasmine Ashwal, "Understanding Accelerationist Narratives: 'There Is No Political Solution,'" Accelerationism Research Consortium, September 2, 2021, https://www.accresearch.org.
84. Quoted in Michael O'Meara, "Toward the White Republic," *Occidental Quarterly* 10, no. 3 (2010): 10.
85. Faye, *Colonisation of Europe*, 5.
86. Guillaume Faye, *Prelude to War: Chronicle of the Coming Cataclysm*, trans. Roger Adwan (London: Arktos, 2021), 133.
87. Quoted in Zúquete, *The Identitarians*, 330. This position is also central to Faye, *Ethnic Apocalypse*.
88. For an overview, see Matthew Kriner, "An Introduction to Militant Accelerationism," Accelerationism Research Consortium, accessed June 24, 2022, https://www.accresearch.org. For a more focused account that situates accelerationism within the contemporary alt-right, see Whitney Jordan Adams and Brian Gaines, "Heil, Twitter: Social Media, Accelerationism, and Extremism," in *Mind the Gap! Proceedings of the Sixth Argumentor Conference*, ed. Rozalia Klara Bako and Gizela Horvath (Oradea, Romania: Partium Press, 2020), 179–96.

89. For a popular account, see Zack Beauchamp, "Accelerationism: The Obscure Idea Inspiring White Supremacist Killers around the World," Vox, November 18, 2019, https://www.vox.com.
90. For an overview of some of these accelerationist groups, see Alex Newhouse, "The Threat Is the Network: The Multi-node Structure of Neo-fascist Accelerationism," *CTC Sentinel* 14, no. 5 (2021): 17–25.
91. Robertson, *The Ethnostate,* 23.
92. See Kamali, *Homegrown Hate,* 160–80.
93. Tarrant, "The Great Replacement," 8.
94. Earnest, "Open Letter," 6.
95. This theme of interpellation is likewise central to Andreas Malm and the Zetkin Collective, *White Skin, Black Fuel: On the Danger of Fossil Fascism* (New York: Verso, 2021).

3. Metapolitics and Demographic Fear

1. Christopher Rufo (@realchrisrufo), "We are no longer going to let the Left set the terms of debate," Twitter, June 18, 2022, https://twitter.com/realchrisrufo/status/1538232677459009537.
2. Christopher Rufo (@realchrisrufo), "So we have to fight at two levels," Twitter, July 7, 2022, https://twitter.com/realchrisrufo/status/1545251012046249984.
3. Krebs, "Metapolitical Rebirth of Europe," 348.
4. For an overview of how the French New Right emerged from the GRECE Institute, see Tamir Bar-On, *Rethinking the French New Right: Alternatives to Modernity* (New York: Routledge, 2013), 10–32. See also Jean-Yves Camus and Nicolas Lebourg, *Far-Right Politics in Europe,* trans. Jane Marie Todd (Cambridge, Mass.: Harvard University Press, 2017), chap. 3.
5. This Gramscian inspiration has been discussed by many commentators on the European New Right. See, for instance, Tamir Bar-On, *Where Have All the Fascists Gone?* (Burlington, Vt.: Ashgate, 2007), 84–90; Karl Ekeman, "On Gramscianism of the Right," Praxis 13/13, November 11, 2018, http://blogs.law.columbia.edu/praxis1313; Roger Woods, *Germany's New Right as Culture and Politics* (New York: Palgrave, 2007), chap. 2.
6. Friberg, *The Real Right Returns,* 4. In a more militant vein, Friberg continues, "Metapolitics is a war of social transformation, at the level of worldview, thought, and culture" (20). A particularly clear rendering of this interventionist logic appears in Krebs, "Metapolitical Rebirth of Europe," 348–50.
7. The influence of new right metapolitics on the contemporary alt-right is explored in Tamir Bar-On, "The Alt-Right's Continuation of the 'Cultural War' in Euro-American Societies," *Thesis Eleven* 163, no. 1 (2021): 43–70. See also Alexandra Minna Stern, "Gender and

the Far-Right in the United States: Female Extremists and the Mainstreaming of Contemporary White Nationalism," *Journal of Modern European History* 20, no. 3 (2022): 322–34.

8. The first passage is quoted in Stern, *Proud Boys and the White Ethnostate,* 22; the second appears in Spencer, "Facing the Future as a Minority." In related interviews, Spencer has explicitly noted the influence of the French New Right on his thought. See "Richard Spencer's Interview with Europe Maxima," *Radix Journal,* February 15, 2017, https://radixjournal.com.
9. See Andrew Breitbart, *Righteous Indignation: Excuse Me While I Save the World!* (New York: Grand Central, 2012).
10. Johnson, *White Nationalist Manifesto,* 108–10. For a mission statement of this "offensive" metapolitics in the alt-right, see George T. Shaw, "Dismantling Anti-white Newspeak," in Shaw, *A Fair Hearing,* 184–98.
11. References to ethnic death and ethnomasochism are particularly prevalent in the work of Guillaume Faye and Pierre Krebs. See Faye, *Colonisation of Europe*; Krebs, *Fighting for the Essence.*
12. Quoted in Zúquete, *The Identitarians,* 131.
13. Richard Hofstadter describes this insistence on a media apparatus captured by "the enemy" as a staple of the "paranoid style." As he notes: "Very often the enemy is held to possess some especially effective source of power: he controls the press; he directs the public mind through 'managed news'; he has unlimited funds; he has a new secret for influencing the mind . . . he is gaining a stranglehold on the educational system." Hofstadter, "Paranoid Style," 32.
14. For a symptomatic case, see Lawrence Auster, *The Path to National Suicide: An Essay on Immigration and Multiculturalism* (Monterey, Va.: American Immigration Control Foundation, 1990).
15. Krebs, *Fighting for the Essence,* 24.
16. Camus, *You Will Not Replace Us!,* 89.
17. Alain de Benoist, *View from the Right: A Critical Anthology of Contemporary Ideas,* trans. Robert Lindgren (London: Arktos, 2017), 16.
18. Gregory Hood, "Excellence over Equality," *American Renaissance,* July 22, 2022, https://www.amren.com.
19. There is a considerable conservative literature that challenges the egalitarian commitments of liberalism. For market-based critiques, see Milton Friedman, *Free to Choose* (New York: Harcourt, 1980); Friedrich Hayek, *The Constitution of Liberty: The Definitive Edition* (Chicago: University of Chicago Press, 2011). For challenges that target the anthropological or moral commitments of egalitarianism, see Samuel Francis, *Beautiful Losers: Essays on the Failures of American Conservatism* (Columbia: University of Missouri Press, 1993); Murray Rothbard, *Egalitarianism as a Revolt against Nature, and Other Essays* (Auburn, Ala.: Ludwig von Mises Institute, 2000). For an overview of

these classic arguments, see John Schaar, "Some Ways of Thinking about Equality," *Journal of Politics* 26, no. 4 (1964): 867–95.

20. In the formula of Jared Taylor: "An important corollary to these beliefs is that since all human populations are identical, they can replace each other without any loss to the groups being replaced. The replaced population is, in effect, being replaced by itself." Taylor, "Race Realism," 118.
21. Chetan Bhatt addresses these connections between equality and population replacement, particularly as they relate to the new right's fears of "white extinction." The present analysis diverges from Bhatt's in that he emphasizes the Nietzschean strains of the new right's equality critique and does not disentangle the competing strains of new right thought with regard to their visions of cultural defense. See Bhatt, "White Extinction."
22. As a broad literature notes, the social ontology of the new right is largely communitarian, drawn from the canonical work of such figures as Ernst Gehlen, Konrad Lorenz, and Joseph de Maistre. For a critical discussion of this point, see Pierre-André Taguieff, *The Force of Prejudice: On Racism and Its Doubles,* trans. Hassan Melehy (Minneapolis: University of Minnesota Press, 2001), 202–4.
23. O'Meara, *New Culture, New Right,* 90.
24. Alain de Benoist, *Beyond Human Rights: Defending Freedoms,* trans. Alexander Jacob (London: Arktos, 2011), 81. Tomislav Sunic provides a similar critique of "human rights ideology" in *Against Democracy and Equality,* 141–57.
25. A canonical expression of this thinking, often cited by the new right literature, comes from Joseph de Maistre: "I have seen Frenchmen, Italians, Russians . . . I know, too, thanks to Montesquieu, that one can be a Persian. But as for man, I declare that I have never met him in my life; if he exists, he is unknown to me." Joseph de Maistre, *Considerations on France* (New York: Cambridge University Press, 2003), 53. In more contemporary terms, Alex Kurtagic argues that within such a social ontology "a person is . . . always a stranger, always a meaningless atom in a sea of formica, PVC, neon, polyester, and reinforced concrete." Alex Kurtagic, "Masters of the Universe," Counter-Currents, September 23, 2011, https://counter-currents.com.
26. Friberg, *The Real Right Returns,* 107. John Bruce Leonard expands on the homogenizing outcomes of liberal universalism: "Racial equality, gender equality, social equality, educational equality, income equality, the eradication of injustices—which in this newfangled language really means the eradication of *differences* and the levelling of the heights. Men and women are dressing in a hideous new fashion, everywhere alike, they are abandoning the worship of their gods and embracing a New Age pseudo-religion, cut and tailored for Everyman; they are emphasizing that in them which is identical to

all their neighbors, and reducing themselves to the lowest common human denominator." John Bruce Leonard, "The Ethnostate, Yesterday and Tomorrow," Arktos.com, August 21, 2019, https://arktos.com.

27. Alain de Benoist, "The European New Right: Forty Years Later," *Occidental Quarterly* 9, no. 1 (2009): 65.
28. Quinn Slobodian, *Globalists: The End of Empire and the Birth of Neoliberalism* (Cambridge, Mass.: Harvard University Press, 2018).
29. It would require considerably more space than is available here to capture the new right relationship to capitalism—particularly given (a) the variance between figures of the new right and (b) how some of their major positions have shifted over time. For a symptomatic effort to highlight the homogenizing effects of neoliberal capitalism, see Sunic, *Against Democracy and Equality,* 158–68. Alain de Benoist offers some symptomatic critiques of market society, along with some suggestions for domesticating market structures, in *Manifesto for a European Renaissance* (London: Arktos, 2012), 42–43. For accounts that extoll the productivity of economic markets while resisting the full saturation of a "market society," see Friberg, *The Real Right Returns,* 30–31; Faye, *Why We Fight,* 124–26, 245–46; O'Meara, *New Culture, New Right,* 91–94.
30. The term "soft totalitarianism" is borrowed from de Benoist. See Bar-On, *Where Have All the Fascists Gone?,* 94.
31. Leonard, "Ethnostate, Yesterday and Tomorrow."
32. For a discussion of the new right's antipathy toward the spread of American "monoculture," see Lindholm and Zúquete, *Struggle for the World,* 57–59. Michael O'Meara argues: "The present globalist impetus of liberal ideology seems aimed at precisely this sort of annihilating deculturation, as the international system of acronyms (the UN, US, WTO, GATT, NAFTA, IMF, *et cetera*) forcibly channels the flow of money, goods, and services into markets favoring the integration of local cultures into a single global (in effect, Americanized) 'culture' that takes functionalization to its ultimate extreme. The whole, as a result, is turned into what some identitarians call a ZOA: a *zone d'occupation américaine,* where everything is subject to the cultural imperatives of Washington's 'cosmo-capitalism.'" O'Meara, *New Culture, New Right,* 72.
33. Spencer, "Spencer Speaks!"
34. These democratic concerns have been raised perhaps most forcefully in the work of Wendy Brown. See Wendy Brown, *Undoing the Demos: Neoliberalism's Stealth Revolution* (New York: Zone Books, 2015).
35. Such concerns about the far-reaching effects of capitalism define a rich vein of conservative literature. For a neoconservative perspective, see Irving Kristol, *Two Cheers for Capitalism* (New York: Basic Books, 1978). For more explicitly paleoconservative arguments, see

Patrick J. Buchanan, *The Great Betrayal: How American Sovereignty and Social Justice Are Being Sacrificed to the Gods of the Global Economy* (Boston: Little, Brown, 1998); Samuel Francis, "Capitalism, the Enemy," *Chronicles: A Magazine of American Culture*, August 2000, 34–35.

36. For example, Richard Spencer argues that globalist economic policies transform previously distinct nations "into great 'nothings' and 'nowheres': indistinguishable, concrete dumping grounds and shopping centers, divorced from culture, people, and history." Richard Spencer, "What It Means to Be Alt-Right: The Charlottesville Statement," Altright.com, August 11, 2017, https://altright.com.
37. Alex Kurtagic offers a particularly bitter indictment of these commitments in "Equality: A Justification of Privilege, Oppression, and Inhumanity," Counter-Currents, February 26, 2013, https://counter-currents .com.
38. Krebs, *Fighting for the Essence*, 92.
39. In Camus's definition: "Undifferentiated Human Matter [UHM]. Man (and woman) such as industrially treated by global replacism, egalitarianism, antiracism. No races, no sexes, no cultures, no nationalities, no origins, no discrimination and no defining borders either, in short a general reversion of history and evolution of human society to what biologists call 'the Primeval Soup.'" Camus, *You Will Not Replace Us!*, 191.
40. For a symptomatic case, see Taylor, "Race Realism and the Alt-Right," 29–34.
41. This line of argument features prominently in much of the French far right. For instance, Marine Le Pen draws from Alain Finkielkraut to indict the "replaceability" and "interchangeability" encouraged by globalist institutions. See Michel Eltchaninoff, *Inside the Mind of Marine Le Pen*, trans. James Ferguson (London: Hurst, 2018), 70–74.
42. Camus, *You Will Not Replace Us!*, 17.
43. See, for instance, Camus's discussion of the "Davocracy" in *You Will Not Replace Us!*, 112–20. Greg Johnson presents a more explicitly anti-Semitic version of the conspiracy in his *White Nationalist Manifesto*.
44. Krebs, "Metapolitical Rebirth of Europe," 349.
45. De Benoist, "European New Right," 65.
46. Guillaume Faye, for instance, has rejected the new right label because of the public embrace of a multiculturalist language on the part of some new right figures. See Faye, *Archeofuturism*, chap. 1. See also Faye, *Why We Fight*, 239–42. A broader account of such critiques from previous allies of the new right appears in O'Meara, *New Culture, New Right*, 263–266.
47. This ostensible right of "cultural defense" has proven instrumental for a variety of ethnopopulist movements inspired by the new right.

Michael O'Meara, for instance, argues that "every people has . . . the right to pursue their destiny in accord with the organic dictates of their distinct identity." O'Meara, *New Culture, New Right,* 104.

48. See, for instance, Buchanan, *Suicide of a Superpower,* chap. 7; Taylor, *White Identity,* chaps. 2–3.
49. In O'Meara's terms, multiculturalism represents a "people-killing dogma," and its proponents work to "impose a system in which Europeans are to be turned into an indifferent multiracial multitude, without roots or collective memories." O'Meara, *New Culture, New Right,* 101.
50. De Benoist, *Manifesto for a European Renaissance,* 28.
51. Camus, for instance, depicts the true defenders of diversity as those nations that enact immigration controls to protect "that most precious form of biodiversity, human biodiversity. The only coherent ecologists are those who fight for the happy conservation of all races, peoples, cultures, languages, ethnic groups and civilisations, as well as for animal and plant biodiversity." Camus, *You Will Not Replace Us!,* 131.
52. See Pierre-André Taguieff's helpful account in "From Race to Culture: The New Right's View of European Identity," *Telos,* nos. 98–99 (1993): 107.
53. This deployment of diversity discourse takes a number of shapes. At an institutionalist level, some new right theorists have argued that cultures can achieve their full efflorescence (i.e., their "destiny") only where ethnically homogeneous peoples engage in an internal practice of governance that approximates direct democracy. See, for instance, de Benoist, *Manifesto for a European Renaissance,* 38–41; Alain de Benoist, *The Problem of Democracy* (London: Arktos, 2011), 93–99. Similar appeals to direct democracy appear in Michael Walker, "Democracy We Presume? Michael Walker Asks Himself What Democracy Really Is in Theory and Practice," *Scorpion* 24 (2006): 3–19.
54. "Preserving Our Ethnocultural Identity," Generation Identity, home page, accessed February 12, 2023, https://www.generation-identity.org.uk.
55. Richard Spencer, "Identitarianism—a Conversation Starter," *Radix Journal,* June 15, 2015, https://radixjournal.com. Pierre Krebs places this vision on a broader stage when he argues that "the future of this world will never stop being many-voiced, multicoloured, multicultural, and multihistorical as long as the human species that bears it remains permanently multiracial, that is to say . . . as long as the *homogeneity of the peoples* remains a guarantee of the *heterogeneity of the world.*" Krebs, *Fighting for the Essence,* 40–41.
56. See, for instance, Faye, *Why We Fight,* 240–41.
57. De Benoist, for instance, cites Johann Gottfried Herder approvingly

in *Manifesto for a European Renaissance,* 18–19. See also Bar-On, *Rethinking the French New Right,* 152.

58. These tropes of difference have found considerable purchase "downstream" in extremist movements for cultural and racial defense. For instance, the Christchurch shooter's manifesto (using an analogy replicated in the manifesto of the Buffalo shooter) states that "the attack was to ensure a preservation of beauty, art and tradition. In my mind a rainbow is only beautiful to due its [*sic*] variety of colours, mix the colours together and you destroy them all and they are gone forever and the end result is far from anything beautiful." Tarrant, "The Great Replacement," 18.
59. See, for instance, Bar-On, *Where Have All the Fascists Gone?,* 201–2. De Benoist has recently proposed a more nuanced vision of how cultural identity is forged necessarily in relation to difference. As he argues: "Difference, moreover, is not an absolute. By definition, it exists only in relation to other differences, for we distinguish ourselves only vis-à-vis those who are different. The same goes for identity: even more than an individual, a group does not have a single identity. Every identity is constituted in relationship to another. This also holds for culture: for in creating its own world of meaning, a culture nevertheless does so in relationship to other cultures." This passage appears in an interview de Benoist conducted with Terre et Peuple, quoted in Michael O'Meara, *Guillaume Faye and the Battle of Europe* (London: Arktos, 2013), 34.
60. In the American context, the identitarian position is captured in Richard Spencer, "Who Are You?," *Radix Journal,* July 23, 2016, https://radixjournal.com. For detailed discussion of this break in the European context, see O'Meara, *New Culture, New Right,* 104–6; Zúquete, *The Identitarians.*
61. Faye, *Archeofuturism,* 24. For more on Faye's break with the "multicultural" turn of GRECE, see Camus, "Guillaume Faye"; O'Meara, *New Culture, New Right,* 101–5.
62. See Zúquete, *The Identitarians,* 157–59. Camus proposes "remigration" in *You Will Not Replace Us!,* 45–50. The phrase "slow cleanse" is from the American identitarian Greg Johnson, who likewise advocates policies of removal in order to forge a white ethnostate. See Greg Johnson, "Restoring White Homelands," Counter-Currents, March 23, 2021, https://counter-currents.com.
63. This charge appears throughout Krebs, *Fighting for the Essence.*
64. This is an example of what Roger Griffin describes as the rhetorical "sleight of hand" that defines new right cultural politics. See Griffin, "Between Metapolitics and *Apoliteia,*" 48.
65. See Bar-On, *Where Have All the Fascists Gone?,* 33–43.
66. Johnson, "Restoring White Homelands"

67. See, for instance, Sunic, *Against Democracy and Equality,* 141–45; Zúquete, *The Identitarians,* 266–319.
68. Krebs, *Fighting for the Essence,* 28, 30. Tomislav Sunic also approvingly cites the importance of biological factors for cultural integrity in *Against Democracy and Equality,* 141–45. Guillaume Faye makes the racial implications clearer yet, by repeatedly figuring white Europeans as specifically targeted for violence and replacement. In Faye's terms, "The underlying purpose is for the system to impose upon ethnic peoples—upon Whites, to be perfectly clear—an invasion at the hands of foreign masses of illegal immigrants and to force them to accept the destruction of their own living environment and culture." Faye, *Ethnic Apocalypse,* 13. On the tensions in the European New Right between racialist and culturalist formulations of ethnopluralism, see Zúquete, *The Identitarians,* chap. 5.
69. On this point, see Bhatt, "White Extinction."
70. As Taguieff argues, the official movement of the European New Right has cycled through a number of distinct stages in which it has progressively attempted to mitigate the reliance on race and biology in its earlier work. See Taguieff, "From Race to Culture," 102–3.
71. See, for instance, Arthur Versluis, "A Conversation with Alain de Benoist," *Journal for the Study of Radicalism* 8, no. 2 (2014): 90.
72. Etienne Balibar, "Is There a 'Neo-racism'?," in *Race, Nation, Class: Ambiguous Identities,* by Etienne Balibar and Immanuel Wallerstein, trans. Chris Turner (New York: Verso, 1991), 17–28.
73. This argument is found in Pierre-André Taguieff, "The New Cultural Racism in France," *Telos,* no. 83 (1990): 117–18. See also Raphael Schlembach, *Against Old Europe: Critical Theory and Alter-Globalization Movements* (Burlington, Vt.: Ashgate, 2014), 97–98.
74. I borrow this phrase from Tamir Bar-On. See Bar-On, *Rethinking the French New Right,* 144–48.
75. Stolcke, "New Boundaries," 4–5.
76. Michel Foucault, "Nietzsche, Genealogy, History," in *Language, Counter-memory, Practice: Selected Essays and Interviews,* trans. Donald F. Bouchard and Sherry Simon (Ithaca, N.Y.: Cornell University Press, 1977), 151.
77. Pierre Krebs argues, for instance, that "to resist the aggressive ideology of human rights, the doctrinal alibi of the totalitarian Western society, it is urgent to draw up a new Declaration of the Rights of Peoples in concert with all the movements that fight on this Earth for the respect of their ethno-cultural identities." Krebs, *Fighting for the Essence,* 115.
78. Taylor, "Race Realism and the Alt-Right," 32.
79. Pierre Krebs, for instance, has called for "the drafting of a Charter of Peoples' Rights, radically antinomical to the Declaration of Human Rights." Krebs, *Fighting for the Essence,* 27.

80. This biological language of vitality or degeneration is typically borrowed from sources such as Konrad Lorenz or Hans Eysenck. See, for instance, Sunic, *Against Democracy and Equality,* 141–47. As Griffin has noted, this narrative of decline draws from the fascist historiography of Julius Evola. See Griffin, "Between Metapolitics and *Apoliteia,*" 40–42.
81. Shaw, "Dismantling Anti-white Newspeak," 194.
82. See Alberto Spektorowski, "The New Right: Ethno-regionalism, Ethno-pluralism and the Emergence of a Neo-fascist 'Third Way,'" *Journal of Political Ideologies* 8, no. 1 (2003): 111–30. Such concerns over the defense of hierarchy are also raised by James Shields, *The Extreme Right in France* (New York: Routledge, 2007), 149–52. The commitment to racial hierarchy is a staple of Jared Taylor's "white advocacy"; see Taylor, "If We Do Nothing." The demand for removal is particularly clear in the work of Faye, who argues that "it is wise to reject in the West multiracial society and think of returning immigrants to their own countries." Quoted in Alberto Spektorowski, "The French New Right: Multiculturalism of the Right and the Recognition/Exclusion Syndrome," *Journal of Global Ethics* 8, no. 1 (2012): 50. Camus explicitly advocates the "remigration" of immigrant populations in *You Will Not Replace Us!,* 45–50. Spektorowski points out that this project of removal is often paradoxically framed as a benefit to those expelled or repatriated; see Alberto Spektorowski, "The French New Right: Differentialism and the Idea of Ethnophilian Exclusionism," *Polity* 33, no. 2 (2000): 283–303.
83. Faye, *Ethnic Apocalypse,* 209.
84. For discussion of the Great Return, see Zúquete, *The Identitarians,* 157–59. Greg Johnson proposes the idea of "racial divorce" in "Irreconcilable Differences."
85. Alain de Benoist, for instance, has forwarded this position, even as he disavows any connection to those who promote nativist themes in their visions of cultural preservation.
86. For some broad overviews of the alt-right's polemical cultural politics, see George Hawley, *The Alt-Right: What Everyone Needs to Know* (New York: Oxford University Press, 2019), 106–28; Angela Nagle, *Kill All Normies: Online Culture Wars from 4Chan and Tumblr to Trump and the Alt-Right* (Winchester, England: Zero Books, 2017).
87. Greg Johnson, "Technological Utopianism and Ethnic Nationalism," Counter-Currents, September 17, 2018, https://counter-currents.com.
88. Taguieff, "New Cultural Racism," 116. In related terms, Richard Wolin argues that through its discursive politics, the new right "cynically appropriated the universalistic values of tolerance and the 'right to difference' for its own xenophobic agenda." Richard Wolin, *The Seduction of Unreason* (Princeton, N.J.: Princeton University Press, 2004), 268.

89. As Corey Robin notes, this strategy of discursive appropriation is not unique to the new right; it also characterizes political conservatism more broadly. See Robin, *The Reactionary Mind,* 49–52.
90. This emphasis on the common as the space of politics is often tracked back to Hannah Arendt. See Arendt, *The Human Condition,* 50–57. For a contemporary defense of the common, see Bonnie Honig, *Public Things: Democracy in Disrepair* (New York: Fordham University Press, 2017). Concerns over common political truths are at the heart of Muirhead and Rosenblum's discussion in *A Lot of People Are Saying.*
91. A significant body of new right literature is devoted to critiquing the premises, value, and defensibility of egalitarian commitments. See, for instance, Alex Kurtagic, "Equality, the Way to a Meaningless Life," Counter-Currents, February 21, 2013, https://counter-currents.com; Rothbard, *Egalitarianism as a Revolt against Nature*; Sunic, *Against Democracy and Equality.*
92. Kevin C. Shelly, "Three Sought after White Supremacist Posters Appear on South Jersey Campus," *Philly Voice,* September 19, 2017, https://www.phillyvoice.com.
93. Christopher Rufo (@realchrisrufo), "This is a perfect example of discourse engineering," Twitter, August 5, 2022, https://twitter.com/realchrisrufo/status/1555610851574292481.
94. Christopher Rufo (@realchrisrufo), "The phrase 'radical gender theory' is catching on," Twitter, August 5, 2022, https://twitter.com/realchrisrufo/status/1555583596232163328.
95. Christopher Rufo, "Anti-CRT Parent Guidebook," accessed September 17, 2022, https://christopherrufo.com.

4. Visions of Escape

1. See, for instance, Edward Blakely and Mary Gail Snyder, *Fortress America: Gated Communities in the United States* (Washington, D.C.: Brookings Institution Press, 1999); Mike Davis, *City of Quartz: Excavating the Future in Los Angeles* (New York: Verso, 1990); Setha Low, *Behind the Gates: Life, Security, and the Pursuit of Happiness in Fortress America* (New York: Routledge, 2003); Elaine Tyler May, *Fortress America: How We Embraced Fear and Abandoned Democracy* (New York: Basic Books, 2017).
2. This is the distinction that David Goodhart famously describes as "somewheres" (those bound to specific local communities) versus "anywheres" (those whose resources allow them to transcend ties to any specific community). David Goodhart, *The Road to Somewhere: The Populist Revolt and the Future of Politics* (London: Hurst, 2017), 19–48.
3. Mike Lofgren, "Revolt of the Rich," *American Conservative,* August 27, 2012, https://www.theamericanconservative.com.
4. Many of these discussions in the popular media find inspiration in

Michael Hart, *Restoring America* (Litchfield, Conn.: VDARE Books, 2015). The theme of polarization and civil war, however, is not limited to figures from the far right. A wide literature has arisen to diagnose the possibility of an impending second civil war in the United States. See, for instance, Stephen Marche, *The Next Civil War: Dispatches from an American Future* (New York: Avid Reader Press, 2022); Barbara Walter, *How Civil Wars Start, and How to Stop Them* (New York: Crown, 2022). The theme has also inspired a significant popular literature, as illustrated by the December 2019 issue of *The Atlantic,* which is devoted entirely to the question "How to Stop a Civil War?"

5. Marjorie Taylor Greene (@mtgreenee), "We Need a National Divorce," Twitter, February 20, 2023, https://twitter.com/mtgreenee/status/1627665203398688768.
6. The concept of "cultural secession" is often tracked to Paul Weyrich, one of the founders of the Heritage Foundation. See Paul Weyrich, "The Culture War Is Lost, Now What?," *Sacramento Bee,* February 24, 1999. See also Buchanan, *Death of the West,* 247–51.
7. Notably, this vision has been promoted by both Jean Thiriart and Guillaume Faye. As Faye argues, it would be the "largest unified political entity in the history of mankind, one extending across fourteen time zones." Faye, *Archeofuturism,* 192.
8. See, for instance, Phil Neel, *Hinterland: America's New Landscape of Class and Conflict* (London: Reaktion Books, 2018), 24–26. This parodic vision of masculine community is exemplified by Jack Donovan, *The Way of Men* (Milwaukie, Ore.: Dissonant Hum, 2012).
9. O'Meara, "Toward the White Republic," 4.
10. As the marketing literature states: "The Citadel Community will house between 3,500 and 7,000 patriotic American families who agree that being prepared for the emergencies of life and being proficient with the American icon of Liberty—the Rifle—are prudent measures. There will be no HOA. There will be no recycling police and no local ordinance enforcers from City Hall." The website for the project can be found in archived form on the Internet Archive, accessed August 22, 2023, https://web.archive.org/web/20170202144111/http://www.iiicitadel.com/index.html.
11. An archived version of the Paulville website can be found on the Internet Archive, accessed August 22, 2023, https://web.archive.org/web/20080516003606/http:/paulville.org.
12. Peter Thiel, "The Education of a Libertarian," Cato Unbound, April 13, 2009, https://www.cato-unbound.org.
13. On the links between seasteading and libertarianism, see Philip E. Steinberg, Elizabeth Nyman, and Mauro J. Caraccioli, "Atlas Swam: Freedom, Capital, and Floating Sovereignties in the Seasteading Vision," *Antipode* 44, no. 4 (2012): 1532–50.

14. Patri Friedman and Brad Taylor, "Seasteading and Institutional Evolution" (paper presented at the Association of Private Enterprise Education Conference, Nassau, April 10–12, 2011), n.p., http://seasteadingorg.wpengine.com/wp-content/uploads/2015/12/FriedmanTaylor_2011_Seasteading_APEE.pdf.
15. For discussion of this vision, see Murray Rothbard, *The Ethics of Liberty* (New York: New York University Press, 2002).
16. Ludwig von Mises, *Liberalism: In the Classical Tradition* (San Francisco: Cobden Press, 1985), 109. Similar reflections are found throughout Hans-Hermann Hoppe, *Democracy: The God That Failed* (New Brunswick, N.J.: Transaction, 2001), 89–94.
17. A canonical account of "exit" as a primary political right appears in Albert Hirschmann, *Exit, Voice, and Loyalty: Responses to Decline in Firms, Organizations, and States* (Cambridge, Mass.: Harvard University Press, 1970).
18. See F. H. Buckley, *American Secession: The Looming Threat of a National Breakup* (New York: Encounter Books, 2020).
19. Donald Livingston, "The Secession Tradition in America," in *Secession, State, and Liberty,* ed. David Gordon (New York: Routledge, 1998), 4.
20. In a symptomatic formulation, Guillaume Faye argues, "The underlying purpose is for the system to impose upon ethnic peoples—upon Whites, to be perfectly clear—an invasion at the hands of foreign masses of illegal immigrants and to force them to accept the destruction of their own living environment and culture." Faye, *Ethnic Apocalypse,* 13.
21. See George T. Shaw, "Introduction: An Alternative to Failure," in Shaw, *A Fair Hearing,* ix–xv.
22. Gregory Hood, "An American Son," Counter-Currents, December 31, 2015, https://counter-currents.com.
23. For illuminating discussions of the United States as a *Herrenvolk* democracy, see Beltrán, *Citizenship as Cruelty*; Olson, *Abolition of White Democracy.* The canonical account of the concept is offered in Pierre van den Berghe, *Race and Racism: A Comparative Perspective* (New York: John Wiley, 1967).
24. Though much of the ethnostate literature insists on ethnic or racial homogeneity, less stringent proposals reserve a place for the *Herrenvolk* model. John Bruce Leonard, for instance, describes the ethnostate as "a political and social order, in which a single ethnicity is granted either an overwhelming democratic majority status or an unchallenged monopoly on political power. The name we give to this condition is sovereignty; the ethnostate is then a political or social order in which a single ethnicity is vested with sovereignty." Leonard, "Ethnostate, Yesterday and Tomorrow."
25. Spencer, "Facing the Future as a Minority."

26. "The NSM 25-Point Plan," National Socialist Movement, accessed April 7, 2022, https://www.nsm88.org.
27. For a discussion of the Order (also known as the Silent Brotherhood), see Belew, *Bring the War Home,* chap. 5.
28. The slogan (in full: "We must secure the existence of our people and a future for White children") is found throughout the white power movement and appears repeatedly in Lane's *Deceived, Damned, and Defiant.* For a discussion of this formula as a galvanizing motto for white extremism, see Kamali, *Homegrown Hate,* 39–82.
29. Lane, *Deceived, Damned, and Defiant,* 98.
30. These passages are drawn from Covington's "Butler Plan." The current presentation of the plan has been edited for greater mainstream appeal. The cited version is Harold Covington, "The Butler Plan: Introduction," available on the Internet Archive, accessed August 22, 2023, https://web.archive.org/web/20100723164038/https://northwestfront.org/about/the-butler-plan.
31. "What Is the National Alliance?," National Alliance, accessed January 7, 2022, https://www.natall.com.
32. For an extended discussion of how place organizes the far right imagination, see Miller-Idriss, *Hate in the Homeland,* chap. 1.
33. Roper is not alone in extending this status to the Ozark area. Various white nationalists have called attention to the region as a particularly suitable location for a white ethnostate, owing to its existing white population share. See, for instance, Neil Kumar, "White Identity Nationalism, Part 3," Counter-Currents, May 27, 2022, https://counter-currents.com.
34. Billy Roper, "What Is the ShieldWall Network Plan? Project New America," Roper Report, available on the Internet Archive, accessed February 20, 2022, https://web.archive.org/web/20200414184850/http://theroperreport.whitenationalists.net/the-shieldwall-network.
35. Stern, *Proud Boys and the White Ethnostate,* 51–60. This sanitized public presentation reflects the "metapolitical" strategies discussed in chapter 3. See Bar-On, "Alt-Right's Continuation of the 'Cultural War.'"
36. In the words of Pierre Krebs: "The notion of 'multiracialism' is, to start with, a mystifying term: for the society qualified wrongly as multiracial is no more tolerant of races or ethnic groups—on the contrary, it encourages their biological eradication, through panmixia—than it is respectful of the different cultural paradigms that it forces to disappear into the egalitarian and uniformising mould of identitarian deracination. This society is in reality *raciophobic* by nature and *culturicidal* by vocation." Krebs, *Fighting for the Essence,* 19. Within the Anglo context, John Bruce Leonard argues: "Racial equality, gender equality, social equality, educational equality, income equality, the eradication of injustices—which in this newfangled

language really means the eradication of *differences* and the levelling of the heights. Men and women . . . are emphasizing that in them which is identical to all their neighbors, and reducing themselves to the lowest common human denominator." Leonard, "Ethnostate, Yesterday and Tomorrow."

37. The most prominent example appears in Hart, *Restoring America,* chap. 7. Hart later conceded that his original vision of partition focused excessively on ideological divides and did not pay sufficient attention to racial and ethnic divides—or the ostensible need for nonwhite homelands. See Michael H. Hart, interview, in *Contemporary Voices of White Nationalism in America,* ed. Carol M. Swain and Russ Nieli (New York: Cambridge University Press, 2003), 184–202. Another effort to distinguish the various ethnostates allotted to differing ethnicities appears in Robertson, *The Ethnostate,* 226–29.
38. The competing ethnostates of Aztlan (for "the Latino population wanting to have their own destiny") and the Free Black State (for "the black population who wants a chance to be free") appear in the literature for the New Albion ethnostate. *Welcome to New Albion,* 9, brochure available on Christopher Cantwell's website, accessed August 22, 2023, https://christophercantwell.net/wp-content/uploads/2020/01/Introduction-to-New-Albion-January-2020-Revision-1.0.pdf. (New Albion does not currently have its own web presence.)
39. Taylor, "What Is the Alt Right?"
40. For example, Richard Spencer describes white homeland projects as safeguards for "true diversity and multiculturalism." Spencer, "Identitarianism."
41. A particularly clear example of such arguments appears in Bill Matheson, "Irreconcilable Differences," in Shaw, *A Fair Hearing,* 136–45.
42. See, for instance, Jared Taylor, interview, in Swain and Nieli, *Contemporary Voices of White Nationalism,* 87–113.
43. See David Duke, interview, in Swain and Nieli, *Contemporary Voices of White Nationalism,* 166–83.
44. Taylor, *White Identity,* 286. This argument appears widely in the movement literature of the far right and has been invoked by those mass shooters whose actions were driven by the Great Replacement narrative. The Christchurch shooter's manifesto, for instance, declares, "DIVERSITY IS WEAKNESS, UNITY IS STRENGTH." See Tarrant, "The Great Replacement," 43.
45. As Wilmot Robertson puts this line of argument: "It is increasingly difficult for a citizen of a multiracial nation to feel he has much in common with a fellow citizen, who, it is increasingly likely, may be of a different race and have emerged from an entirely different cultural

background. The more people differ racially and culturally within a country, the more difficult it becomes for members of these different races to believe they share a common peoplehood. As a result, in a heterogeneous state the basic psychological need of every human being, the firm sense of belonging, is in short supply." Robertson, *The Ethnostate,* 19.

46. Johnson, *White Nationalist Manifesto,* 86.
47. For examples of the laments over the ostensible decline of community, see Patrick Deneen, *Why Liberalism Failed* (New Haven, Conn.: Yale University Press, 2018); Robert Putnam, *Bowling Alone: The Collapse and Revival of American Community* (New York: Simon & Schuster, 2000).
48. Hood, *Waking Up from the American Dream*; Spencer, "Spencer Speaks!"
49. As Daniel Martinez HoSang and Joseph Lowndes observe about this strategy, "Disavowal of open white supremacy allows the far right to draw in more recruits and allows participants a certain racial innocence—a plausible deniability of open racism." HoSang and Lowndes, *Producers, Parasites, Patriots,* 104. This is what Leonard Zeskind has described as the tactical shift from a "vanguard" to a "mainstream" approach. Zeskind, *Blood and Politics.*
50. The community of New Albion was promoted most vigorously by Tom Kawczynski, a town planner from Maine who resigned from his job after his ethnostate advocacy became public. The public literature for the New Albion ethnostate persistently avoids appeals to race, instead stressing concerns about a disappearing culture and care for the environment. Though much of the public presence of the New Albion plan has been withdrawn, the project's guiding documents can be found on the Internet Archive, accessed August 22, 2023, https://web.archive.org/web/20180213173812/http://newalbion.org.
51. These quotations come from another brochure titled *Welcome to New Albion,* which is available on the Internet Archive, accessed August 22, 2023, https://web.archive.org/web/20180123125928/http://newalbion.org/archives/400.
52. Spencer, "Facing the Future as a Minority."
53. For a discussion of how the alt-right borrows from Nietzschean (and Heideggerian) sources, see Ronald Beiner, *Dangerous Minds: Nietzsche, Heidegger, and the Return of the Far Right* (Philadelphia: University of Pennsylvania Press, 2018).
54. See, for instance, Andersen, *Rising from the Ruins,* 1–47.
55. For a clear instance of this elite-driven vision, see John Bruce Leonard, "Metapolitics and the Right—Part 2," Arktos.com, October 23, 2018, https://arktos.com.
56. Wilmot Robertson offers a symptomatic rendering of this position:

"The heroes of history are the men who lift their people out of a morass of anarchy and social chaos. . . . Ethnostates need heroic founding fathers whose labors will transform, possibly even transfigure, world politics." Robertson, *The Ethnostate,* 102.

57. Robertson, *The Ethnostate,* 223. Robertson goes on to state this vision of racial supremacy in even clearer terms: "The human record certifies that the race that has lifted itself higher above the ape than any other is the one that has a patent on white genes. This is where the ethnostate enters the picture. It is perhaps the only peaceful and sensible means of assuring white survival in an increasingly antiwhite, nonwhite world" (223–24).
58. For a discussion of Robertson's project, see Stern, *Proud Boys and the White Ethnostate,* 57–60.
59. Robertson, *The Ethnostate,* 223.
60. In the bald terms of David Lane: "The fact is, all races have benefitted immeasurably from the creative genius of the Aryan People." Lane, *Deceived, Damned, and Defiant,* 97.
61. For a discussion of the "carnal homeland," see Zúquete, *The Identitarians,* 109–13.
62. These arguments are well represented in Leonard, "Ethnostate, Yesterday and Tomorrow."
63. As Miller-Idriss renders this point: "For the far right . . . national geographies are foundational for imagining collective pasts as well as imagined futures." Miller-Idriss, *Hate in the Homeland,* 29. She offers fruitful reflections on space, the ethnostate, nostalgia, and white reaction politics as well (see 29–41).
64. Alexandra Minna Stern helpfully renders this constellation of hope and yearning in the ethnostate literature: "The potential emotional appeal of the white ethnostate should not be underestimated. . . . As a construct soaked in ultranationalism, the ethnostate arouses romanticism, sentimentality, and the promise of comfort and fellowship." Stern, *Proud Boys and the White Ethnostate,* 55.
65. A clear statement of this logic appears in Brett Stevens, "Ethnic Self-Determination," Amerika, December 25, 2019, https://www.amerika.org.
66. Don Black, interview, in Swain and Nieli, *Contemporary Voices of White Nationalism,* 157. This sentiment is expressed across the racialist right. Brett Stevens states: "In the twenty-first century, we seek social order again, and that requires separating into our groups so each group can rule itself. . . . We do not hate the other groups, nor do we scorn them, nor do we even dislike them. We however recognize that each group needs its own path, and this only happens through separation." Brett Stevens, "No Future under Diversity," Amerika, December 5, 2019, https://www.amerika.org.
67. Johnson, *White Nationalist Manifesto,* 57.

68. Richard Spencer, for instance, argues against market individualism in the following terms: “These institutions do not want you to have a sense of yourselves. They do not want you to have identity and rootedness. They do not want you to have duties to your people. They do not want you to think of yourself as part of an extended family that is bigger than any single individual, because the moment you have those duties, the moment you have that identity, is the moment that you are no longer the perfect, passive consumer-citizen that they want to create.” Spencer, “Spencer Speaks!”
69. Matt Lewis, “The Insidious Libertarian to Alt-Right Pipeline,” Daily Beast, August 23, 2017, https://thedailybeast.com.
70. Leonard, “Ethnostate, Yesterday and Tomorrow.”
71. As Greg Johnson argues: “We are being subjected to a slow, cold process of genocide. Yet we are managing to ‘live with it,’ largely because we are narcotized and distracted by individualism, careerism, consumerism, hedonism, and all-round selfishness.” Johnson, *White Nationalist Manifesto,* 40–41.
72. See, for instance, Francis, “Capitalism, the Enemy”; Peter Kolozi, *Conservatives against Capitalism: From the Industrial Revolution to Globalization* (New York: Columbia University Press, 2017).
73. For a symptomatic case, see Rothbard, *Ethics of Liberty.*
74. There is an expansive literature on the recent growth of the militia movement. See, for instance, Belew, *Bring the War Home*; Chip Berlet and Matthew N. Lyons, *Right-Wing Populism in America: Too Close for Comfort* (New York: Guilford Press, 2000), 287–304; Matthew N. Lyons, *Insurgent Supremacists: The U.S. Far Right’s Challenge to State and Empire* (Oakland, Calif.: PM Press, 2018); D. J. Mulloy, *American Extremism: History, Politics, and the Militia Movement* (New York: Routledge, 2005); Evelyn Schlatter, *Aryan Cowboys: White Supremacists and the Search for a New Frontier, 1970–2000* (Austin: University of Texas Press, 2006).
75. The white nationalist group Patriot Front, for instance, captures this idea in its advertising of a movement of “the nation against the state.” The organization asserts that “the State that governs us is wholly resistant to the change that is required to save the nation as it convulses and devours itself with unprecedented corruption.” “Manifesto,” Patriot Front.
76. In a symptomatic formulation, Michael O’Meara proposes: “Imagine, then, for a moment, a White homeland in North America, free of the Jew-ridden US government, with its colored multitudes and parasitic institutions: In my mind, this one image says everything, explains everything, promises everything.” O’Meara, “Toward the White Republic,” 17.
77. “What Is the National Alliance?”
78. For some clear instances of this break from libertarian strains of the

right, see Aedon Cassiel, "The Alt Right and National Greatness," in Johnson, *The Alternative Right,* 74–79; Gregory Hood, "The End of Libertarianism and the Rise of the Alt-Right," in Johnson, *The Alternative Right,* 68–73.

79. Johnson, *White Nationalist Manifesto,* 99–100.
80. In doing so, ethnostate advocacy draws from some central commitments of the paleoconservative tradition—particularly its efforts to "take back" the nation. A clear rendering of this project appears in Samuel Francis, "A Message from MARS: The Social Politics of the New Right," in *Beautiful Losers,* 60–78.
81. "What Is the National Alliance?"
82. For instance, in its "Manifesto," the Patriot Front argues, "The State has long since ceased to advocate for the interests of the descendants of its creators, and thus a State which will be, above all else, a reflection of the national interest must be implemented fully and absolutely."
83. Greg Johnson, "Restoring White Homelands," Counter-Currents, June 24, 2014, https://counter-currents.com. See also Stern, *Proud Boys and the White Ethnostate,* 53–56. The far right American Freedom Party also stresses a "gentle" approach, claiming that the removal of nonwhite citizens and their children will be accomplished through "generous grants as part of a voluntary repatriation program that will return them to their ancestral homelands, with the means to start a new life in their home country." "Demographics," American Freedom Party, accessed July 27, 2021, https://amfreeparty.org.
84. Johnson, *White Nationalist Manifesto,* 95–103.
85. Faye, *Ethnic Apocalypse,* 211.
86. Faye particularly inclines toward Islamophobia in his fears of "replacement"—though the Islamophobic currents of anti-immigration literature run considerably broader. See, for instance, Bawer, *While Europe Slept*; Phillips, *Londonistan*; Ye'or, *EurAbia.*
87. "What Is the National Alliance?"
88. "Manifesto," Patriot Front.
89. The recent literature on populism is considerable. For some readings of this populist logic, see John Judis, *The Populist Explosion* (New York: Columbia Global Reports, 2016); Müller, *What Is Populism?*; Norris and Inglehart, *Cultural Backlash*; Revelli, *New Populism.* As Aurelien Mondon and Aaron Winter have helpfully argued, it is necessary to use this category carefully, as the "populism" label has helped to legitimate and mainstream a variety of far right positions and movements. See Mondon and Winter, *Reactionary Democracy.*
90. A particularly informative account of how the contemporary far right draws (or does not draw) from the traditional repertoire of fascist commitments appears in Malm and Zetkin Collective, *White Skin, Black Fuel,* chap. 7.

91. Appeals to fascism run through much of the contemporary far right. See, for instance, the anonymous work *Path of Gods: Handbook for the 21st Century Fascist* (Wewelsburg Archives, 2017); IronMarch, *Next Leap: An IronMarch Anthology* (IronMarch Publication, 2015).
92. "Strength through Unity," Vanguard America, March 25, 2017, available on the Internet Archive, https://web.archive.org/web/20170720053851/https://bloodandsoil.org/2017/05/09/strength-through-unity.
93. See Roger Griffin, *A Fascist Century: Essays by Roger Griffin,* ed. Matthew Feldman (New York: Palgrave Macmillan, 2008), chaps. 1–2.

5. The Reproductive Politics of a Nice, White Nation

1. Tarrant, "The Great Replacement," 4.
2. Greg Johnson, *Toward a New Nationalism* (San Francisco: Counter-Currents Publishing, 2019), 17.
3. According to Patrick Buchanan, the paleoconservative and two-time candidate for the GOP presidential nomination, the replacement of white majorities "is not a matter of prophecy, but of mathematics." Buchanan, *Death of the West,* 24. References to the mathematical certainty of such predictions appear regularly in the literature of demographic panic. During the "race suicide" panic of the early twentieth century, for instance, Theodore Roosevelt claimed: "If all our nice friends in Beacon Street, and Newport, and Fifth Avenue, and Philadelphia, have one child, or no child at all, while all the Finnegans, Hooligans, Antonios, Mandelbaums and Rabinskis have eight, or nine, or ten—it's simply a matter of the multiplication table. How are you going to get away from it?" Quoted in Spiro, *Defending the Master Race,* 99.
4. Spencer, "Facing the Future as a Minority."
5. Daily Stormer, accessed August 24, 2023, https://dailystormer.in.
6. "National Alliance Fliers," National Alliance, accessed August 23, 2023, https://www.natall.com.
7. Much critical attention has focused on the paramilitary Minuteman Project, though a variety of such groups have patrolled the southern border of the United States, claiming authority to detain or assault migrants in the border area. See Brown, *Walled States, Waning Sovereignty,* 87–90; Harel Shapira, *Waiting for José: The Minutemen's Pursuit of America* (Princeton, N.J.: Princeton University Press, 2013); Ryan Devereaux, "The Bloody History of Border Militias Runs Deep—and Law Enforcement Is Part of It," The Intercept, April 23, 2019, https://theintercept.com.
8. This is well illustrated by the "Defend Europe" initiative pursued by the Generation Identity organization. For a discussion of these measures, see Zúquete, *The Identitarians,* 142–45.
9. Tarrant, "The Great Replacement." 68. Demands for higher reproductive rates have a long, significant history in white power movements.

In the stark terms of the white supremacist William Pierce, "We either start having and raising more healthy White babies, or we die. Our race dies. Our country dies." William Pierce, "Marriage and Survival," *National Vanguard,* March 31, 2022, https://nationalvanguard.org.

10. Faye draws this connection explicitly in *Why We Fight,* 86.
11. The canonical discussion is found in Michel Foucault, *The History of Sexuality,* vol. 1, trans. Robert Hurley (New York: Vintage Books, 1978).
12. Foucault, *History of Sexuality,* 145–50.
13. Quoted in Douglas Murray, *The Strange Death of Europe: Immigration, Identity, Islam* (London: Bloomsbury Continuum, 2017), 147.
14. The far right author Wilmot Robertson argues that what he calls "competitive breeding" is "perhaps the most destructive means" of "disrupting the peace and stability of countries with low birthrates." Robertson, *The Ethnostate,* 48.
15. Paul Ehrlich, *The Population Bomb* (New York: Ballantine Books, 1968). Ehrlich followed up his dire set of predictions with a revised vision of overpopulation in Paul Ehrlich and Anne Ehrlich, *The Population Explosion* (New York: Simon & Schuster, 1990).
16. See Buchanan, *Suicide of a Superpower,* 162–89; Kathryn Joyce, *Quiverfull: Inside the Christian Patriarchy Movement* (Boston: Beacon Press, 2010), 189–202.
17. These fears are given exemplary voice in the 2008 documentary film *Demographic Winter: The Decline of the Human Family,* written and directed by Rick Stout, YouTube, https://www.youtube.com.
18. Buchanan, *Suicide of a Superpower,* 166.
19. For a symptomatic version of this lament, see Murray, *Strange Death of Europe.*
20. Grant, *Passing of the Great Race,* 47.
21. For a discussion of the historical debates and currents leading to the fears of race suicide, see Spiro, *Defending the Master Race.* Laura Lovett details how the historic debates over race suicide went beyond the register of immigration panic to address a variety of concerns about female autonomy and the "natural order" of the nation. See Laura Lovett, *Conceiving the Future: Pronatalism, Reproduction, and the Family in the United States, 1890–1938* (Chapel Hill: University of North Carolina Press, 2007), 77–108.
22. Lothrop Stoddard, *The Rising Tide of Color against White World-Supremacy* (New York: Charles Scribner's Sons, 1920), 9.
23. Stoddard, *Rising Tide of Color,* 162.
24. For overviews of these experiments, see Simone Caron, *Who Chooses? American Reproductive History since 1830* (Gainesville: University of Florida Press, 2008), chap. 3; Adam Cohen, *Imbeciles: The Supreme*

Court, American Eugenics, and the Sterilization of Carrie Buck (New York: Penguin Books, 2016); Roberts, *Killing the Black Body,* chap. 2.

25. In Grant's terms: "The American sold his birthright in a continent to solve a labor problem." Grant, *Passing of the Great Race,* 12.
26. For discussion of these eugenics campaigns, see Nancy Ordover, *American Eugenics: Race, Queer Anatomy, and the Science of Nationalism* (Minneapolis: University of Minnesota Press, 2003), 3–58.
27. Grant, *Passing of the Great Race,* 53.
28. In the revealing formula of Guillaume Faye, an ethnonationalist "future biopolitics" would need "to address two major issues: reinvigorating the European birth-rate and reversing the Third World invasion." Faye, *Why We Fight,* 86.
29. This discussion is found on the Stormfront website, accessed April 19, 2022, https://www.stormfront.org/forum/t1359208.
30. Payton Gendron, "You Wait for a Signal While Your People Wait for You," 2022, 1, Anna's Archive, https://annas-archive.org.
31. See, for instance, Shaun Walker, "Viktor Orbán Trumpets Hungary's 'Procreation Not Immigration' Policy," *The Guardian,* September 6, 2019, https://www.theguardian.com. For a useful discussion of how this "birthrate agenda" plays out more broadly across European nations, see Sophia Siddiqui, "Racing the Nation: Towards a Theory of Reproductive Racism," *Race & Class* 63, no. 2 (2021): 3–20.
32. See Philip Bump, "Rep. Steve King Warns That 'Our Civilization' Can't Be Restored with 'Somebody Else's Babies,'" *Washington Post,* March 12, 2017, https://www.washingtonpost.com.
33. See Belew, *Bring the War Home,* 158–61.
34. There is a considerable literature on the film that stresses its raciopolitical anxieties. See, for instance, Deborah Barker, *Reconstructing Violence: The Southern Rape Complex in Film and Literature* (Baton Rouge: Louisiana State University Press, 2015), 25–63; Michael Rogin, *Ronald Reagan the Movie: And Other Episodes in Political Demonology* (Berkeley: University of California Press, 1987), 190–235.
35. A variety of authors have addressed this more active, militant role for women in white power organizations. See, for instance, Seyward Darby, *Sisters in Hate: American Women on the Front Lines of White Nationalism* (New York: Little, Brown, 2020); Nancy S. Love, "Shield Maidens, Fashy Femmes, and TradWives: Feminism, Patriarchy, and Right-Wing Populism," *Frontiers in Sociology* 5 (2020): 1–3. For insights into the syncretic mythology of white supremacy movements, see Kamali, *Homegrown Hate,* 57–62; Goodrick-Clarke, *Black Sun.*
36. For discussion of these varied forms of participation, see Stern, "Gender and the Far-Right."
37. Symptomatic examples can be found in the newsletter published by the Women for Aryan Unity, *Morrigan Rising.* See WAU Sisterhood, accessed September 7, 2023, https://www.waul4.com.

38. On this point, see Darby, *Sisters in Hate,* 56–57.
39. Belew, *Bring the War Home,* 160–61. See also Kathleen M. Blee, *Inside Organized Racism: Women in the Hate Movement* (Berkeley: University of California Press, 2002), 118–19; Darby, *Sisters in Hate,* 140–43; Durham, *White Rage,* 83–98.
40. In the classic literature, Ragnar Redbeard, a pseudonymous white supremacist figure, makes this imperative clear in a statement about what women can contribute to a white nation: "A woman is primarily a reproductive cell-organism, a womb structurally embastioned by a protective, defensive, osseous framework. . . . Sexualism and maternity dominate the lives of all true women." Ragnar Redbeard, *Might Is Right, or the Survival of the Fittest* (Chicago: Adolph Mueller, 1896), 148–49. This passage is cited and discussed in Kamali, *Homegrown Hate,* 128–29. For broader reflections on this gender binary, see Barbara Perry, "'White Genocide': White Supremacists and the Politics of Reproduction," in *Home-Grown Hate: Gender and Organized Racism,* ed. Abby L. Ferber (New York: Routledge, 2004), 79–80.
41. "On Fascism," Vanguard America, February 15, 2017, available on the Internet Archive, https://web.archive.org/web/20170326023916/https://bloodandsoil.org/2017/03/25/on-fascism. Or, in the more blunt terms of Bre Faucheux: "Women build the nest. Men reshape the world. And men are more successful at reshaping the world because women build them a strong nest." Bre Faucheux, "How the Alt-Right Benefits Women," in Shaw, *A Fair Hearing,* 92.
42. This "white baby challenge" has been widely discussed. See Darby, *Sisters in Hate,* 158–60; Stern, *Proud Boys and the White Ethnostate,* 99–102.
43. Quoted in Sian Norris and Heidi Siegmund Cuda, "The Long Backlash against Abortion in America," *Byline Times,* May 5, 2022, https://bylinetimes.com.
44. "Flyers for Guerrilla Marketing—Invite Especially Women!," WhiteDate.net, accessed April 2, 2023, https://www.whitedate.net.
45. "Get White-Verified," WhiteDate.net, accessed April 2, 2023, https://www.whitedate.net.
46. Quoted in Darby, *Sisters in Hate,* 142.
47. Friberg, *The Real Right Returns,* 60. Elsewhere, Friberg ups the reproductive ideal for those who hope to "retake" Europe through their reproductive labor: "We are fighting a demographic war which we have been losing. . . . Get married as early as possible and have four children or more, thus ensuring that future Europeans are *our* descendants, rather than those of colonizing minorities or deranged political opponents." Daniel Friberg, forward to Andersen, *Rising from the Ruins,* xii.
48. Stern addresses this regressive temporality of the far right in *Proud Boys and the White Ethnostate,* 33–49. As Michael Kimmel has rightly

argued, these themes of racial melancholia are shot through with frustrated ideals of masculinity, where racial displacement overlaps with a rage stemming from the displacement of males from the top of the social hierarchy. See Kimmel, *Angry White Men.*

49. The racial subthemes of this slogan have been brought to the fore by the ubiquitous "Make America White Again" flyers and stickers distributed by white nationalist organizations, which imitate the style used by the Trump campaign.
50. See Sinead, "Top Five Reasons Our Cause Needs Women," *National Vanguard,* November 14, 2015, https://nationalvanguard.org.
51. Lane, *Deceived, Damned, and Defiant,* 6. For a discussion of the formula, see Kamali, *Homegrown Hate,* chap. 1.
52. "What Is the National Alliance?"
53. Lane, *Deceived, Damned, and Defiant,* 100.
54. In the terms of the white supremacist William Pierce: "Any sort of racial mixing was abhorrent to us. We looked on miscegenation with the same disgust and disapproval as on bestiality or necrophilia. We didn't tolerate it." See William Pierce, "Race Suicide," *National Vanguard.* July 1, 2021, https://nationalvanguard.org.
55. These assumptions about biological essences are reflected in the far right's frequent recourse to the concept of "bioculture"—the assertion that distinct cultures reflect not only historical experiments by distinct peoples but also the expression of their biological capacities, as inflected by historical and geographic factors. For discussion of this point, see Bhatt, "White Extinction."
56. See, for instance, Perry, "'White Genocide,'" 82–84.
57. Kevin Strom, "Racemixing—Worse Than Murder," *National Vanguard,* May 3, 2015, https://nationalvanguard.org. See also Perry, "'White Genocide,'" 84. In similar terms, David Lane asserts that "miscegenation, that is race-mixing, is and has always been, the greatest threat to the survival of the Aryan race." Lane, *Deceived, Damned, and Defiant,* 99.
58. See Blee, *Inside Organized Racism,* 116–18. The phrase "bedroom genocide" appears throughout the far right literature to describe interracial reproduction. See, for instance, H. Millard, "Do Whites Have a Right to Exist?," *National Vanguard,* October 10, 2016, https://nationalvanguard.org.
59. Andrew Macdonald, *The Turner Diaries* (Hillsboro, W.Va.: National Vanguard Books, 1978).
60. A helpful discussion of these projects appears in Scott Burnett and John Richardson, "'Breeders for Race and Nation': Gender, Sexuality and Fecundity in Post-war British Fascist Discourse," *Patterns of Prejudice* 55, no. 4 (2021): 331–56.
61. Neil Kumar, "White Identity Nationalism, Part 2," Counter-Currents, May 26, 2022, https://counter-currents.com.

62. For David Lane, homosexuality represents a "crime against nature," as the "purpose of the instinct for sexual union is reproduction and thus, preservation of the species." Lane, *Deceived, Damned, and Defiant,* 101.
63. *Morrigan Rising,* no. 13 (2010): 3. I have addressed this argument in Michael Feola, "The Conspiracy Theory at the Center of the Far Right's Violence against LGBTQ+ People," *Slate,* June 16, 2022, https://slate.com.
64. The panic over race suicide at the beginning of the twentieth century, for instance, was inspired by immigration and the declining birthrates of the "higher" Nordic race, but it was also energized by anxieties over women's increasing autonomy, which could lead to neglect of their reproductive and domestic duties. These anxieties reached beyond the increased role for women in public life and the formal workforce to target the burgeoning technologies of birth control that permitted this independence at the cost of the nation's reproductive output. See, for instance, Linda Gordon, *The Moral Property of Women: A History of Birth Control Politics in America* (Urbana: University of Illinois Press, 2007), 86–104; Ordover, *American Eugenics.*
65. Buchanan, *Death of the West,* 24.
66. A characteristic account is offered by the manosphere blogger Roosh Valizadeh, "The End Goal of Western Progressivism Is Depopulation," RooshV (blog), November 18, 2015, https://www.rooshv.com.
67. Johnson, *White Nationalist Manifesto,* 18.
68. David Sims, "Feminism Is a Weapon," *National Vanguard,* February 6, 2022, https://nationalvanguard.org.
69. For instance, one flyer from the white nationalist Patriot Front claims that "the beating heart of America lies not in the marble halls of government, but in the strength and prosperity of its families." See Khalida Sarwari, "Racist Posters Popping Up in South Bay," *Mercury News,* July 5, 2018, https://www.mercurynews.com.
70. *Morrigan Rising,* no. 14 (2014): 28. Henry Makow renders this argument in symptomatic terms: "In the case of human beings, the female must be prepared for motherhood and honored for her contribution to society. The male must be shown that the standard of manhood is to provide leadership and sustenance for mother and children. Both mother and father must be able to give their children intellectual and spiritual guidance. Instead, in schools and universities, the tender shoots of feminine sexuality are crushed under the feminist jackboot. Young women are taught that heterosexual sex, marriage and family are inherently oppressive. Homosexuality on the other hand is an act of rebellion that is 'chic' and 'normal.'" Henry Makow, "Feminism Is a Depopulation Program," January 29, 2017, https://www.henrymakow.com.
71. Love, "Shield Maidens, Fashy Femmes, and TradWives," 2.

72. For discussion of the far right's derision of feminism and feminists, see Stern, *Proud Boys and the White Ethnostate,* chap. 3.
73. For instance, George Shaw defines the "cat lady" as "a woman who is an especially fanatical liberal because her adoption of feminism early in life has stranded her, at the end of her fertile years, without a proper family. . . . The cat lady, having no hope of attaining happiness according to traditional/conservative standards, and with a great deal of time on her hands, fills the void in her existence by doubling down on liberal dogma, 'mothering' all of the world's victims and dutifully hissing at all the (white male) villains at which Marxist social engineers point her." Shaw, "Dismantling Anti-white Newspeak," 195.
74. Wolfie James, "A Place for Women in the Alt Right," Counter-Currents, January 24, 2017, https://counter-currents.com.
75. Darby, *Sisters in Hate,* 140–44. This line of argument runs throughout the antifeminism of the far right. See, for instance, David Duke, *My Awakening* (Covington, La.: Free Speech Press, 1998), chap. 14.
76. See, for instance, Vicky Spratt, "Why Are Members of the Alt-Right Sending Me Pictures of Empty Egg Boxes?," Refinery29, March 6, 2020, https://www.refinery29.com/en-gb.
77. David Sims, "Jews and Feminism: Nexus of Anti-White Hate," *National Vanguard,* February 6, 2019, https://nationalvanguard.org.
78. For an informative guide to the subgroups of the manosphere, see Ann-Kathrin Rothermel, Megan Kelly, and Greta Jasser, "Of Victims, Mass Murder, and 'Real Men': The Masculinities of the 'Manosphere,'" in *Male Supremacism in the United States: From Patriarchal Traditionalism to Misogynist Incels and the Alt-Right,* ed. Emily K. Carian, Alex DiBranco, and Chelsea Ebin (New York: Routledge, 2022), 117–41.
79. For a discussion of the incel world and its roots in the manosphere, see Lisa Sugiura, *The Incel Rebellion: The Rise of the Manosphere and the Virtual War against Women* (Bingley, England: Emerald Group, 2021).
80. Hypergamy has become a central article of faith in the manosphere, thanks to its pseudoscientific appeal to evolutionary biology. For canonical renderings by male supremacist authors, see F. Roger Devlin, *Sexual Utopia in Power: The Feminist Revolt against Civilization* (San Francisco: Counter-Currents Publishing, 2015), chap. 1; Paul Elam, "A Primer on Hypergamy," Paulelam.com, December 10, 2019, https://paulelam.com.
81. For an account of this violence, see Megan Kelly, Alex DiBranco, and Julia R. DeCook, "Misogynist Incels and Male Supremacist Violence," in Carian et al., *Male Supremacism in the United States,* 164–80.
82. In the notorious formulation of Tom Metzger: "Very little abortion should be tolerated, among our White race, while at the same

time, abortion and birth control should be promoted as a powerful weapon, in the limitation of non-White birth. . . . Covertly invest into non-White areas, invest in ghetto abortion clinics. Help to raise money for free abortions, in primarily non-White areas." Tom Metzger, "What We Believe as White Racists," in Kaplan, *Encyclopedia of White Power,* 539. This sentiment is widespread across the far right, where many figures argue that a white homeland would abolish abortion, but abortion access should be preserved for tactical reasons in the present, given the racially mixed state of liberal democracies. See, for instance, Greg Johnson, "Abortion and White Nationalism," Counter-Currents, April 11, 2016, https://counter-currents.com.

83. Andrew Anglin, "Stupid Whores Want to Spend Time Guzzling Cock Rather Than Producing Children," Daily Stormer, August 7, 2018, https://dailystormer.in.
84. Elsewhere, Anglin put this logic in even more direct terms when he asserted: "It's OUR WOMB. It belongs to the males in her society." Quoted in Darby, *Sisters in Hate,* 9.
85. The widespread use of eugenics and surrogacy technologies (i.e., "pregnancies in incubators") is a conspicuous feature of Guillaume Faye's vision of a repopulated Europe. See Faye, *Archeofuturism.* One of the more notorious appeals to surrogacy and reproductive technologies appears in the manifesto that the Norwegian white supremacist Anders Breivik wrote to accompany his 2011 act of mass murder. For a discussion of Breivik's vision, see Kaiser, *Political Masculinity,* 113–20.
86. "The Meaning of Life Is Life Itself," WhiteChild.net, accessed April 4, 2023, https://whitechild.net.
87. Home page, WhiteChild.net, accessed April 4, 2023, https://whitechild.net.
88. Kaiser, *Political Masculinity,* 120–23. See also Laura Bates, *Men Who Hate Women: From Incels to Pickup Artists* (Naperville, Ill.: Source Books, 2021), chap. 1.
89. Sacco Vandal, "Why We Need White Sharia," Vandalvoid.com, August 3, 2017, available on the Internet Archive, https://web.archive.org/web/20170808170949/http://vandalvoid.com/why-we-need-white-sharia.
90. "NSM 25-Point Plan." Idealization of the family is common across far right movements. For instance, the Patriot Front frequently parades at antiabortion events carrying banners that read "Strong Families Make Strong Nations."
91. See Annie Kelly, "The Housewives of White Supremacy," *New York Times,* June 1, 2018, https://www.nytimes.com; Stern, "Gender and the Far-Right"; Stern, *Proud Boys and the White Ethnostate,* 105–9.

92. See, for instance, Julia Ebner, *Going Dark: The Secret Social Lives of Extremists* (New York: Bloomsbury, 2020), chap. 3. The imperative for sexual service is well captured by the book that is often cited as a guide for aspiring tradwives, Laura Doyle's *The Surrendered Wife: A Practical Guide to Finding Intimacy, Passion, and Peace* (New York: Fireside, 2001).
93. For a helpful engagement with tradwives—particularly in their social media performances—see Eviane Leidig, *The Women of the Far Right: Social Media Influencers and Online Radicalization* (New York: Columbia University Press, 2023), esp. chaps. 3 and 4; Catherine Tebaldi, "Tradwives and Truth Warriors: Gender and Nationalism in US White Nationalist Women's Blogs," *Gender & Language* 17, no. 1 (2023): 14–38.
94. On this point, see Darby, *Sisters in Hate,* 123–24.
95. The specifics of this imagined past vary across the "tradlife" movement. For many, the ostensible "golden age" of the American republic demands a return to a parodic vision of the 1950s. For others, the past to be reclaimed is something closer to a back-to-nature pioneer vision, set further back in the history of the nation. See, for instance, Darby, *Sisters in Hate,* 153–54.
96. See Darby, *Sisters in Hate,* 153–58.
97. See Ashley Mattheis, "#TradCulture: Reproducing Whiteness and Neo-fascism through Gendered Discourse Online," in *Routledge Handbook of Critical Studies in Whiteness,* ed. Shona Hunter and Christi van der Westhuizen (New York: Routledge, 2022), 91–101.
98. See William Lind, *Retroculture: Taking America Back* (London: Arktos, 2019).
99. Lind, *Retroculture,* 12–14.
100. See, for instance, Spencer, "Spencer Speaks!"
101. On this point, see Miranda Christou, "#TradWives: Sexism as Gateway to White Supremacy," OpenDemocracy.net, March 17, 2020, https://www.opendemocracy.net.
102. As Kathryn Joyce argues, in connection with the "Quiverfull" movement, such a politics "requires a world of women to dedicate their lives and wombs to demographic battle . . . with the maternity ward as battleground." See Joyce, *Quiverfull,* 201–2.
103. This point is also made by Kaiser, *Political Masculinity,* 28.

Coda

1. See Gustaf Kilander, "Ex-Fox Reporter Lara Logan Unleashes Bizarre Conspiracies Including UN Plan to Flood US with Immigrants and Elites Drinking Blood," *The Independent,* October 20, 2022, https://www.independent.co.uk.
2. For a historical overview of this trope, see Magda Teter, *Blood Libel:*

On the Trail of an Antisemitic Myth (Cambridge, Mass.: Harvard University Press, 2020).

3. For an overview of Carlson's many references to replacement theory, see Nicholas Confessore, "How Tucker Carlson Stoked White Fear to Conquer Cable," *New York Times,* May 4, 2022, https://www.nytimes.com.
4. Marjorie Taylor Greene (@RepMTG), "We have no idea who or what is coming across our Southern border," Twitter, March 15, 2023, https://twitter.com/RepMTG/status/1636081567566102531.
5. See Binoy Kampmark, "Giorgia Meloni: The Great Replacement Moves In," International Policy Digest, October 13, 2022, https://intpolicydigest.org.
6. See Erin Clare Brown, "Tunisia's President Embraces the 'Great Replacement Theory,'" *New Lines Magazine,* February 27, 2023, https://newlinesmag.com.
7. "Tunisia: President's Racist Speech Incites a Wave of Violence against Black Africans," Amnesty International, March 10, 2023, https://www.amnesty.org.
8. Pamela Paul, "The Far Right and Far Left Agree on One Thing: Women Don't Count," *New York Times,* July 3, 2022, https://www.nytimes.com.
9. On this point, see Philip Gorski and Samuel Perry, *The Flag and the Cross: White Christian Nationalism and the Threat to Democracy* (New York: Oxford University Press, 2022).
10. For instance, the far right agitator Matt Walsh, who writes for the Daily Wire media outlet, recently claimed that "we hear so much about groups of people being erased . . . that's only actually happening to one group and that is white men. . . . And then people that are being erased in another sense, women, by . . . by . . . the trans activism." See Jason Campbell (@jasonscampbell), "Matt Walsh complains white men are 'erased,'" Twitter, March 3, 2023, https://twitter.com/JasonSCampbell/status/1631753809822187546.
11. For in-depth discussion of the rhetoric of white male victimhood, see Paul Elliott Johnson, *I, the People: The Rhetoric of Conservative Populism in the United States* (Tuscaloosa: University of Alabama Press, 2022).
12. Roosh, "Kill Whitey," in *Best of Roosh,* vol. 2 (self-pub., 2019), 208.
13. For discussion of this trend toward victimhood on the alt-right, see Simon Strick, "The Alternative Right, Masculinities, and Ordinary Affect," in *Right-Wing Populism and Gender: European Perspectives and Beyond,* ed. Gabriele Dietze and Julia Roth (Bielefeld: Transcript Verlag, 2020), 207–30. For a characteristic expression of such charges from within the far right, see Val Koinen, "The 'Other War' (The Ongoing War against White People)," Occidental Dissent, November 16, 2010, https://occidentaldissent.com.

14. This inversion is what Ruth Wodak terms the "victim–perpetrator reversal" of much far right rhetoric. See Wodak, *Politics of Fear*. Helpful reflections on the right-wing politics of victimhood also appear in Jeremy Engels, *The Politics of Resentment: A Genealogy* (University Park: Pennsylvania State University Press, 2015); Kelly, *Apocalypse Man*; Jason Stanley, *How Fascism Works: The Politics of Us and Them* (New York: Random House, 2020).
15. On this point, see Robert B. Horwitz, "Politics as Victimhood, Victimhood as Politics," *Journal of Policy History* 30, no. 3 (2018): 552–74. Casey Kelly describes this strategy well: "Victimhood remains a refuge for white men to, when cornered, turn the tables on the marginalized when they demand justice." Kelly, *Apocalypse Man,* 157.
16. This strategy is what Lee Bebout terms a "weaponized" victimhood. Lee Bebout, "Weaponizing Victimhood: Discourses of Oppression and the Maintenance of Supremacy on the Right," in *News on the Right: Studying Conservative News Cultures,* ed. Anthony Nadler and A. J. Bauer (New York: Oxford University Press, 2020), 64–83.
17. Andreas Malm and the Zetkin Collective term this the far right logic of *palindefense* (playing on the myth of *palingenesis* that rests at the heart of the fascist political imagination). See Malm and Zetkin Collective, *White Skin, Black Fuel,* 255–314. Sara Kamali also places a narrative of victimhood at the center of contemporary white extremism. See Kamali, *Homegrown Hate,* esp. chaps. 1 and 3.
18. Simon Stow, *American Mourning: Tragedy, Democracy, Resilience* (New York: Cambridge University Press, 2017), 2–3.
19. Stow reflects on the "restoration of an imagined past." Stow, *American Mourning,* 150.
20. Stow, *American Mourning,* 15–16.

INDEX

Page numbers in italics refer to illustrations.

Abercrombie & Fitch, 62
abortion, 121, 123, 194n82; access to, 124; legalized, 120; opposition to, 119
accelerationism, 50, 51, 168n88
activism, 58, 76, 97; alt-right, 74; anti-trans, 134; men's rights, 122; white homeland, 86, 88; white power, 118
Ahmed, Sara, 158n84
Alexander, Jeffrey, 14
Alfred the Great, 42
Allen, Danielle, 9, 152n29
alt-right, 57, 62, 74, 76, 86, 126, 168n88, 169n7
American Conservative, 79
American Freedom Party, 186n83
American Nazi Party, 86, 126
American Renaissance, 35
"American Son, An" (Hood), 79
Anderson, Carol, 157n67
anger, xvi; action and, xvii; gestures of, vii; justice and, 148n32; male, 123; racial, xvii
Anglin, Andrew, 124, 194n84
Angry White Men (Kimmel), 148n35
anti-Blackness, 133, 158n74
antiegalitarianism, 59, 65, 76
antifeminism, 118–24, 127
anti-immigration measures, 105, 106
antiliberalism, 64, 65, 69
anti-Semitism, 1, 16, 97, 132; far right, 52, 156n61
antiwhite hatred, xiv, 36, 111
anxiety, ix, xx, 16, 133; consumerism and, 96; cultural, 52; demographic, xix, 164n34, 166n52; far right, 134; political, 52; racial, 31; range of, 118; white, 21
Arendt, Hannah, 159n85, 168n81, 178n90
Arktos, 57, 62
Aryans, 87, 88, 89, 113, 119, 159n84, 184n60
Atlantic, The, 160n1
Atomwaffen Division, 51
autonomy: nonwhites and, 6; reproductive, xxii, 120; sexual, 118, 124; women's, 192n64
Aztlan, 89, 182n38

Balibar, Etienne, 71
Bar-On, Tamir, 176n74
Bauman, Zygmunt, 162n15
Belew, Kathleen, 39, 113, 156n60
Benawah County, planned community in, 81–82
Bhatt, Chetan, 163n30, 164n38, 171n21
Biden, Joe, 132
bioculture, 66, 72, 191n55
biodiversity, 44, 66, 72, 174n51
biology, 33, 34, 35, 36, 40, 44, 49, 67, 70, 191n55; facts of, 91; New Right and, 176n70
biopolitics, xxi, 11, 106, 107, 118, 128, 189n28; far right, 124, 127; racism and, 162n16
birth control, 120, 121, 192n64, 194n82
Birth of a Nation, The (Griffith), 112
birthrates, xxi, 103, 113, 119, 120,

188n14, 189n31; anxieties over, 106, 121; death rates and, 108; declining, 192n64
Black, Don, 95
Blackness, 8, 157n67
Boogaloo Bois, 51
Boumediene, Houari, 107
Braddock, Kurt, xix
Branch Davidian compound, 97
Breitbart, Andrew, 57
Breivik, Anders, 39, 194n85
Brexit, 80
Brown, Wendy, xvi, 148n36, 155n50, 155n51, 172n34
Buchanan, Patrick, xiv, 10, 28, 187n3; on autogenocide, 119; ethnomasochism and, 152n33; on existential crisis, 108; sadness/melancholy and, 151n14
Buffalo, shootings at, viii, xvii, xx, 111, 175n58
Butler, Judith, 156–57n63, 157n66

Camus, Renaud, ix, 1–2, 59, 63, 84, 150–51n14, 153n36, 162n18, 166n60; UHM and, 173n39
capitalism, 61, 63, 172n35; anxieties toward, 62; entanglements of, 160n94; neoliberal, 172n29; new right and, 172n29
caravans, xi, 74
Carlson, Tucker, 132, 147n22, 195–96n3
Carrying Capacity Network, 34
Castells, Manuel, 149n40
catastrophes, 28, 52, 161n4; narratives of, 35–40, 43–45
Charlottesville, 16, 48, 88, 113, 125; far right gathering in, viii, 1
Charter of Peoples' Rights, 176n79
Cheng, Anne, 156n63, 157n66
Christchurch, 46, 49, 51, 175n58; shootings at, xvii, xx, 38, 103, 165n46, 165n47, 182n44
Church of the Creator, 40
Citadel Community, 82, 179n10
citizen rule, process of, 9, 75
citizenship: axis of, 7; democratic, 9; languages of, 65; racial, 5, 8, 18, 60, 151–52n22; space of, 9, 30
civic breakup, 27, 28, 79, 91
civilization, 101; European, ix, xiv, 92; restoring, 111–12
civic life, 7, 9, 80, 141
civic memory, 139, 140
civil rights, 8, 27
civil society, 22, 38, 57, 59, 71, 72, 73, 91, 135; cultural politics and, xxi; white citizenship and, 7
civil war, 25, 80, 112; cold, 27; second, 27, 160n1, 179n4
Cold War, xiii
collaborationism, 32, 55, 97; replacement and, 162n21
colonization, 18, 32, 46, 52, 163n26; biological, 35; cultural, 35; demographic, 38; far right and, 19; reverse, 11, 43, 45, 104; rhetoric of, 37
communities, 58; civic, 91; experimental, 81–85; idealized, 140; racialized vision of, 95
competitive breeding, 107, 188n14
Confederacy: memorializing, 160n99; racial values of, 25
conflict, 30, 56; mechanistic vision of, 46
conservationist movement, 34, 49, 66
conspiracy theories, 52, 147n21; anti-Semitic, xii, 43, 97, 120; demographic, xi
consumerism, 93, 185n71; anxiety and, 96
Cooper, Brittany, 148n34
corruption, 31, 34, 97, 117, 138
cosmopolitans, 16, 68, 155n50
Counter-Currents, 57, 104
Covington, Harold, 87

Creativity movement, 43, 166n56
Crimp, Douglas, 18
critical race studies, 151n18
critical race theory, xvii
Crow tribe, 157–58n71
Crusaders, 40
Crusius, Patrick, 39
cultural change, ix, 22, 37, 138
cultural crisis, 18, 28, 35, 45, 46, 48, 67, 89, 93
cultural defense, 46, 64, 66, 69, 70, 71, 75, 173n47, 175n58
cultural differences, 63, 66, 67, 68; equal right to, 73; framing of, 28
cultural groups, ix, 29, 67, 72, 95
cultural politics, 57, 64, 75, 77; alt-right, 177n86; civil society and, xxi; liberal categories within, 65; new right, 59, 175n64
cultural totality, 65, 70–71, 72
culture, 1, 3, 9, 26, 33, 36, 44, 57, 60, 61, 73, 75, 85, 92, 94, 98; appeal to, 23–24; bygone, 25; consumer, 64; contemporary, 128; death sentence for, 70; defenders of, 28; demographic, 58; distinct, 89; diversity of, 65, 66; environment and, 176n68, 183n50; equivalence of, 154n44; European, xi, xix, 115; extremist, 149n41; far right, 53; hybridization of, 117; identity and, 117; liberal, 68; pagan warrior, 81; political, ix, xix, 16, 59; population change and, 59; traditional, 80; vision of, 28
culturecide, 35, 164n31, 181n36
culture war, 28

Daily Stormer, x, 104, 124
Daily Wire, 196n10
Darby, Seyward, 113
Davis, James, 28
Davocracy, 64, 173n43
Day of the Rope, 118
death rates, birthrates and, 108
de Benoist, Alain, 61, 66, 67, 70, 174–75n57, 175n59, 177n85; on ENR, 65
Declaration of Human Rights, 176n79
Declaration of the Rights of Peoples, 176n77
"Defend Europe" initiative, 187n8
degeneration, 28, 72, 177n80
de Maistre, Joseph, 171n22, 171n25
democracy, 50, 75, 93; direct, 174n53; false dreams of, 92; liberal, 74; psychological pressure and, 152n29
Democratic Party, xiii, 147n22
demographic change, x, xxiii, 5, 10, 11, 29, 46, 52, 64, 75, 137, 138, 139; anti-white, 153n35; egalitarian commitments and, 60; intentional aspect of, xiv; iron law of, 108; large-scale, 45, 63; reactions to, xviii–xix, 2
demographic fear, 2, 48; far right politics of, xiv, xviii, xxiii; politics of, xii, 32, 33, 49, 55, 58, 59, 77, 81, 103, 111, 113
demographic majorities, xviii, 36, 58
demographic panic, xv, 10–11, 109, 147–48n28, 187n3; politics of, 30, 35, 38
demographic war, 30, 38, 106
demographic winter, x, xxi, 108, 146n9
Demographic Winter: The Decline of the Human Family (Stout), 188n17
demography, 29, 33, 36, 81; destiny and, 109
depopulation agenda, 119
depopulation bomb, 108
Devi, Savitra, 167n67
difference, 134, 175n59; equality and, 64; eradication of, 182n36;

legacy of, 68; national, 60–61; right to, 65, 67, 72, 73; values of, 71
differences: human, 134; racial, 31, 60–61, 66, 153n40
discourse, 57, 75; diversity, 65, 70; ecological, 33, 163n27; engineering, 76; militant, 38; political, 27–28, 74; replacement, 29; trauma, 158n72
discrimination, 22, 27, 173n39; antiwhite, 164n39, 164n41
Disney World, 2
displacement, xv, 16, 19, 138; discourse of, 137; narrative of, 13
dispossession, 7, 26, 79, 141, 159n89; Indigenous, 6; theme of, xii–xiii, 35; white, 10, 12, 19
diversity, xxi, 12, 16, 19, 30, 44, 52, 59, 65, 68, 74, 75, 92; biocultural, 66; ethnic, 58; language, 66; natural, 66; racial, 90; stand of, 89; true, 67
divorce: civic, 80; national, 80; racial, 38, 68, 167n64, 177n84
DuBois, W. E. B., 7, 151n20

Earnest, John, 52, 165n52
ecofascism, 33, 34
ecology, 34, 49, 50, 66, 134; media, xviii, xix, 39, 51, 65, 112, 121, 135; thought, xxiii, 51, 53, 126, 136
economic losses, 13, 51, 108
economic restructuring, 12, 24, 36
ecosphere: conservative, 73–74; far right, 57, 113, 137; media, xvi–xvii, 73–74
education, 24, 90, 98, 170n13; antiwhite, 87; physical, 107
egalitarianism, 60–64, 68, 75, 170n19
Ehrlich, Paul, 108, 188n15
elites, xii, xiii, 55, 141, 146n17; financial, 58; Jewish, 16, 64; media, 58; natural, 93; political, 15, 16, 50
El Paso, shootings at, xvii, xx
emergency, 40, 43, 53; perception of, 37; rhetoric of, 46; state of, 48, 50
ENR. *See* European New Right
entitlement, xv, 122; aggrieved, 18, 148n35; animus for, 148n30; loss of, 19; whiteness and, 23
environment: culture and, 176n68, 183n50; social, 116
equality, xvi, xxi, xxii, 19, 58, 59, 75, 93, 136; civic, xvii, 10, 23; critique of, 65; difference and, 64; educational, 171n26, 181n36; false dreams of, 92; fungibility and, 60–64; gender, 113, 171n26, 181n36; income, 171n26, 181n36; legacy of, 68; LGBTQ+, 76; material, 140; moral commitment to, 63; overhaul of, 73; population replacement and, 171n21; reformed vision of, 65; social, xvii, 171n26, 181n36; values of, 71; women's, 122
"Equality Is a False God" (poster), 76
erasure, 56, 134; charges of, 135; discourse of, 136, 137; Indigenous, 8; white, xiii, 32, 36, 104
Esposito, Roberto, 162n15
ethnic cleansing, 46
ethnic competitors: reproduction of, 21; tide of, xii
ethnic core, xii, 2–3, 32, 151n14
ethnic groups, ix, 11, 29, 50, 71, 73, 84, 90, 99, 111, 181n36; native, 38
ethnicity, 3, 99, 180n24, 182n37; appeal to, 4; distinct, 89; race and, 107–8; white, 101
ethnic mixing, 64, 99
ethnic war, xx, 43
ethnocide, 29, 35

ethnomasochism, 35, 164n34, 170n11
ethnonationalism, xv, 3, 4, 9, 22, 51, 60, 66, 71, 146n14, 150n9
ethnopluralism, 67, 176n68
ethnopopulism, 74, 173n47
ethnostate, 21, 180n24, 181n33, 182n38, 184n57, 184n63; advocacy of, 98, 186n80; dream of, 85–91, 94, 97–98; natalist imperative of, xxi; pattern for, 86; tensions of, 91–95; violent sovereignty of, 96–101
Ethnostate, The (Robertson), 93–94
ethnosuicide, 35, 110, 164n34
eugenics, 34, 100, 189n26, 194n85
Eurabia, xv
European Action, 40
European New Right (ENR), 56, 61, 65, 68, 70, 73, 74, 169n5, 176n68, 176n70
European Union, secession from, xii, 80
Eurosiberia, 80
Evola, Julius, 28, 45
extermination, xiii, 30, 36, 37, 46, 56
extremism, 46, 49, 51, 52, 111, 126, 167n70, 175n58; scholarship on, xxii; white/nativist, xxii

fantasy, 18, 40, 55, 97; attachment, 154n44; gendered, 15; race, 8, 103, 155n58
far right, xi, xiv, xv, xxiii, 10, 22, 23, 30, 34, 45, 63, 186n89; actors, xxiii, 40, 77; defining, xxii; geographic schools of, xxiii; history of, xxii; organizations, 1, 44, 77; terms/phrases on, 55
fascism, 32, 33, 96–101; appeals to, 187n91; European, 31; political imagination of, xxi; political mobilization and, 101; themes of, 100; tradition of, 70; ultranationalist, 101
Faucheux, Bre, 190n41
Faye, Guillaume, ix, 32, 38, 43, 55, 68, 73, 161n4, 162n21, 165n46, 176n68, 177n82; biological identity of, 3; biopolitics and, 189n28; born leader and, 167n76; on de-migration, 99; ethnocide and, 29; Islamophobia and, 186n86; militaristic stance and, 166n60; multiculturalist language and, 173n46; race war and, 166n61; rootedness and, 163n24; violent action and, 50
female life, biological meanings of, 134
#femininenotfemininist, 127
feminism, 16, 120, 155n50, 156n59; adoption of, 193n73; far right and, 193n72; gender-critical, 134; hostility toward, 121–22; language of, 127; reproduction and, 124
feminist society, 80, 120, 122, 124, 135
fertility: ambivalence about, 112; anxieties, xii; comparative rates of, 11
fertility rates, x, xii, 111; drop in, 29, 108
Finkielkraut, Alain, 173n41
Foucault, Michel, 31, 71, 106; permanent purification and, 32; on racism, 162n14, 162n16; sexuality and, 107
Fox News, 11, 132, 147n22
Free Black State, 89, 182n38
Freud, Sigmund, 13
Friberg, Daniel, 57, 115; on alien masses, 162n21; reproductive ideal and, 190n47; on universalism, 61
Friedman, Patri, 83

Front National, 73
futurity, xviii, xx, 6, 21, 127, 128, 159n85; white, 111–13, 115–18, 127

Gehlen, Ernst, 171n22
gender, xvi, 106, 123, 135, 190n40; anxiety over, 134; distinction, 126; natural order of, 129; race and, 15; roles, 121, 128, 138; separate purposes of, 113
gender-affirming care, 119
gender flexibility, technology of, 134
Gendron, Payton, 111
Generation Identity, 12, 50, 67, 187n8
genetics, 34, 40, 70, 93
genocide, 29, 46, 49, 52, 56, 185n71; bedroom, 117, 191n58; cultural, 37; fascist campaigns of, 34; fighting, 103; physical, 37; by replacement, 11; soft, 39, 166n52; white, xiii, xx, 10, 11, 36, 46, 65, 153n35, 155n59
geopolitical spaces, xxi, 12, 37, 63, 80, 87
Gilroy, Paul, 18
globalism, 16, 22, 44, 62, 105, 133
globalists, xii, 16, 22, 99, 132, 155n50
globalization, ix, 9, 32, 35, 61, 67, 68, 89; conditions of, 29; economic, xv, 13; neoliberal, 62; political, xv; population changes and, xxi; social, xv
golden age, 26, 128, 138, 195n95
Goodhart, David, 178n2
Gramsci, Antonio, 56
Grant, Madison, xi–xii, 109, 110
Great Replacement, ix, x, xi, xv, xvii, xix, 40, 52, 55, 59, 69, 103, 131, 182n44; appeals to, 133; invoking, 33; liberal democracies and, 2; narrative of, xviii, xix, xx, 30; rage and, 22; tropes of, 132
"Great Replacement, The" (Tarrant), 38
Great Return, 68, 73
GRECE Institute (Groupement de Recherche et d'Études pour la Civilisation Européenne), 56, 57, 169n4
GreekIdentitarian, 55
Greene, Marjorie Taylor, 80, 132
grievance, viii, xiii, xix, 11, 122, 136, 140; core, 18–19; economic, 24; racial, xviii, 141; rage of, 138; white, 4, 5, 6, 23, 45
Griffin, Roger, 45, 175n64, 177n80
Griffith, D. W., 112
Guénon, René, 28

Hage, Ghassan, 8
Harari, Yuval, 131–32
Hardin, Garrett, 34
Harris, Cheryl, 8, 151n17
Hart, Michael H., 182n37
Herder, Johann Gottfried, 174–75n57
heritage, 7, 12, 21; white national, 25
Heritage Foundation, 179n6
Herrenvolk, 86, 180n23, 180n24
Heyer, Heather, viii
historical differences, 60–61, 72
history, 29, 67, 85; cyclical nature of, 45; narratives of, 94; nonwhite/nonmale, 136; racial, 12, 84; teaching, xvii; war on, 136
Hitler, Adolf, x
Hochschild, Arlie, 11, 13, 155n54
Hofstadter, Richard, xiii, 147n21, 170n13
homelands: carnal, 94, 184n61; colored, 109; ethnic, xxi, 88, 94; homogenous, 71; racial, 85, 94. *See also* white homelands

homeownership, 7–8, 24, 82
Homo economicus, 61
homophobia, 119
homosexuality, 192n62; as act of rebellion, 192n70; condemnation of, 119
Hood, Gregory, 79, 85, 167–68n77; on egalitarianism, 59; on race, 3
Hooker, Juliet, 4, 23, 158n74
Hooton Plan, xi
Hopf, G. Michael, 168n78
HoSang, Daniel Martinez, 24, 183n49
HuffPost, 62
humanity, 37, 60, 61, 66, 70
Huntington, Samuel, 11

Identitare Bewegung, sticker from, *41*
identitarians, 68, 70, 73, 105, 106
identity, 13, 36, 40, 62, 90; abstract, 7; appeal to, 23–24; biological, 3, 70, 117, 163n24; cultural, 20, 29, 33, 68, 117, 163n24, 176n77; ethnic, 45, 68, 176n77; gender, 135; genetic, 117, 163n24; group, 67; national, 33, 70, 106; primordial site of, 12; racial, 36, 155n5, 164n33; traditional markers of, 60; Tunisian, 133; white, 4, 7, 20, 157n66
Identity England, poster from, *42*
ideology, 49, 79, 84; anti-Semitic, 43; antiwhite, 120; gender, 135; human rights, 171n24; replacement, 133, 135; universalist, 65
Ignatiev, Noel, 159n88
imaginary: antiliberal political, 73; extremist, 86; far right, 48; fascist, 32, 45; gender, 113; mythic, 113; political, 49, 57, 72
imagination: civic, 140, 141; conservative, 28; ethnonationalist, 108; extremist, 55; far right, 25, 30, 50, 83, 118, 128, 181n32; melancholic, 26; political, 3, 21, 23, 96, 115, 129, 138, 161n12; secessionist, 84, 85; technological, 82
immigrants, xiv–xv, 7, 73, 104; flood of, 131; invasion by, 112; violence against, 133
immigration, ix, 34, 40, 59, 60, 108; controlling, 104, 110, 120; cultural integrity and, 33; debates over, 133–34; global age, 67; increase in, xii; internal, 79; lightning rod of, 2; mass, 19, 161n4; Muslim, xv; non-white, 153n35; patterns of, xi, ix; policies, 21, 33, 104; reproduction and, 110; warnings about, 131; white reproduction and, 111
incels, 122–23
Indigenous population, 31; dispossession of, 6
individualism, 52, 75, 98, 100, 128, 185n71; critique of, 96
Inglehart, Ronald, 159n93
Ingraham, Laura, 11–12
injustice, eradication of, xvi, 171n26, 181n36
integration, 85, 87; cultural, 44; ethnic, 65, 90; racial, 65, 90, 156n59
International Monetary Fund, xii
invaders, 32, 165n46; cultural, 35, 37–38; ethnic, 35; Islamic, 40
invasion, 46, 52, 74; demographic, 162n18; rhetoric of, 10–11
irreplaceability, 4, 9, 61, 94; logic of, 10; politics of, 5
Islamophobia, xv, 99, 125, 148n28, 164n32, 186n86
"It's OK to be white" campaign, 4

Jackson, Paul, 46
James, Wolfie, 121
Jews, 16, 64, 97, 156n60
Johnson, Greg, 36, 38, 57, 95, 98, 99, 104, 120, 155n59, 173n43,

175n62; genocide and, 153n35, 185n71; habitat loss and, 33; national identity and, 70; on white nationalism, 90–91; white separatism and, 167n64
Joyce, Kathryn, 129, 195n102

Kalergi Plan, xi, 146n14
Kali Yuga, 45
Kamali, Sara, 197n17
Kaufmann, Eric, 2
Kawczynski, Tom, 183n50
Kelly, Casey Ryan, 156–57n63, 197n15
Kimmel, Michael, 18, 148n35, 159n91
King, Steve, 111
Klassen, Ben, 43
Kohl, Erlung, 44
Krebs, Pierre, 33, 39, 44, 63, 64, 70, 164n31, 174n55, 176n77, 176n79; on egalitarian ties, 58–59; on multiracialism, 181n36; race and, 36
Ku Klux Klan, 95
Kumar, Neil, 27, 37, 150n10
Kurtagic, Alex, 36, 146n17, 171n25, 173n37

labor, 189n25; global flows of, 63; outsourcing of, 24
Lane, David, 87, 116, 117, 184n60; formula of, 86; on homosexuality, 192n62
language, 33, 59; as battleground, 64–69; civic, 72; race war, 46; replacement, 45–46, 48–53
language war, 75, 77
Lebensraum, 88
Lebout, Lee, 197n16
Le Camp des saints (Raspail), x
Lee, Robert E., 25
Le Grand Remplacement (Camus), ix, 2
Leonard, John Bruce, 62, 96, 171n25, 180n24; on equality, 181n36
Le Pen, Jean-Marie, 73
Le Pen, Marine, 173n41
LGBTQ+ movement, vii, 134
liberal democracies, xiv, 36, 37, 58, 73, 74, 194n82; far right and, 29; Great Replacement and, 2
liberalism, xx, 59, 63, 65; egalitarian commitments of, 170n19; legacy of, 60
libertarianism, 82, 83, 84, 97, 98, 185–86n78
liberty, 6, 82, 179n10
literature: antireplacement, 58; conservative, 28, 170n19, 172n35; demographic, x, 146n10; estrangement, 12; ethnonationalist, 2, 8, 67; ethnostate, 88, 95, 180n24, 184n64; movement, 20, 46, 126; new right, 60; panic, 36; racialist, 40, 112; right-wing, 91; seasteading, 83; separatist, 89; trauma, 158n72; white extremist, 16; white nationalist, 23; white supremacist, 88, 112, 113, 163n26
Livingston, Donald, 84
Lofgren, Mike, 79
Logan, Lara, 131
Lokteff, Lana, 146n18
Lorde, Audre, xvi
Lorenz, Joseph, 171n22
loss: civic, 141; memory of, 140; narrative of, xix; pathos of, 15; politics of, 5, 140; rage and, 10–16
Lost Cause, 25, 84, 160n98
Lovett, Laura, 188n21
Lowndes, Joseph, 24, 183n49

“Make America White Again,” 4, 23, 191n49; advertisement, *5*
Makow, Henry, 192n70
Malm, Andreas, 197n17

Manhattan Institute for Policy Research, 56
"Manifesto" (Patriot Front), 186n82
Manne, Kate, 157n63
manosphere, 122, 123, 125, 136, 193n79, 193n80
market society, 62, 172n29
marriage, 192n70; interracial, xi, 99
Marxism, 76
masculinity, 80, 106; aggressive politics of, 157n63; ideals of, 191n48; institutional structures of, 15; militant, 168n78; toxic, 122
mass murder, 38, 132, 153n35, 194n85
Matrix, The (film), 52
Mattheis, Ashley, 128
media, viii, xxiii, 116; campaigns, 106; common, 75; conservative, xiii, 136; far right, 57, 149n40; global, 64
media ecosystem, vii, xix, 74
melancholia: political, 5, 10–16; postcolonial, 18; psychodynamics of, 22; racial, 18, 191n49; social, 14, 157n63; subjecthood and, 156n63. *See also* white melancholia
melancholy, 14, 21, 151n14, 155n51, 157n63; aggressive, 156n63
Meloni, Giorgia, 74, 132
memes, 67, 74
metapolitics, 55, 56, 57, 58, 69–77; as counteroffensive, 64–69; new right, xx, 64, 66, 75, 76, 169n7
migrants, 35, 176n68, 180n20; assault on, 187n7; influx of, 104; rescue of, 162n21
migration, xi, xii, 34, 67; ethnocide and, 29; global flows of, 63
militias, 51, 97, 185n74
Millard, Martin H., 166n59
Miller-Idriss, Cynthia, 94, 149n42, 184n63
Mills, Charles, 20
Minassian, Alek, 123
Minuteman Project, 105, 187n7
miscegenation, 117, 156n59, 163n25, 163n26, 191n54, 191n57; ban on, 120
Mises, Ludwig von, 83
Mises Institute, 96
misogyny, 123, 124
Mitscherlich, Alexander, 18, 158–59n82
Mitscherlich, Margarete, 18, 158–59n82
modernity, 60, 62, 101; end of, 93; global, 2, 63, 89; industrial, 1; liberal, 59, 61; pathologies of, 128
Moglen, Seth, 14
Mondon, Aurelien, 186n89
monoculture, 67, 84, 85, 89; antipathy for, 172n32; global, 65
monuments: Confederate, viii, 25, 136, 137; contested politics of, 160n96; cultural, 37; removal of, 1
moral decline, 29, 48, 61
motherhood, 120, 192n70
mourning, 4, 13, 21, 139, 144, 158n82
Mudde, Cas, xxii
Muirhead, Russell, 178n90
multiculturalism, 4, 12, 16, 18, 19, 22, 30, 35, 36, 43, 44, 58, 63, 68, 85, 155n50, 174n49, 174n55; diversity of, 52; experiments in, 90; hierarchical, 73; liberal, 67; sickness of, 88; true, 67
multinational corporations, xiii, 32, 62
multiracialism, 90, 164n31, 174n49, 181n36
Muslims, 16, 35, 67, 104, 108; murder of, xvii

mythology, 21, 112–13, 118, 122, 126; antistate, 97; far right, 53

narrative, xviii, 22, 138; catastrophe, 35–40, 43–45; change, 29; civic, 141; crisis, 33; demographic, 52; displacement, 13; far right, xxiii, 20; fascist, 92; global, 39; history, 94; loss, xix; melancholic, xx; nationhood, 139; reaction, 20; replacement, x, xiii–xiv, xix, xx, xxii, 30, 32, 132, 133, 135, 137; social, 155n55, 157n63; threat, 167n70; victimhood, 137, 197n17
natalism, xxii, 106
natalists, 21, 118, 121, 125
nation-state, 62, 81, 84
National Alliance, 87, 99, 104, 113, 116; flyer from, *105, 114*; public platform of, 98
nationalism, 74; ethnic, 2; melancholic, 6, 18, 20, 21, 151n15; racialized, 23; radical, 128; resurgent, 2; white, xx, 22, 90–91, 98, 154n46, 156n60
nationalists, white, 1, 48, 62, 100, 115, 135, 181n33, 185n75, 191n49, 192n69
National Policy Institute, 8
National Socialist Movement, 18, 86, 126
National Vanguard, viii–ix, 116, 117
nationhood: definition of, 70; fascist approach to, 31, 92; narratives of, 139; white, 88–89, 125, 128
nativism, xii, 74, 177n85
Nazism, 92
neighborhoods: degradation of, 90; occupation of, 11; White, 88
neo-Confederates, 25, 81, 84
neoliberalism, 24, 62, 140
neo-Nazis, 51, 88
neo-racism, 71, 74
New Age, pseudo-religion of, 171n26
New Albion, 21, 80, 89, 92, 182n38, 183n50
New America, 88
New Century Foundation, 19, 20, 35, 44, 72, 89
New Class, 64
new right, 57, 58, 61–67, 73, 77, 161n2, 171n22, 177n88; biology and, 176n70; capitalism and, 172n29; cultural insights of, 64; culturalist wing of, 71; defining, 56; egalitarian commitments and, 64; human biodiversity and, 66; language and, 64–65; monoculture and, 172n32; projects, 71, 74; race and, 176n70; theory, 61. *See also* European New Right
Newsmax, 131
New World Order, 156n60
New York Times, 135
Nietzsche, Friedrich, 93
nonwhites, vii, xiii, xviii, 16, 37, 89, 99, 109, 118; autonomy and, 6; exclusion of, 88; immigration of, 99; invasion of, x; removal of, 186n83; repatriating, 21; reproductive rates of, 11; responsibility to, 24; sexual assaults by, 112
Nordic race, xi, 109, 192n64
Norris, Pippa, 159n93
Northwest Front, 87; promotional sign for, *87*
Northwest Territorial Imperative, 21, 87
nostalgia, 23, 93, 116, 139, 184n63

Obama, Barack, 13, 74
Olson, Joel, 7
O'Meara, Michael, 60, 81, 174n47; multiculturalism and, 174n49; white homelands and, 185n76

open borders, 131, 132
Orbán, Viktor, xv, 74, 111
Ozarkia, 21, 80, 88

Pacific Northwest Territorial Imperative, 80
paleoconservatism, 10, 63, 172n35, 186n80
palingenesis, 45, 197n17
panic, xi, 36, 187n3; immigration, 188n21; moral, 76; race, xii. *See also* demographic panic
panmixia, 35, 89, 164n31, 181n36
paramilitary groups, 105
Passing of the Great Race, The (Grant), xi–xii, 109
pathology, 5, 28; political, 22; social, 90
patriarchy, 92, 126, 129
Patriot Front, 48, 100, 167n77, 185n75, 192n69, 194n90
Paul, Pamela, 135
Paul, Ron, 82
Paulville, 82, 179n11
peoplehood, 154n44, 183n45
persecution, xxii, 15, 136, 137, 138
Pierce, William, 118, 188n9, 191n54
Pioneer Fund, 44
pluralism, 9, 67, 68, 75, 89, 136
polarization, 27, 52, 75, 80, 179n4
political change, ix, 37, 57
politics, xiii, 30, 57, 58, 80, 91; border, 131; closure of, 45–46, 48–53; conflict/rhetoric and, 56; cultural, 63, 75; democratic, 6; demographic, 14; egalitarian, 75; far right, xvi, xxiii, 5, 9, 81, 85; grievance, 5, 6, 23, 158n74; melancholic, 18–22, 25; natalist, xxii, 115, 124; naturalized reduction of, 128; racial, 4, 34, 115; reproductive, 119; transphobic, 134; white reaction, 15, 25, 184n63
Political Theory, 158n73
popular media, 160n1, 178–79n4
Population Bomb, The (Ehrlich), 108
population change, 22, 62, 72, 108, 111; culture and, 59; globalization and, xxi; narrative, 29
population mixture, xiii, 67
populism, 3, 140, 150n8, 186n86; racial, 100; upsurge in, vii
power, 71, 81; coercive, 97; cultural, 64, 134, 136; hierarchies of, xvi, 20; institutional, 56; material, 136; natal, 123; political, 56, 134, 180n24; racial topography of, 13, 20; social, 134, 137. *See also* white power
Practical Idealism (von Coudenhove-Kalergi), xi
Prager, Jeffrey, 2, 159n83
preservation, 20, 43, 175n58, 192n62; cultural, 66, 73, 89, 137, 177n85; racial, 94, 124, 137
Primeval Soup, 173n39
progressives, vii, 76, 110
Proud Boys, 76
psychoanalytic theory, 13, 21
psychodynamics, 5, 11, 13, 60
public goods, 79, 80, 82
public spaces, 26, 72, 79, 165n46; invaders in, 32
purebloods, 55
purity, 33, 46, 87

queer movements, 18
"Quiverfull" movement, 195n102

race, xvi, 3, 53, 75, 89, 94, 117, 124; assassination of, 36; axis of, xviii; biological foundations of, 91; entanglement of, 160n94; ethnicity and, 107–8; facts of, 91; fixation on, 70; gender and, 15; New Right and, 176n70; positional logic of, 151n16; real differences between, 166n62;

social body and, 162n14; as status of power, 151n18
race realism, 44, 48, 90
race science, 44
race suicide, xi, xii, xxii, 10, 109, 110, 187n3, 188n21, 192n64
race theory, fascist, 55
race traitors, 55, 117, 118
race war, xx, 39, 51, 53, 112, 149n38, 162n20; fear of, 161n12; language of, 46; political imagination of, 30–35
racial core, 32, 34, 151n14
racial defense, 64, 69, 75, 175n58
racial groups, 71, 90, 95, 99, 111, 156n63
racial hierarchy, 19, 25, 95, 112
racial holy war (RAHOWA), 43, 166n59
racial hygiene, 32
racialist right, xi, 96, 108, 117, 146n9, 165n46
racial mixture, xi, 11, 86, 91, 118, 191n57; anxiety about, 109; crime of, 117
racial nation, 51, 124
racial relations: nature of, xx; realistic approach to, 44
racial replacement, viii, xi, 1, 2, 53, 110, 134, 157n63, 176n68; collaboration and, 162n21; demographic, 29, 58, 107; discourse of, 136, 137; ethnic, xix, 5, 36; far right and, ix; fear of, x, 26, 109, 147n22; genocide by, 11; narrative of, xiv, 137; process of, 109; rage of, xvi
racial separation, 94, 100, 158n79, 166n58
racial survival, 39, 117
racism, 32, 70; antiwhite, xiv, xvii; biopolitics and, 162n16; classic, 71; differentialist, 71; indignities of, xvi; reaction to, xvi; reverse, 164n41; state-sanctioned, 76
radical right, xxii; conspiracies and, 147n21; metapolitical strategies of, 181n35
rage, vii, xv–xxii, 117–18; capturing, 2; currents of, xiv; far right and, xxii, 22; gestures of, vii, viii; Great Replacement and, 22; loss and, 10–16; melancholic, 23, 26; politics of, xvi, 19, 24, 25, 145n2
Ragnar Redbeard, 190n40
RAHOWA. *See* racial holy war
Rana, Aziz, 6
rapefugees, 112
Raspail, Jean, x
reconquest, 39, 40, 50, 73, 99
Reconstruction South, 7, 112
Réflechir & Agir, cover of, *47*
remigration, 68, 73, 177n82; sticker for, *69*
repatriation, 37, 186n83
replacement, 45–46, 48–53, 133, 135; collaboration and, 162n21; discourse, 29; ethnic, 30, 39, 46, 48, 111; genocide and, 11; population, x, 61, 110, 121, 145n8, 171n21; social, 2; white, ix, xiii, xx, 5, 6, 18, 126, 156n61. *See also* Great Replacement; racial replacement
replacement fears, psychodynamics of, 10
replacement rates, white nationalists, and, 115
replacement theory, 132–33, 134, 136, 137
reproduction, 106, 107; biological function of, 128; Black, 153n40; decline in, 120; defensive vision of, 118; emphasis on, 115; enhancing, 125; feminism and, 124; immigration and, 110; interracial, 99, 117, 119; Latinx, 153n40; nonwhite, 11, 123; as racial combat, 111–13, 115–18;

rates of, x, 29, 125; refusing, 119; sexuality and, 108; wellspring of, 126. *See also* white reproduction
reproductive ownership, 124
reproductive threats, 118–24
resentment, xvii, xviii, 11, 13, 16, 22, 45, 77, 122, 141, 155n50; nativist, 18; private, xix; racial, viii, ix
right to exit, 84
Rising Tide of Color against White World-Supremacy, The (Stoddard), 109
Roberts, Dorothy, 153n40
Robertson, Wilmot, 4, 51, 93–94, 158n79, 159n89, 182n45, 183–84n56, 184n57, 188n14
Robin, Corey, 161n7
Rockwell, Norman, 23
Rodger, Elliot, 123
Roof, Dylann, 39, 149n38
Roosevelt, Theodore, 187n3
rootedness, 163–64n30, 185n68
Roper, Billy, 88, 181n33
Rosenblum, Nancy, 178n90
Ruby Ridge, 97
Rufo, Christopher, 56, 76

Saied, Kais, 133
sameness, 59, 61, 65, 93
Sartre, Jean-Paul, 157n63
Schwidetzky, Ilse, 33
seasteading, 83
Seasteading Institute, 82
secession, 79, 96, 100; cultural, 80; dreams of, 81–85, 98; far right, 84–85; vision of, 81, 85
segregation, racial, 120, 166n48
settler colonialism, xii, 6, 36, 158n71
sexual activity, 119, 123
sexual assaults, 112
sexual depravity, 120, 122
sexual freedom, 124, 125
sexuality, 106, 107, 112, 123; anxiety over, 134; female, 125, 192n70; nonreproductive, 108; reproduction and, 108
sexual relations, 122–23
Shaw, George, 73, 193n73
shield maidens, 112
Shield Wall Network, 88
Shklar, Judith, 151–52n22
Silent Brotherhood, 181n27
slaves, 30, 151n17; chattel, 6; racial difference of, 30
social benefit, calculus of, 15
social change, ix, xiii, 4, 22, 72, 137, 138; vision of, 136
social conflicts, 30, 49, 50, 51
social Darwinism, 166n48
social engineers, 21, 100, 193n73
social media, xvii, 126, 127; tradlife, 128; white nationalist, 115
social order, 121, 180n24, 184n66; traditional, 127; white supremacy and, 31
solidarity, 22, 140; civic, 98, 138; class-based, 7; human, 91; racial, 96; toxic forms of, xvi; white, 148n29
sovereignty, 62, 82, 152n29; cultural, 84; nation-state, 162n20; national, 63; political, 18; regional, 84; violent, 96–101
Spektorowski, Alberto, 73, 177n82
Spencer, Richard, 57, 62, 86, 104; alt-right and, 8; diversity/multiculturalism and, 182n40; on erasure, 32; French New Right and, 169n4, 170n8; globalist economic policies and, 173n36; market individualism and, 185n68; national identity and, 70; white homelands and, 67
Spengler, Oswald, 28, 93
Stanley, Jason, 197n14

Stern, Alexandra Minna, 88, 181n35, 184n64, 190n48
Stewart, Ayla, 115
Stoddard, Lothrop, 109, 110
Stolcke, Verena, 49, 71
"Stop the Great Replacement" (Kumar), 150n10
Stormfront, 95, 111, 189n29
Stout, Rick, 188n17
Stow, Simon, 138–39, 197n19
Strom, Kevin Alfred, 117
strong men, 48, 53, 93, 98
substitution, 71, 134; ethnic, ix, xii, xiii, 2, 30, 132; racial, xiii, 110, 111
Sunic, Tomislav, 171n24, 176n68
supremacy: male, 122, 193n80; political, 9, 94; racial, 30, 50, 89, 91–92, 184n57; separatism and, 91–95. *See also* white supremacy
surrogacy, 125, 194n85
symbols, 26, 33, 57, 59, 69

Taguieff, Pierre-André, 71, 74, 176n70
Tarrant, Brenton, 38, 49, 51, 52, 106, 165n46; on ethnic replacement, 48; murders by, 103
Taylor, Brad, 83
Taylor, Jared, 19, 35, 44, 72, 89, 90, 154n42, 154n44, 157n70; on celebrate diversity, 156n62; on demographic forces, 164n33; European man/European civilization, xiv; national identity and, 70; white advocacy and, 177n82; on whites/aliens and, 153n34
Tea Party, 148n30
technology, 24, 192n64; eugenics/surrogacy, 194n85; reproductive, 125, 194n85
Terre et Peuple, 37–38, 175n59
thanatopolitics, 157n63, 162n16
Thiel, Peter, 82
Thiriart, Jean, 49, 179n6, 179n7
Those Who Remain: A Post-apocalyptic Novel (Hopf), 168n78
Thule-Seminar, 33, 56
Todorov, Tzvetan, 158n83
totalitarianism, soft, 62, 172n30
tradfamily, 127, 128
tradlife, 126, 127, 128, 195n95
tradwife, 126, 127, 128
trans-exclusionary radical feminists (TERFs), 134
transgenderism, 119, 134, 135
trauma, 158n72; historical, 19; reverberations of, 21; social, 14
true nation, xxi, 85, 97
Trump, Donald, 74, 116; criminal indictment of, 27; white grievance politics and, 25; white nationalists and, 191n49
Tunisian National Security Council, 133
Turner Diaries, The (Pierce), 118
Tyler, Rick, 4, 23; advertisement for, *5*

Undifferentiated Human Matter (UHM), 63, 173n39
unions, 7, 24
"Unite the Right" rally, 1, 2, 15, 88, 101, 113, 125; advertisement for, *3*
United Nations (UN), xii, 107, 131
universalism, 61, 146n17, 171n26
U.S. Census, xii
U.S. Congress, 4

vaccines, 27, 55, 107, 125
Valizadeh, Daryush "Roosh," 136, 192n66
Valkyries, 112
values, 35, 65, 69, 75; egalitarian, 59; extramarket, 63; liberal, xxi, 74; moral, 60, 71; nonwhite/nonmale, 136; political, 71
Vandal, Sacco, 125, 126

Vanguard America, 15, 100–101, 113, 155n57; poster from, *17*
Venner, Dominique, 58
Vial, Pierre, 37–38, 162n18
victimhood, 136, 156n63, 197n15; alt-right, 196n13; discourse on, 136; logic of, 137; male, 122, 196n11; narrative of, 137, 197n17; weaponized, 197n16; white majorities and, xxii
violence, xx, 19, 30, 90, 103; agent of, 83; anti-immigrant, 133; campaign of, 46; committing, 51; ethnocidal, 70; extremist, 48, 51, 53, 137, 166n53; geopolitical, 157n66; historic, 158n77; mobilization against, 18; online technology and, 165n47; outcomes of, 35–40, 43–45; promoting, 50; racial, xvii, xviii, 20, 25, 38, 39, 51, 52, 137; rise of, 46; sexual, 112; social frustration and, 46; white, 8, 20, 137, 166n53
virtual reality, 52
vision, 75, 85; conspiratorial, ix; expansionist, 88; racial, 81, 92, 95; social, 81
vocabulary, 69; civic, 73, 74, 75; liberal normative, 73; political, 65
von Coundenhove-Kalergi, Richard, xi

Waco, 97
Walker, Francis Amasa, xii
Walmart, shootings at, xvii, 39
Walsh, Matt, 196n10
Weaver, Randy, 97
Weyrich, Paul, 179n6
White Baby Boom, 111
white baby challenge, 115, 190n42
WhiteChild.net, 125
white children, 86, 117; future for, 116; producing, 111
white citizens, viii; native-born, xiv; political mastery and, 23
white culture, xix, 21, 25, 45, 85, 87, 96; threat to, 19
WhiteDate.net, 115, 125
white dominion, 19, 20, 23; far right claim to, 10; politics of, 6–10
White Ethno-State, 86
white extinction, 36, 153n35, 164n38, 171n21
white extremism, viii, x, xiv, xviii, 39, 106, 118, 146n14; militant, 50; practice of, xx; xenophobia of, 123
white homelands, 67, 81, 86, 91–92, 93, 98, 126, 185n76; advocacy, 87–88; creating, 38; pathologies of, 96
"White Identity Nationalism, Part I" (Kumar), 27
White living spaces, 98; nonwhite penetration of, 88, 153n35
white majorities, 2, 4, 38, 45, 53, 58, 86, 104, 109, 111, 127; decline of, viii, xii; displacement of, 22; ethnocide against, 29; replacement of, xix, 36, 187n3; settler colonialism and, xii; threat to, 19; victimhood and, xxii
"WhiteMan," 103
White Man's Bible, 163n25
white melancholia, 10–16, 116; full depth of, 24; material resonance of, 22–26
white men, 15, 22, 73, 128, 136, 167n77, 196n10; aggrieved, 137; angry, 1; surplus, 121; war against, xv
white nation, xxi, xxii, 8, 45, 81, 88, 101, 119, 126, 128; eulogy for, 4; reproductive rate of, 125
whiteness, xviii, 6–10, 18, 24, 25, 116; abandoning, 23; assertion of, 13; bearers of, 26; bonds of,

xxi, 140; class structure and, 6; enemies of, 19, 119; entitlement and, 23; gendered order of, 15; historical meaning of, 20; language of, 133; logic of, 140; politics of, xix, 7, 19; subject of, 5; upper-middle-class, 128
white people, 20, 23, 85, 100, 180n20; aliens and, 153n34; demographic eclipse of, 37; dominance of, 21; integrated, 101; race conscious, 125; reducing percentage of, ix; as refugees, 154n42; war against, 136; White nationalism and, 91
white population, 21, 29, 70, 106, 116, 159n89; decline of, x, xii, 111; destiny of, 94; displacement of, xvii; reproduction by, 107–8; sacrifice of, 37
white power, 30, 81, 89, 92, 118, 181n28, 187n9; reproduction and, 113; women and, 189n35
white race, 43, 93, 104; concentration of, 99; demographic flood and, 118; eclipse of, x, 109; extinction of, 153n35; Jews and, 156n60; preserving, 94
white reaction, xiii, xiv, 18, 48, 107, 148n36; far right politics of, 9–10; gender imaginary of, 113; narratives of, 20; politics of, 21, 22, 24, 25, 115, 123
white reproduction, 118; diminishment of, 119; immigration and, 111; significance of, 117
white separation movements, 85, 92, 95, 96, 167n64
white sharia, 125, 126
white supremacy, ix, xvii, 1, 4, 10, 11, 43, 86, 88, 92, 94, 95, 96, 103, 111, 115, 116, 118, 135; disavowal of, 183n49; logic of, 8; mythology of, 189n35; reverberations of, xvii; social order and, 31
white working class, xv, 24
Why We Fight: Manifesto of the European Resistance (Faye), 55
Willinger, Markus, 50
Winter, Aaron, 186n89
Wodak, Ruth, xix, 196n14
Wolin, Richard, 177n88
womanhood, 112, 135
women: authentic, 135; domestication and, 128; as gatekeepers, 116; natural tendencies of, 128; proper places for, 127
Women for Aryan Unity, 115, 119, 120, 189n37
World Church of the Creator, 40
World Economic Forum, 132

xenophobia, xi, xii, 39, 71, 73, 74, 123, 132, 148n29, 177n88

Ye'or, Bat, xv
Young Europe, 49

Zemmour, Eric, 40, 145n8
Zetkin Collective, 197n17
Zionist Occupational Government (ZOG), 97, 156n60
zone d'occupation américaine (ZOA), 172n32

Michael Feola is associate professor of government and law at Lafayette College and author of *The Powers of Sensibility: Aesthetic Politics through Adorno, Foucault, and Rancière.*